RAILWAYS OF THE WORLD

RAILWAYS OF THE WORLD

Boat trains at Ostend in the early 1900s — Vienna express with type 12 at front and type 11 at rear; type 17 (Dunalastair II) No. 2415

RAILWAYS OF THE WORLD

4 *Railways of*
Western Europe

O.S. Nock

B.SC., C.ENG., F.I.C.E., F.I.MECH.E.
HONORARY FELLOW AND PAST PRESIDENT,
INSTITUTION OF RAILWAY SIGNAL ENGINEERS

WITH 80 PHOTOGRAPHS
AND 31 MAPS AND DIAGRAMS

ADAM & CHARLES BLACK · LONDON

FIRST PUBLISHED 1977
A. & C. BLACK LIMITED
35 BEDFORD ROW, LONDON WC1R 4JH

© 1977 O.S. NOCK

ISBN 0 7136 1686 5

Nock, Oswald Stevens
    Railways of the world
    4: Railways of Western Europe.
    1. Railroads
    I. Title
    385   HE1021

    ISBN 0-7136-1686-5

TYPESET BY COMPUTACOMP (UK) LTD
FORT WILLIAM, SCOTLAND
PRINTED AND BOUND IN GREAT BRITAIN AT
THE PITMAN PRESS, BATH

Contents

Illustrations

32   MODERN FRENCH POWER

(A)   PASSENGER TRAIN NEAR LISIEX

(B)   TWO 200 KM./H. FLYERS AT THE AUSTERLITZ
        STATION

(C)   ONE OF THE LATEST THYRISTOR CONTROLLED
        A.C. ELECTRIC LOCOMOTIVES

MAPS AND DIAGRAMS

Acknowledgements

The author and publishers thank the following for permission to use photographs:

Austrian Federal Railways for 15c, 17a, 18a.
Bern-Lötschberg Simplon Railway for 20b, 22a, 22b, 22c.
Beyer, Peacock & Co. Ltd. for 2a, 2b, 2c.
C.R.L. Coles, Esq., for 5c, 7b, 11a.
Monsieur G.F. Fenino for 7a, 29a, 29b, 29c, 32a.
French National Railways for 27b.
German Federal Railways for 12a, 14a, 14b, 14c.
Integra AG for 21b.
Italian State Railways for 23b, 25a, 25b.
Jungfrau Railway for 21a.
Locomotive Publishing Co. Ltd. for 4, 16a, 19c.
Netherlands Railway Museum for 1a, 3b, 3c.
O.S. Nock, Esq., for 1b, 3a, 8b, 8c, 9b, 13d, 15a, 15b, 17b, 18b, 20a, 23a, 24b, 31, 32b, 32c.
North British Locomotive Co. Ltd. for 9a.
P. Ransome-Wallis, Esq., for 5a, 5b, 6a, 6b, 6c, 10a, 10b, 11b, 12d, 13a, 13b, 13c, 16b, 24a, 24c, 27c.
Siemens Co. (Germany) for 11b.
Swiss Federal Railways for 19a, 19b.
La Vie du Rail (Paris) for 26a, 28a, 28b, 30a, 30b.

Plates 8a, 12b, 12c, 26b, 27a are from the collection of the late Lord Monkswell.

The coloured frontispiece is from a painting by Jack Hill.

The maps and line diagrams were drawn by Mrs. C. Boyer, of Chippenham, from data in the author's collection.

Preface

In this series of books on Railways of the World it seems that with each succeeding volume I have an ever-greater canvas on which to work. In Western Europe I certainly have not such a vast expanse of territory to cover as in Australia or Canada, but looked at historically the diversity of origin and development could indeed be bewildering — even though the scope of the book, as in previous volumes in this series, is confined to the routes and countries in which I have travelled personally. So far I have not been into Scandinavia, nor at the opposite end of the map, into Portugal. But elsewhere I have been, and seen, and made many friends who between them have 'filled me in', as they say in Canada, with many details of history and operation.

While this book takes the form of a series of separate essays I have tried not to make them too separate, arranging them in the form of a zig-zagging journey that opens at Parkeston Quay, Harwich and proceeds via Holland, Belgium, a brief initial excursion into France, a dip into Rhineland history and thence to Austria, almost to the borders of Jugoslavia. Then back to Switzerland for a welter of mountain climbing and tunnelling, into Italy, down to Naples and back to the Cote d'Azur, and so finally into France to relive the greatest days of her steam locomotive prowess, and to be suitably impressed by the startling efficiency of her 200 km./h. electrics.

In looking back over the many notebooks that I have filled full of details of journeys in these fair lands, and of visits I have made to railway establishments, museums, and technical meetings, it is a delightful experience to recall one by one the good friends who have contributed to my enjoyment and enlightment, and in some cases made me and my wife so very welcome in their homes. Olivia my wife has indeed been my companion on most of these journeys in Europe, and if through the painful disability of increasingly severe arthritis she is no longer able to type my books, she is still happily there as constant adviser and literary critic.

Among those who have helped me, in addition to the senior railway managements in the countries we have visited, I must mention particularly Baron Gerard Vuillet, and his wife Monique; Monsieur Y. Paris, of the

Jeumont Schneider Company, his wife Janot, and their daughters; Baron van Hemstra, of Utrecht; Mrs. Asselberghs of the Netherlands Transport Museum; Monsieur Louis Devillers, former Director of Electrical Engineering of the Belgian State Railways; Herr Helmuth Calmbach of the Deutsches Bundesbahn, Frankfurt; Dr. Adolf Giesl-Gieslingen, of Vienna, and his family; Dr. Karl Oehler of Zurich, and his son; and finally Herr Heinz Studer, and his wife Hedi, of Zurich. To all of them my best thanks are due.

Silver Cedars
High Bannerdown
Batheaston
BATH

O. S. NOCK

April 1976

CHAPTER ONE

Outward bound from Harwich
Holland — a first look round

The London and North Eastern Railway had a splendid coloured poster called *The Night Parade*, showing the departure of three giant packet steamers in line ahead from Parkeston Quay, some little distance up the River Stour. One could stand on the waterfront at Harwich and watch this stately procession steam slowly by. The first was bound for the Hook of Holland, the second was for Antwerp, and the third was the Danish steamer for Esbjerg. In the period between the two world wars, which corresponded roughly with what could be called the 'normal' life of the London and North Eastern Railway, there was a day time service from Parkeston Quay to the rival Dutch packet station of Flushing, on the island of Walcheren, and behind this lies a fascinating piece of transport history that can well open this story of railways in Western Europe. It extends back to the year 1861, when an Englishman with strong Dutch connections, James Staats Forbes, was appointed General Manager of the half-finished, potentially insolvent East Kent Railway. He was already Manager of the Dutch Rhenish Railway, and how under his somewhat chimerical leadership the East Kent blossomed into the London Chatham and Dover Railway is no part of the present story, except in respect of the packet station that was established at Queensborough, in the Isle of Sheppey.

Forbes was not content with snatching the Government mail contract on the Dover-Calais route from under the very noses of the rival South Eastern Railway; he must do the same for the Dutch and German mails. In view of the close family ties between the British and German Royal houses at that time, the mail service was very important. Using every influence that could be brought to bear through his Dutch connections Forbes secured a mail contract for the route from Queensborough to Flushing. Unlike that operated from Dover to Calais however, the sea passage was made by foreign steamers, those of the Zeeland Company, which the writer of a popular handbook on Holland described as 'no doubt the largest and finest that cross that ever-vexed bit of sea, which often tries the inner consciousness more than the Atlantic itself'. The latter part of the nineteenth century was however a time when national sentiments at home took the form of 'England first, and the rest nowhere', and the fact that so important a mail service from England was carried in Dutch ships rankled, particularly with the management of the Great Eastern Railway, which was actively developing its continental services via Harwich.

At this same time the railway situation in the Netherlands was complex, to say the least of it. In that small country there were no less than five main line companies, and a map (see page 8) is necessary for their various extents and interconnections to be clearly grasped. It would be no surprise to the visitor to find that trains connecting with the steamers at the Hook of Holland and Flushing were run by different administrations, but on reaching Utrecht he would find the trains of *four* companies entering the one central station! In 1910 Baedecker describes the Hook of Holland as 'an insignificant village', but qualifies this statement by adding that it has 'since 1892 been an important place for the passage to England'. This of course was when the Great Eastern Railway began to compete seriously with the Queensborough–Flushing route for the German traffic. At the Hook the trains were those of the Dutch Rhenish Railway, which had a main line from west to east across Holland, and at the turn of the century was distinguished by some handsome British-built express locomotives. The opinions of travellers seemed to differ on the merits of Dutch railway travel at that time. One such, writing in *The Railway Magazine* of 1898, showed a lack of discernment, and a general aim to draw unfavourable comparisons with contemporary British standard — one of the 'England first and the rest nowhere' school; and one can turn with more interest to Foxwell and Farrer's classic of 1888: *Express Trains English and Foreign*.

After having made some rather scathing remarks about travel in Belgium, the joint authors continue:

The management displays a brisker air in Holland. The engines are finer, mostly by English makers. Passengers and their luggage are tackled more rapidly, and there is less tendency to official hysterics when emergencies disturb the prescribed routine. In Holland the stations are 'open' as in England, the refreshment rooms are both frequent and good, and comfort is everywhere more prominent than red tape. In small items of fittings of carriages, etc., Dutch thoroughness comes out. Thus the noiselessness of their windows, and the very neat arrangement for 'dowsing' the light during sleep, are two instances of detail which we in England are at present far behind.

In a country whose railways have been so thoroughly modernised in the past thirty years, one could hardly expect to find many relics of earlier days, and at the Hook on the short run up to Rotterdam there are no traces. But if we go further over the tracks of the one-time Dutch Rhenish Railway through Gouda to Utrecht, there is, within pleasant walking distance of the station, one of the most delightful railway museums I have ever seen; and there, by full-sized exhibits, models, and a collection of exquisite pictures one is indeed carried back to the early days of the Dutch railways, and can begin to absorb something of their unique character, and stoutly individual origins. On the platform outside one can stand beside one of the splendid 'Rhine-bogie' engines that hauled trains of the 'nineties' from the Hook, and walk a little further to admire the elegant 2–4–0 of the State Railway that took the rival trains from Flushing. But locomotives are no more than a part of the vivid contemporary railway scene that is gradually unfolded by a leisurely walk round this most tastefully arranged museum.

Having progressed thus far it is time to go back still further, to the very origins of railways in Holland, and to the inception and building of the line from Amsterdam, through Haarlem and The Hague, to Rotterdam — known in the 'nineties' as the Holland Company. Work started as early as 1837, but the first engineer got into such difficulties that he had to resign within two years having made very

3

little progress in building the line westwards from Amsterdam towards Haarlem. It may be wondered why pioneer railway construction proved so difficult in Holland. The country is level, and there would be no occasion to blast deep excavations or drive long tunnels; but the very fact that it *was* so level created problems. And then of course there was the geographical phenomenon that much of those level innocent-looking polders was actually below sea level, and protected from inundation by the elaborate system of defensive earthworks. So much of the land was spongy and unstable — far from ideal for providing the solid foundation needed for a railway. In more than a hundred years of railway operation, and all the experience that has been gained with it, the permanent way in Holland is not one of the best in Europe. This does not disparage a railway administration of the highest efficiency, but merely emphasises the physical difficulties with which they have to contend. Shortly before commencing to write this book I had occasion to travel by a through fast express train from The Hague to Paris, in a modern French corridor coach. It was most noticeable how the riding improved from the oscillation and slight hunting over the Dutch part of the journey to Rotterdam, and across the low marshy land of the Rhine delta when we got on to more 'solid' ground south of Brussels, to the perfection of travel that one now takes for granted in France.

When the first engineer of the Holland Railway got 'bogged down' — literally! — west of Amsterdam the Government of the day called in the very distinguished civil engineer F.W. Conrad, and he managed to get the first 17 kilometres, to Haarlem, open by September of 1839. Most students of railway history will have heard of Chat Moss, that notorious stretch of bog land near the eastern end of the Liverpool and Manchester Railway, where George Stephenson had such difficulty in getting a firm foundation. Conrad experienced much the same difficulty but in a far greater and more treacherous form. While Stephenson had no more than a few miles, practically the whole length of the Holland Railway had to be laid on this spongy, unstable ground. The road bed was formed, for almost the entire distance on faggots, and there were places where one, two, or even three layers were not enough, and the layers of faggots were alternated in depth with beds of rubble. These layers, sometimes as

4

many as seven of each, were held together with stakes and wattle, and then the roadbed, consisting of sand from the seashore covered with turf, was formed on the surface of the faggots. Sand and turf was hardly an ideal foundation for the track of a railway, but it was the best that could be done.

Then of course there were innumerable waterways to be crossed. Holland is famous for its system of canals, and at the time the first railways were built practically all the traffic was conveyed in sailing barges. Seeing how difficult it was to form a railway across such country, it can well be imagined that Conrad carried his track level at a height very little above the ground, and the crossing of those waterways presented him with a host of different problems. It was just not practicable to raise the level of the railway so that the underside of a bridge could be high enough to clear the masts of those sailing ships, and so the bridges had to be made with at least one section that could be moved, or lifted clear, to permit the passage of ships. Between Amsterdam and The Hague there were no less that 58 localities where moveable bridges were required. Conditions varied to such an extent that no standard design was possible. Every case had to be treated on its merits: in some cases a swinging span, pivoted about its centre point; in some a lifting span like a castle drawbridge; in others an arrangement for rolling one span lengthwise or slantwise to afford the necessary clearance from the navigable waterway. Conrad himself laid down the basic design; potential contractors were then required to submit their detailed proposals.

The design of these bridges was in every case so important that tenderers were required to submit, with their price for the job, a working scale model so that Conrad himself and all local interests concerned could see exactly what was proposed. It was one of the conditions of contract that the successful tenderer made a present of his model to the company. By the greatest good fortune some of the most interesting of these models have been preserved and are now on display in the museum at Utrecht. They are not only masterpieces of the modeller's art in themselves, and most ingenious mechanisms, but in a marvellous state of preservation, seeing that they are now well over a hundred years old. They range from the familiar type of swing bridge, to others in which the moveable portions were slid sideways, or diagonally. Perhaps the most extraordinary was a folding bridge, on the section between The Hague and Rotterdam. It would need pages to describe, even in the merest outline, the working of these bridges; but Conrad described many of them in complete engineering detail, with working drawings, in a paper before the Institution of Civil Engineers in London, April 1844 to which those interested in the finer points of these fascinating structures may be referred.

More recent structures have now replaced the majority of these early bridges, and like the locomotives of steam days traces of them have long disappeared. The onrush of modernisation has however not yet obliterated everything that belonged to an older and more spacious age. When travelling to and from Zandfoort-am-Zee recently, in the course of an engineering convention, I had to change trains several times at Haarlem, and noticed the truly magnificent block of buildings in the centre of the station. Those through stations that still remain in their original form, have all the station offices on an island block, like the still-surviving London and North Western stations at Rugby and Preston, with an arched roof covering all lines used by passenger trains. But at Haarlem, and to a lesser extent at The Hague, the central timber buildings are of a height and elegance of detail that is a sheer delight. The all-over roof was a popular form of station covering in Holland, though not always with the 'island' block of offices in the centre.

Until the First World War the premier sea route from Holland to England was undoubtedly that via Flushing, and the station on the quayside was appropriately equipped. It was a route of Royal patronage, and has a most tastefully decorated Royal waiting room. A pleasing touch of publicity to the route from Germany was given at the time of the marriage of Queen Wilhelmina, at the turn of the century. The first Dutch station on the North Brabant German Railway, entering Holland from Wesel, was Gennep on the River Maas. A dining car was attached to the Flushing boat train at 7.15, and an attractive montage postcard was produced showing Gennep station with a train running in, one of the packet steamers, and portraits of the Queen and the Crown Prince. They bore the following quaintly worded legend, in English:

From the Continent to England
(via Vlissingen)
Breakfast in the train

(one hour for to eat)
Coffee and milk or tea
bread and butter, cold dishes
Price: 1 sh. 9d.
Railway guards receive the orders please

The dining car was conveyed only on the North Brabant section of the journey, and the 'one hour for to eat' related to the run from Gennep to Boxtel.

The North Brabant German Railway had a main line little more than 80$^1/_2$ kilometres long, as will be seen from the map (on page 8), and the remarkable thing was that nearly half of that distance was on German territory. It remained a stoutly individual concern for many years, and as will be told in the next Chapter had some locomotives equally distinctive in the early 1900s. In the latter part of the nineteenth century it was not exactly a high speed route — nor for that matter were any other main lines on the continent of Europe. When Foxwell and Farrer produced their celebrated statistical work they chose an overall speed of 64 km./h. inclusive of stops as the hallmark of an 'express' train. But while this was all very well so far as Great Britain was concerned, the standard had to be lowered to 47 km./h. for the Continent, otherwise there would not have been very many runs to chronicle! The North Brabant ran a train over the 61 kilometres from Goch, just on the German side of the frontier, to Boxtel in 67 minutes, a leisurely average of 55 km./h.; and this train, in 1888, conveyed only first and second class passengers. It was nevertheless considered a prestige route, and in the early 1900s its handsome royal blue locomotives could have been taken as a mark of affinity with the Great Eastern in England, even though the North Brabant engines gave place to the highly embellished grass green engines of the Netherlands State Railway, at Boxtel, for the remainder of the run to Flushing — (Vlissingen, to give it the Dutch spelling). But I must not at this stage anticipate the subject matter of

7

the next Chapter, and will travel instead northwards to that veritable 'grand junction' of the Dutch railways, Utrecht.

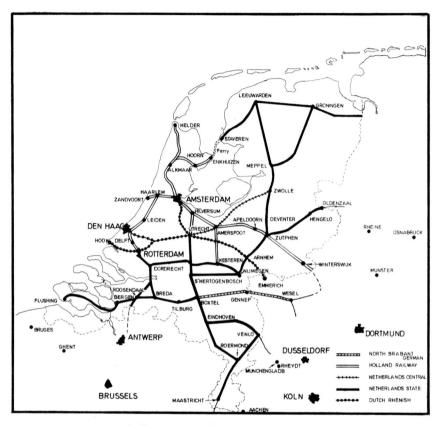

1. Railways in Holland — about 1890

No fewer that six express routes converged here, in the days before the various amalgamations. Working round the compass clockwise and starting with the line running due west, there was the principal main line of the Dutch Rhenish to Gouda, which forked there with its principal route turning south west for Rotterdam, and thence to the Hook. Northwards from Utrecht there were two alternative and rival routes to Amsterdam, one of the Rhenish and the other of the Holland Railway. The main line of today is the latter, which runs via Hilversum. The next route out of Utrecht was that of the Netherlands

8

Central — again a relatively small concern, but forming a major and indispensible link in the main line to north-eastern Holland, and to the cities of North Germany. As if to underline its independence the Netherlands Central also had some highly distinctive locomotives. Eastwards from Utrecht went the main line of the Dutch Rhenish, heading for Arnhem and an entry into a northern part of the heavily industrialised area of the Rhineland, while due southwards from Utrecht ran the State Railway, leading first to Nijmegen.

Amsterdam has one of the most strikingly sited stations in the world. Arriving by train, either from Haarlem or from Utrecht, one is intensely conscious of approaching a great maritime capital city. There are not merely glimpses of docks, busy waterways, great ships, and innumerable intersecting canals; one has a grandstand panoramic view of the whole activity. Then, the study of a map reveals that the entire complex is built on a veritable archipelago in the estuary of the River Ij. Not all main line traffic was originally routed into the Central station, it was used only by the trains of the Holland Railway; the Dutch Rhenish came in at the Weesperpoort station, to which there was a connecting line to the Central. Although the opening of the first railway in the Netherlands between Amsterdam and Haarlem in 1839 was made the occasion of much festivity, in 1845 the Weesperspoort line was also opened under Royal patronage, with the Prince of Orange in attendance. The original station of the Holland Railway in Amsterdam soon proved inadequate for the international traffic that began to flow into it, and towards the end of the nineteenth century the present magnificent station was built, and opened in 1885.

St. Pancras, the terminus of the Midland Railway in London, with its great single arch span has its platforms in the roof, as it were. Amsterdam Central is a much larger version, but with a very important difference. St. Pancras is built on solid ground and has, in the main building, two storeys below the platforms used for warehousing and such like, whereas at Amsterdam the station is virtually built over the water, and as the map shows it is reached by bridges over the Open Haven. The station facade is in keeping with the impressive surroundings: it is built in the Dutch renaissance style, and was designed by the celebrated architect, P.J.H. Cuypers. The

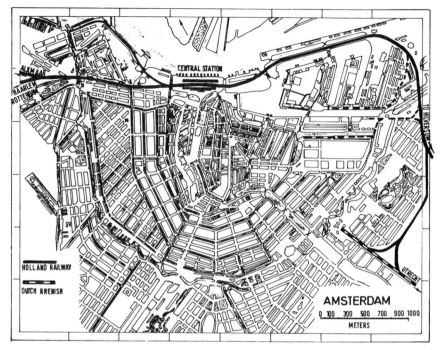

2. Railways in Amsterdam

first thing a passenger sees when coming out of the station building is the lofty Roman Catholic Cathedral of St. Nicholas, while on the river side of the station is the De Ruyter-Kade — the quay from which there are steamer services to practically every other Dutch port. The Central Station was built with a view to future expansion of traffic. The area under the great roof was originally much larger than contemporary business required. The platforms from which the longer distance trains departed were very wide, and were liberally provided with bookstalls, and refreshment kiosks from which drinks, sandwiches and such like were served to tables on the platform. In the main station building, apart from purely railway offices there were palatial restaurants, and a Royal waiting room which is still in use and is a private showpiece among Dutch railway officers and their visitors.

The geographical position of Amsterdam at the south-western extremity of the Zuider Zee renders it less of a railway junction than

Utrecht or Amersfoot; but it is the starting point for an important group of branch lines in the narrow strip of land that extends northwards between the inland Zuider Zee, and the North Sea. A number of fascinating places are to be found there, that even today retain an atmosphere of the past while fulfilling an important niche in the business economy of the country as a whole; Zaandam, Alkmaar, Hoorn, Enkhuizen, and Den Helder. In that area the business of railway working was carried on in even more leisurely style than in the rest of nineteenth century Holland. Even in the 1930s vintage steam locomotives trundled short rakes of ancient non-corridor carriages along. Stations like Hoorn and Enkhuizen were a delight to the photographer seeking after some of the early British-built specimens of Dutch steam power; but in the days when Foxwell and Farrer collected their voluminous blocks of data the line to Enkhuizen was one of those in Holland over which express trains ran. There was evidently at least one train that made an overall average speed of more than 46 km./h. on the run to and from Amsterdam.

It is a long detour by train from Amsterdam round the Zuider Zee to its north eastern extremity. The Dutch people need little encouragement to take to the water, and in the latter part of the nineteenth century the quickest way to Leeuwarden was to take an 'express' train of the Holland Railway to Enkhuizen, and then cross the Zuider Zee by steamer to Stavoren. Foxwell and his collaborator were charmed by this particular run. They wrote:

The little 'cross-country' service from Amsterdam to Leeuwarden, including a passage of 12 miles over the Zuider Zee, is worked as admirably as if it were a Continental service at 'express' fares. The boat has electric lights throughout, with a mere handful of passengers to appreciate them.

They were certainly far removed from ferry boats, and at both Enkhuizen and Stavoren on the eastern shore there was nothing more than a 'cross platform' interchange between train and steamer. This cross country service was interesting in that it involved co-operation between two different Dutch railways on either side of the Zuider Zee. From Stavoren the train was worked by the Netherlands State system.

The map of the nineteenth century railways of Holland shows how the State system made its way from Flushing by Tilburg, Nijmegen, Zutphen, and Zwolle to the north-east, encircling as it were the Rhenish and the Central on the way. But the Netherlands Central had an important function in the working of another cross-country service. In providing through trains from Rotterdam to the north-east it was the practice to run these over the Rhenish system to Utrecht, and there add to them a portion from Amsterdam. The combined train then went forward over the Central line to Zwolle, where it was again divided, one portion going to Leeuwarden and the other to Groningen. Before the absorption of the Dutch Rhenish system into the State Railway a passenger from Rotterdam to the north-east would be hauled by locomotives of three different railways in this relatively short journey, with the red-brown engine of the Rhenish as far as Utrecht, a yellow Central engine to Zwolle, and finally a grass-green State 2–4–0 to finish the journey, either to Leeuwarden or to Groningen.

The people of the Netherlands showed great discernment in the location of their railways, or perhaps I could put it another way and explain that railways were built so as to cause the least possible disturbance to existing houses, thoroughfares and such like. There was none of the steam-roller tactics that blasted a way for the London Chatham and Dover into the heart of the City of London, earning it the unenviable nickname of 'destroyer of houses'. In Holland the larger towns and the ancient cities were so linked up with canals that any disturbance would have a 'chain reaction' of subsidence and collapse, and generally speaking the railways and their stations were kept clear of the old town centres. Of this tendency there is perhaps no more interesting a case than that of Groningen. The history of this ancient town goes back to the 9th century, and its central area is ringed by a system of canals. There are others cutting through the busiest part of the town. It is rather like a watery version of the city walls of Paris, though on a smaller scale. When the State Railway came to Groningen it was kept entirely outside this central nucleus, and although the town had little more than 50,000 inhabitants a magnificent station was built on the outer bank of what is known as the Provincial Canal, and faced by pleasant gardens. The effects of this fine building, mirrored in the still waters of the canal, is very impressive.

The great majority of Dutch stations remain in their original form today, even though the track layouts, signalling, and methods for moving trains have necessarily been modernised. There is however one very significant exception. The original station at Rotterdam was not one of the most distinctive in Holland, and it was completely destroyed in the fearful aerial bombardment by which the Nazi attack on the Netherlands opened in May 1940. Although this is carrying the story far beyond the general period of this Chapter, it is interesting to see how the Dutch railway planners have adopted a layout that is so very similar to those of British and other stations that have been completely modernised, by having a large number of through platforms, connected for passenger use by a very commodious subway, and individual awnings for each platform rather than the all-over roof of earlier days. The result is starkly utilitarian — thoroughly characteristic of building in the second half of the twentieth century — though ideal for the mass-handling of railway passengers.

CHAPTER TWO

Dutch steam locomotives

In the early days the Holland Railway Company purchased most of their locomotives from Germany, while the State Railway, the Dutch Rhenish, and the North Brabant strongly favoured British manufacturers. The English firm of Beyer, Peacock and Company developed a series of standard designs capable of adaptation to suit a variety of different running conditions, and by the 1850s examples of both the 2–2–2 and the 2–4–0 type were giving fast and reliable service in several different countries. Unlike many British-built locomotives of that period the frames were entirely inside, while the driving wheel splashers had no side protection at all. Locomotives of both wheel arrangements were at work in the 1850s on most of the constituent companies that were amalgamated to form the Great Northern Railway of Ireland and about the year 1860, the Netherlands State Railway being in need of some new engines went to Beyer, Peacocks in Manchester, and bought some of the standard 2–2–2s and 2–4–0s virtually 'off the shelf'. They were excellent engines, and from the transaction there sprang a long and fruitful association between the firm and the railway company.

The Irish engines, and those the firm supplied to other countries have long since disappeared; but in Holland the memory of them is venerated. In 1863 the first deliveries consisted of four 2–2–2s and four 2–4–0s, and they were used on the Breda-Tilburg, Roosendaal-Bergen-op-Zoom, and Harlingen-Leeuwarden lines. The 2–4–0s became the backbone of the State Railway services in early days and between 1865 and 1872 another 70 were imported from England. As a tribute to the service they rendered in those formative years one of them has been restored to its original condition and style of painting, and is preserved in the Railway Museum at Utrecht. That is not all. Among the many beautiful scale models in the museum there is a Beyer, Peacock 2–2–2, engine No. 1. These neat, typically English designs make an interesting contrast to the German-built 'Nestor', also in the museum. This latter was one of a batch of 29 built by Borsig in Berlin in 1878–1883, of characteristically gaunt appearance, and having a large wooden cab. Although looking so different they were equally good engines as the Beyer, Peacocks.

While Borsigs were building locomotives for the Holland Railway the cordial association between the State Railway and Beyer Peacocks was carried an important stage further in 1880 with the production of the P/3 class of 2–4–0. This was not a standard product of the firm, but a design worked out jointly to meet the special requirements of the railway. It was one of the most beautiful and successful of all locomotives exported from England in the nineteenth century. Unlike the early 'standard' engines the P/3 had outside frames throughout, and these were painted in light red, admirably showing off the basic grass green livery of these engines. They had coupled wheels of no less than 2133 mm. diameter; the typical Beyer copper-capped chimney; and a large polished brass dome with a bell-mouthed top. No fewer than 176 of these splendid engines were supplied in the years 1880–1895, and it is not surprising to find a fully restored representative of so widely appreciated a design in the museum at Utrecht. Three of them were allocated to the North Brabant Railway, for working the German mail trains on the Flushing-Wesel route.

At the same time as Beyer, Peacocks were turning out the first of the P/3 2–4–0s for the State Railway, another famous British firm, Sharp Stewart & Co., then also operating in Manchester built ten very fine 4–4–0 locomotives for the Dutch Rhenish Railway. Except for their cabs, which were large and rather closed in, they were of typically British appearance, and very distinguished in a chocolate brown livery with red frames and red wheels. They were the first engines in Holland to have a leading bogie, but did not remain long in their original ownership. In 1890 there was a take-over, and the 'Rhenish' was acquired jointly by the Holland and the State Railways. At first the 'Rhine-bogies' as they were known were parcelled out, four to the 'Holland' and five to the State administrations; but later they were all allocated to the Holland. They did so well that a further 50 were built between 1891 and 1903 for general service on the Holland Railway.

One of the original engines of 1890, restored and painted in the old Rhenish livery, is in the museum at Utrecht. Some of these engines were still in regular passenger service up to the time of the Second World War. I photographed one of them at Hoorn in 1936, modified only as to colour, and having a later standard chimney instead of the original stovepipe one. It is however delightful to be able to walk round the museum at Utrecht and see so many examples of nineteenth century Dutch locomotives in the flesh. In view of the wholesale slaughter of railway equipment and rolling stock that took place in Holland during the closing stages of the Second World War, it is astonishing that any museum pieces survived. Another example of a vintage locomotive type that I saw and photographed at Hoorn in 1936 was a Beyer, Peacock 4–4–0 with outside frames, developed from the celebrated P/3 2–4–0 of 1880. This was another graceful design of which much more is to be said later. The 2–4–0 type in general survived much longer in Holland than in England, and in the late 1920s and early 1930s a remarkable number of the old outside-cylindered engines were still at work. In addition to the German-built examples, of which the preserved 'Nestor' is typical, there were quite a few of the still earlier Beyer, Peacock engines — distinguishable generally from the Germans by their shapely copper-capped chimneys, and the famous circular brass nameplate on the leading coupled wheel splasher. Engines of the outside-cylindered 2–4–0 type, both of English and German build, were to be seen at The Hague and at Hoorn at this time.

To those in search of old Dutch engines in the period between the two world wars however it was Zwolle that could prove a veritable treasure trove. For it was there that many old engines were sent after withdrawal to await scrapping, and in the 1930s it became a positive graveyard for the Beyer, Peacock outside framed 2–4–0s of the P/3 class. Having mentioned those beautiful engines it is now time to refer to their successors on the State Railway system. The 'Rhine-bogie' 4–4–0 locomotives built by Sharp Stewart & Co. for the Dutch Rhenish Railway created something of a sensation in Holland and

16

when, as previously mentioned, the nine of them were temporarily divided between the Holland and the State Railways, the latter were quick to appreciate the superior tracking qualities of a 4–4–0 over a 2–4–0; and when the five Rhenish engines were transferred to the Holland company it was decided that future State Railway express engines should be of the 4–4–0 type. But while the Holland Railway adopted the Sharp Stewart 'Rhine-bogie' as their future standard, without any modifications, the State Railway took their existing standard P/3 2–4–0, with its good steaming boiler, 457 mm. by 660 mm. cylinders and 2133 mm. coupled wheels and developed it from a 2–4–0 into a 4–4–0. As previously the new design was prepared in close consultation with Beyer Peacocks, and a most graceful and elegant new engine resulted. The first 15 were shipped from Manchester in 1899, and between that year and 1906 no fewer than 125 were added to the stock. It continued to be a completely standard design, and with further units needed urgently, ten additional engines to the same design were built by Werkspoor of Amsterdam in 1906–1907, bringing the total of the class up to 135.

These engines perpetuated the ornate green livery of the State Railway, with all its embellishments, though a curious change was to be noted in the external style of the chimney. The 2–4–0s of the P/3 class had the traditional Beyer shape tapering upwards from the base, and looking very handsome. Of course this was only so much outward show, for the 'business' interior of the chimney would need to be tapered the opposite way to suit the outward spreading cone of exhaust steam. Now the 'Rhine-bogies' had a striking and purely functional stovepipe chimney tapering outwards from the base, and this idea was followed in the new State Railway 4–4–0s of 1899 except that they had an ornamental copper top. The only thing that tended to detract from their otherwise very handsome appearance was the large main reservoir of the Westinghouse brake system, carried on the running plate on the left-hand side of the smokebox. This was however no more than a minor point. The engine crews took a great pride in their appearance, and the turn-out was usually immaculate; from contemporary accounts the same could not always be said of the express locomotives of the Holland Railway.

While the numerous additions were being made to the stud of

17

4–4–0 express locomotives a haulage problem had arisen with the very heavy German mail trains to and from Flushing. These regularly needed double-heading and before the turn of the century S. E. Haagsma, Chief Mechanical Engineer of the State Railways consulted Beyer, Peacock & Co. regarding still larger engines. The main problem was that of providing greater steam raising capacity, and it so happened that intense interest had been created in England about that time by the introduction of large passenger engines of the 4–4–2, or 'Atlantic' type on the Great Northern and on the Lancashire and Yorkshire Railways. Whether these events had any influence upon the decision of Mr. Haagsma to adopt the same type we do not know; but the performance of the L. & Y.R. 'Atlantics' were certainly the talk of the engineering community of Manchester at the same time. Be that as it may, an order for five very large 'Atlantic' engines was given to Beyer, Peacocks specially for the Flushing mail trains, and these most imposing machines were put into service in 1900. In appearance they were a very much enlarged and elongated version of the State Railway 4–4–0s, with all their salient characteristics of outside frames, much embellished boiler mountings, and a very large Belpaire firebox.

They proved powerful and free-running engines, though unfortunately prone to unsteady riding. As mentioned in the foregoing chapter, however, the railway system of the Netherlands was generally a difficult one to maintain because of the spongy nature of the ground; and what might have been a very successful engine elsewhere was found to have certain limitations. In the ordinary way engines of such tractive power could have been 4–4–0s, but the limitation of axle loading at the time to 15 tonnes made it necessary to use five rather than four axles, and this was in some ways thought to contribute to their unsteady riding. Nevertheless these engines were popular with their crews — more so than with the civil engineer who had to maintain the tracks they ran over! For travellers from England they were certainly a most impressive introduction to locomotive power on the continent of Europe though, as discerning visitors would realise later, very far from a characteristic one — either in the elegant appearance or the immaculate turn-out. At one time the mail trains were run non-stop over the 138 kilometres between Flushing and Boxtel in 110 minutes; and it is now time to refer to the various ways in which they were taken forward into Germany

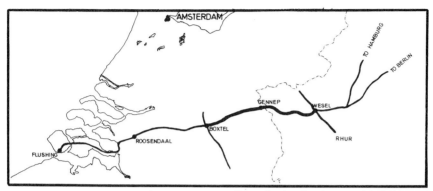

3. Position of the North Brabant German Railway in Anglo-German Mail Route

In the years before the First World War there were three definite channels of mail, passenger and tourist traffic from England to Germany via Flushing: to Hamburg and the Baltic cities; to Berlin; and to Cologne and the south. In appreciation of the build-up of train services, and of the locomotives needed to operate them the position of the North Brabant German Railway must now be described. Its highly strategic location is indicated on the accompanying sketch map. It was a remarkable concern, having no more than a single main line, nearly half of which was actually in Germany. Its relations with the State Railway system were not always friendly, and as the latter company had exclusive control of the key route west of Tilburg, the situation of the North Brabant could at times be slightly delicate. East of Tilburg the State system had two routes that were exclusively its own: north-eastwards, via Nijmegen, Arnhem and Zutphen; south-east, through Eindhoven and Venlo. This latter was good for the South German route, because once the frontier was crossed and Kaldenkirchen passed, one headed straight for Cologne. But when relations between the State Railway and the North Brabant were not so friendly the mail traffic for Berlin was routed via Venlo, and then over the circuitous and complicated line through Kempen and Crefeld to reach Oberhausen. While the State system kept the traffic to itself

19

by this route, they derived little benefit from it; the trains were subjected to much delay, and there was little opportunity for making up lost time.

In 1892 however matters were re-arranged, and all the mail trains for north and central Germany were routed via the North Brabant line, while in 1897 the South German mail from Flushing was also changed to run via Wesel, and thence to Cologne via Duisberg and Dusseldorf. This was a triumph for the North Brabant company, but it found them without suitable locomotives to haul these heavy and important trains. They obtained from Beyer, Peacock & Co. three 2–4–0 express engines of the standard State Railway's type, and these bore the heat and burden of the day for several years. But that section of the line east of the German frontier included some heavy gradients, and with increasing loads on the mail trains these 2–4–0 locomotives were unable to cope, when there was late running. It was considered not merely a point of honour but imperative to make up time in such conditions, and this the 2–4–0 engines could not do. The company had not sufficient of them to indulge in regular double heading, as the State Railway had done before the introduction of the 'Atlantics' on the Flushing route. So, as Dutch locomotive engineers had done several times previously, the North Brabant went to Beyer, Peacocks. Once again the enterprise of one of the smaller Dutch railways came to have a lasting influence upon the motive power position in the country as a whole. Just as the introduction of the 4–4–0 type by the Rhenish, in 1889, led to its general adoption, so also did the action of the North Brabant, with the 4–6–0.

No more British-looking locomotives were ever exported from England than the six big 4–6–0s that Beyer, Peacocks built for the North Brabant in 1908. They were neat, compact, and had boiler mountings that were a direct copy of the extremely graceful styles then in vogue on the Great Central Railway, and produced at the neighbouring works at Gorton, Manchester. They were finished in a gorgeous livery of royal blue, which happily has been preserved for all interested posterity to see in one of the fine models in the Dutch Railway Museum, at Utrecht. Technically they were a very simple, straightforward design, with cylinders 482 mm. diameter by 660 mm. stroke, and coupled wheels 1981 mm. diameter; but they carried

20

a boiler pressure of 14 kg. per sq. cm. which was high in Holland at that time. Their success was little short of sensational. They handled train loads of 457 tonnes with ease over the steep gradients of 1 in 120 that existed east of the German frontier. They worked the mail trains not only over their own line to its eastern extremity at Wesel, but took the North German mail as far east as Holtern, and the Berlin and South German mails to Oberhausen. The remarkable extent of this penetration will be apparent from the map.

The success of these beautiful engines attracted the attention of the State Railway and arrangements were made for one of them to be loaned for trial running between Amsterdam and Emmerich, again a heavy and important service to Germany. These trials convinced the State Railway that it would be to their advantage to introduce the 4–6–0 type, for although the main lines in the Netherlands do not include any gradients so severe as on the German section of the North Brabant, train loads were very much on the increase, and with nothing larger than 2–4–0 and 4–4–0 locomotives with 457 mm. by 660 mm. cylinders, and 2133 mm. coupled wheels tractive power was certainly limited. The five 'Atlantic' engines used on the Flushing mails were in a class by themselves, and not one suitable for adoption as a general standard. The State Railway in deciding to adopt the 4–6–0 type did not however follow the precedent set by the Holland Railway in the 1890s when it took the Rhenish 4–4–0, just as it stood. The North Brabant 4–6–0 would certainly have done the job, but there were other considerations that influenced the State Railway. Whereas the German mails over the North Brabant line involved relatively long non-stop runs the State Railway required a locomotive capable of rapid acceleration, and thus having a higher tractive effort and greater adhesion weight. Therein lay the difficulty, for the civil engineer was not prepared to allow higher axle loads.

While the State Railway's locomotive department had hitherto worked in close collaboration with Beyer, Peacock & Co., and continued to do so for many years afterwards, Dutch engineers had also friendly associations with the German manufacturers of the day, and it was indirectly through the work of the Bavarian firm of Maffei of Munich, that the solution came. That company had developed a form of 4-cylinder compound 4–6–0 that was not only giving

21

excellent service in South Germany but which, through the arrangement of its machinery, eliminated the harmful effects on the track that arose from the disposition of the balance weights in an ordinary 2-cylinder locomotive. The North Brabant 4–6–0 was a conventional 2-cylinder job, on which balance weights were placed in the wheels to balance the effects of the reciprocating and revolving parts. But these balance weights, while resulting in a smooth riding engine at express speed produced a 'hammer blow' effect on the track, so that while the dead weight per axle was only about 14 tonnes, when running at speed this was increased by the 'hammer blow' to 22 or 23 tonnes. In the Maffei 4-cylinder compounds all four cylinders drove on to the leading coupled axle, and the machinery balanced itself. There was no hammer blow. The civil engineer of the Netherlands State Railway was prepared to accept an axle load of 16 tonnes if it was not augmented by hammer blow at speed; and so Beyer, Peacocks were given the task of designing a powerful new 4–6–0, with four cylinders, all driving on the leading pair of coupled wheels.

It so happened that Maffei were also building some new 4–6–0s for the Dutch Central Railway, and they too were designed as 4-cylinder machines. They, like the English-built engines for the State Railway, were single expansion not compounds. This was all taking place in 1909–1910, and the helpful understanding between the civil and mechanical engineers in Holland was in some contrast to what happened on the English London and North Western Railway. At Crewe the Chief Mechanical Engineer, C. J. Bowen Cooke, was planning a large new express passenger locomotive and, being aware of the merits of the Maffei layout of machinery, designed a 4-cylinder 4–6–0 with all four cylinders driving on to the leading pair of coupled wheels, and no hammer blow. He hoped to get the civil engineer's agreement to an axle load, static, of about 21 tonnes; but the civil engineer was deaf to all the arguments that had such happy results in Holland, and Bowen Cooke had to re-design his big engine to have a smaller boiler and reduce the axle load to a maximum of 20 tonnes.

The Dutch 4–6–0s of 1910 were extremely successful engines, and a total of 120 were eventually built. The four cylinders were 408 mm. in diameter, by 660 mm. stroke, and the coupled wheels were 1854 mm. diameter. They had the Walschaerts valve gear, arranged inside, and the valves of the outside cylinders were actuated through a rocking shaft mechanism. The first 36 were built by Beyer, Peacock in 1910–1914, but construction of them continued by various Dutch and German manufacturers until the last five, which were put into service in 1928. One of these splendid engines, No. 3737, has been preserved and until early in 1973 was a static exhibit in the Railway Museum at Utrecht. But it has since been restored to a fully operable condition, and is now used on occasions for special excursion trips. No finer example of a European steam locomotive of the 1900–1910 decade could be imagined. The contemporary 4-cylinder 4–6–0 of the Netherlands Central Railway, built by Maffei was an equally distinctive design, especially in respect of its striking livery. This was an exact replica of the Stroudley style on the London, Brighton and South Coast Railway, in bright yellow; but there was little else remotely English about these engines. They were a very typical German design of the period, though in their long and useful service, particularly after the 'Central' had become part of the State system, they underwent several changes that made them look slightly more Dutch, than originally.

The standard 4-cylinder 4–6–0s of the State Railway remained the most powerful passenger engines in Holland until 1929 when a considerably larger and more powerful version was introduced. This was the '3900' class, also a 4-cylinder 4–6–0 but with larger boiler and firebox, cylinders 419 mm. in diameter, instead of 408 mm. and a boiler pressure of 14 kg. per sq. cm. By the time these fine engines were introduced the basic engine livery had been much simplified, to a plain olive green, but still retaining polished brass dome covers and copper-capped chimneys. These engines were followed by a series of huge 4–8–4 tank engines, having interchangeable cylinders and machinery with the 4–6–0 passenger engines, but with a reduced size coupled wheel. These engines were all built by German firms; one of them has been preserved, and is among the full-sized static exhibits at the Railway Museum in Utrecht. This 4–8–4 tank was the last type of steam locomotive to be designed for the Netherlands Railways, and it certainly was a worthy termination of a notable history.

Dutch steam locomotives did not have to run at the speeds that

23

were later customary in England, France or Germany, but they certainly had to pull heavy loads, and they had their own particular problems of operation. The Dutch Central 4–6–0s, the yellow engines, were originally designed to work only on their own system between Utrecht and Zwolle, but at a slightly later period arrangements were made for reciprocal working with State Railway 4–6–0s. The Central engines on some trains worked through from Utrecht to Groningen, while by way of balance State Railway 4–6–0s worked southwards over the Central line to complete the entire run from Groningen to Utrecht. After the absorption of both the Central and the North Brabant into the amalgamated State Railway system, which included the Holland company, the individual locomotives, although repainted, underwent little change otherwise in their appearance. The maximum limit of speed in the later steam days was 109 km./h., though this was rarely approached in ordinary service.

CHAPTER THREE

Holland — the great metamorphosis

It is now nearly forty years since I first went to Holland; although not on a purely railway safari, I travelled a good deal and saw the Dutch railways at the beginning of a marked stage of transition. Some sections of the line had been electrified on the 1500 volt direct current system, with pick-up from overhead line. Electric trains were running into the Hook; the line from Rotterdam was then the most recent section to be electrified, and the local trains were extremely fine. They were made up of two-car articulated sets, and finished in a handsome colour scheme of grey and scarlet. The interior effect was entirely grey, relieved by a liberal amount of chromium plating. They ran very smartly, with speed rising to 88.5 km./h. in about 1.2 km. from each start from a station; and when a new one of these units was driven all-out for test purposes, between Rotterdam and Amsterdam, it reached a speed of 160 km./h. But this very pleasant introduction to Dutch electric trains was short lived. The train for the north into which I changed at Schiedam was very different. It was a dull and uninviting thing, one of the older multiple-unit type, rather like the earlier rolling stock on the Metropolitan District Railway in London but in a dull, dingy dark green style of painting. I found they nipped along quite smartly, but to a railway lover they were about as inspiring as an old style omnibus or tram with no upholstery on the seats into the bargain. But I had left the Harwich steamer and breakfasted in time to see two international express trains leave the Hook; and with the memory of that new 'electric' also I was largely reassured. Both the North German and the South German expresses were steam hauled by the earlier type of 4-cylinder 4–6–0. It was in the very height of the tourist season, and both trains were heavy; and

25

although neither of the locomotives was immaculate the cleaners had not neglected to shine up those polished brass domes.

The journey to Amsterdam, broken by sightseeing visits to Delft and The Hague rather savoured of the Southern electric service at home, except that most of the Dutch multiple-unit electric trains were not so smartly kept; but I saw also that the signalling was almost entirely mechanical, with both semaphore arms and points operated by the double-wire system. Over much of the continent of Europe this latter was the standard method of actuation before the days of electric operation and colour light signals. The method can be most simply described as that of an endless rope passing round wheels at both the signal box end, and at the function to be operated. In practice the 'rope' is not continuous, but is anchored to the wheels at each end. The operating wheels in the signal box are connected to the levers. The latter stand normally at much the same angle as in a conventional British interlocking frame; but instead of needing a pull through a relatively small angle the levers in a double-wire interlocking machine have to be pulled through a half-circle, and finish up pointing downwards, diametrically opposite to the position from which they started. The double-wire system obviates the need for having a solid rodding for working the points, and it was generally favoured in Holland, Belgium, and Germany. Today however with the rapid introduction of electrical methods of signalling and point operation, it is being replaced. The Dutch semaphore signals are of the upper-quadrant type, and although they can still be seen at many busy junctions they are gradually giving way before the all-conquering colour lights.

Once I arrived in Amsterdam there was evidence, even as long as 40 years ago, of more pronounced changes. It is true there was still much steam to be seen, with the largest 4-cylinder 4–6–0 locomotives on the international express trains from Germany and the south, but amongst these there were some startling newcomers in the form of streamlined three-coach diesel electric multiple-unit trains, in the same striking livery of red and grey as I had seen on the electric trains running between the Hook and Rotterdam. Although few of us realised it at the time this was the first step towards a new philosophy of passenger train operation within Holland itself and the eventual elimination of locomotive haulage of any kind, steam, diesel, or electric. At the time of my first visit there were two very special international express trains that will figure again in this account of European railways. One was the 'Edelweiss Express', which then left Amsterdam at 8.06 and made its way south via Brussels, Luxembourg, Strasbourg and the Alsace-Lorraine main line into Switzerland. It was composed entirely of Pullman cars, and although conveying only four cars from the start it received many substantial additions on the way south. The other all-Pullman celebrity was 'L'Etoile du Nord' which then, as now, ran non-stop from Brussels to Paris. In Holland in those pre-war days both trains were hauled by the older 4-cylinder 4–6–0 locomotives.

The changes in passenger traffic operating policy, of which I had seen some of the beginnings in the late 1930s, were accompanied by the embodiment of some advanced techniques in locomotive and rolling stock design; and the trials of one of the new streamlined electric trains up to a maximum of 160 km./h. was only one manifestation of the fact that the Dutch railway administration was not thinking merely of changes in the traction system. I should explain also that while an arrangement for pooling traffic between the two principal systems, the 'Holland Railway' and the 'State', had been in operation since 1917 full amalgamation took place from January 1, 1938, and the new organisation then took the title of 'Netherlands Railways'. By that time the introduction of new multiple-unit electric and diesel-electric trains had progressed to such an extent that a very thorough revision of timetables was made in the summer of 1938. While up to that time most passenger train services had been leisurely to a degree the new services included no fewer than 227 runs timed at 96 km./h. and over from start to stop, representing a total of 6214 kilometres. This was remarkable in itself for so relatively small a country, but to lovers of the old order it was significant that all these runs were made either by electric, or diesel-electric multiple-unit trains. The fastest steam runs at that time — $66^1/_2$ kilometres between Amersfoort and Zwolle in 45 minutes (89 km./h.) — showed a remarkable advance over previous standards, but the diesel-electrics were doing the same run in 38 minutes, at 105 km./h.!

This splendid transformation scarcely had time to settle into its stride however before war came again, in September 1939. At first, as in 1914, Holland was not directly involved, but the sudden invasion of the Low Countries in May 1940 changed everything. In the first hours of the attack the fearfully concentrated bombardment of Rotterdam virtually destroyed all existing railway facilities around the city centre, though the early collapse of military resistance in Holland made it unnecessary to repeat such tactics elsewhere. It was in the interests of the Nazi invaders to keep the railway system in good shape; but of course this enemy occupation brought to a temporary end all ordinary railway development in Holland. It was not until the year 1944 that Dutch railwaymen were called upon to play an active and terrible part towards the re-entry of Allied troops on to the continent of Europe. In September of that year all personnel concerned with the running of trains ceased work and 'went underground'. The Nazi invaders had to carry on as best they could, providing footplate crews and signalmen from among their own troops. Destruction of trains and fixed equipment by sabotage and Allied bombing was tremendous, while the great battles following the British airborne landings at Arnhem and Nijmegen resulted in the virtual destruction of all railway property in those areas, including unfortunately the magnificent station at Nijmegen, one of the finest in Holland. The end of the war left the Netherlands Railways in a shockingly crippled condition as will be appreciated from the following comparative statistics of locomotives and rolling stock in 1939 and 1945.

Rolling Stock Totals

	Sept. 1939	July 1945
Steam Locomotives	865	334
Streamlined electric multiple-unit trains	430	80
Diesel-electric trains	82	36
Steam train passenger carriages	1,908	233
Goods wagons of all kinds	30,453	1,073

Such figures simply make one gasp! And when I add that the workshops of the Locomotive Carriage and Wagon Department at Utrecht, Rotterdam, Haarlem and Amsterdam were mostly reduced to fire-blackened empty skeletons, stripped by the retreating enemy of any machinery that remained serviceable, one can indeed wonder how on earth the Netherlands Railway began to rebuild.

The task of rehabilitation was however tackled with the utmost vigour and determination. While the war was at its height, indeed while the Government of the Netherlands was resident in London, something of the situation that eventuated in 1945 was foreseen and orders were placed with the Swedish firm of Nydqvist & Holm of Trollhatten, for 35 goods and 15 passenger locomotives for delivery after the war. Extensive damage to the electrified system was also foreseen, and it was generally agreed that the quickest way to get things moving again would be with steam. The locomotives ordered from Sweden were of the 3-cylinder simple type, 0–8–0 for goods and 4–6–0 for passenger. They were delivered in 1946, by which time the railway shops in Holland were building more of the successful 4-cylinder 4–6–0s of the '3900' class. This of course was not enough to secure a return to anything near normality, and in 1947 22 compound 4–6–0s were purchased from the Swiss Federal Railways. These latter were veterans, having been built as long ago as 1907–1915; but they were a design of excellent repute, and were still in good condition. Because of the increasing spread of electrification they were surplus to requirements in Switzerland. As 4-cylinder locomotives with all four cylinders driving on to the leading coupled axle, these Swiss veterans would no doubt have appealed, by tradition, to steam locomotive men in Holland. This use of steam was no more than an interim stage in the rebuilding of the Dutch railway system, and in the meantime important discussions were taking place towards more permanent facets of modernisation.

The success of the electric and diesel-electric multiple-unit trains in the first phase of the transition, in 1938, had confirmed the view that the entire internal network of passenger services in Holland could profitably be operated by such trains, and that locomotive haulage could be confined to the international trains and to freight. The fact that the system of traction, at 1500 volts direct current, was the same as that which had been recommended for main line electrification in Great Britain, and which was in course of installation on the Manchester-Sheffield line of the London and North Eastern Railway, led to discussions between British and Dutch locomotive engineers, and arrangements were made for the pioneer LNER electric locomotive, No. 6000, to be shipped over to Holland for trial running. The successful working of this locomotive led to a decision to purchase units of similar tractive capacity of the Bo + Bo type, and these were eventually obtained from the French firm of Alsthom, 'off the shelf' so to speak, which had a standard design that could be readily adapted to Dutch use.

The most interesting and important features of railway modernisation in the Netherlands have taken place in the realms of signalling and traffic controls. Lovers of the old-time railways must make a sojourn in the museum at Utrecht to satisfy their abiding fancy; and I can say from several visits there that it can be a very satisfying experience. One has to look behind the scenes as it were to find the real fascination of a modern railway system composed of little more than swarms of multiple-unit electric and diesel-electric trains speeding, with effortless ease and the punctuality of chronometers, through a busy and complicated national network. Holland provides a very interesting example of the process of evolution that has taken place in the use of colour light signals. In the first phase of reconstruction after the war, a novel but rather complicated code of indications was devised. Unlike long established practice in Great Britain, the Dutch considered it essential to advise the driver, by signal, of the speed at which he must travel — 'maximum', 'medium' and 'low' speed — with variations according to the particular line over which he was travelling. In 1952 however when the General Manager of the day asked the Signal Engineer to draw up a comprehensive plan for the colour-light signalling of the entire network, the magnitude of the project led to some intensive re-thinking. As the distinguished signal engineer, H.A.E. de Vos tot Nederveen Cappel, once said:

We realised that if millions of guilders should be invested in a modern signalling system it would not be possible to modify it in the next ten years.

30

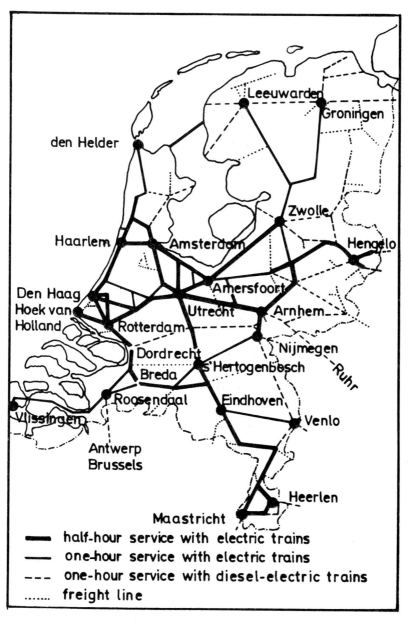

4. Network of the Netherlands Railways

Under his direction an extremely simple system was evolved to replace the isolated instances of the older more complicated plants, and to be provided as standard for the future. The three basic colours of green, yellow and red were to be used for their internationally understood functions of 'travel at maximum permissible speed of the line'; 'slow down', and 'stop'; but they were to be elaborated by the addition of illuminated figures displayed below the signal, reminding the driver of what the maximum permissible speed over the section concerned actually was, when less than the normal. In the last mentioned case the signal was a green light, and nothing else; but if on such a line there was a section where speed had to be reduced, say to 70 km./h. the driver would first be presented with a yellow light, with an illuminated figure 7 below it by way of warning, and at the point where the restriction began he would see a green light once again, but flashing instead of steady and again with the figure 7 below it. These principles, with a few variations to deal with special cases, were adopted for the national resignalling plan put into effect from 1954 onwards.

Concurrently with this new signalling plan there was developed one of the most methodical regular systems of passenger train service ever devised in any country. On the busiest routes there was to be a half hour service of electric trains throughout the day. On the less busy electrified lines the service frequency was to be hourly, supplemented by an hourly service of diesel-electric trains on the non-electrified routes. The effect of this remarkably enterprising development will be apparent from the accompanying map. This also shows the purely freight lines, and one can note in particular that the one-time crack North German mail route from England, via the North Brabant line, is now used only for freight. Superimposed upon these purely Dutch services are the important international trains: these include frequent connections to Belgium and Germany, together with the longer distance trains to France, Switzerland, South Germany, and Scandinavia.

The intensity of working over certain sections and the experience of a serious accident in 1962 led to the decision to install automatic train control, and again after studies of systems currently in use in various parts of the world, it was decided to adopt one that provided *continuous* indication in the driver's cab. Having been associated for many years with the British intermittent system, and had the privilege of seeing other intermittent systems in operation, it is interesting to find that the Dutch have invested in the more elaborate and expensive continuous system. One of the reasons for their choice was the undoubted superiority of the information given to the driver in conditions of bad visibility. During the winter, railway working in Holland has often to be conducted when heavy sea fogs envelop much of the low-lying country, and from an early date in Dutch railway history an aid to signal sighting in bad weather was provided by the inclined warning boards, known as *baaks*. These are long wooden planks sloping gradually upwards, roughly at driver's eye level, painted white on the top surface with a series of horizontal black stripes across. These were mounted at the line side on the approach to signals, and were of great help to drivers in establishing their position in respect to an important signal they were approaching in fog.

Nevertheless the *baak* was all very well in the days of steam and more leisurely running. Nowadays the multiple-unit electric and diesel-electric trains have to run at speeds of more than 129 km./h. to keep their schedules, and as every effort is made to run normally, whatever the weather, the adjunct of continuously displayed signals in the driver's cab is invaluable. On the dashboard is a panel with six illuminated indications, which are displayed in the appropriate circumstances as follows:

Green	maximum permissible speed, 140 km./h.
Yellow, with figure 13	maximum 130 km./h.
Yellow, with figure 8	maximum 80 km./h.
Yellow, with figure 6	maximum 60 km./h.
Yellow (no figure)	maximum 40 km./h. be prepared to stop at next signal
Blue, with letters BD	the train control apparatus is switched off, but is ready to come into operation when you enter train control territory

In automatic train control territory the panel indications in the driver's cab are continuously displayed, changing according to the

33

state of the line ahead and for any permanent speed restrictions that might apply. The control is effected through an inductive electrical link between a receiver on the train and coded currents flowing in the track rails. A bell is rung when there is any change in the cab signal indication and if, within a brief pre-determined time, the driver has not braked sufficiently to bring the speed down to the lower figure required, control is taken out of his hands and the train is stopped. I had an opportunity of riding in the cab of a fast train on the main line running down to the most southerly point of Holland from Utrecht, through 's-Hertogenbosch and Eindhoven to Roermond and Maastricht, and found the indications arrestive and most helpful in their aid to the driver.

In other respects the methods of regulation of railway traffic in Holland are now among the foremost in the world. It is said that today on all the most thoroughly modernised of railways the signalman is going increasingly hand in hand with the computer. This is certainly so in some of the largest installations on the Netherlands Railways. The density of passenger traffic in the peak hours is constantly increasing, imposing a load far greater than the regular pattern imagined from a study of the basic timetable represented by the map on page 31, and while train movement can be planned to a high degree of precision in such busy areas as Amsterdam, Utrecht, and Rotterdam, a factor that becomes of ever greater concern is the disturbance that can be caused by the late running of no more than a single train. While the purely domestic services may run with clock-like punctuality, some of the international trains arrive in Holland after travelling many hundreds of kilometres across Europe, and a variety of dissimilar causes may affect their punctuality.

The signal engineers of the Netherlands Railways have constantly been seeking ways to improve control of a situation that could lead to wide disturbance of train running if allowed to proceed unhindered. An example will make the beginnings of such a disturbance clear. There is a regular timetable plan of train movement in a large station like Amsterdam Central, with each train having its appointed platform during its stop there, and its recognised route through the maze of tracks into and out of the station. Then for example, an

34

important international express train, for reasons outside Holland, draws near to this central area 15 or 20 minutes late. Its appointed platform would then be occupied by another train. If the normal path were kept clear there might be widespread disturbance. An improvisation has to be made, and the problem is to decide what improvisation will cause the least all-round disturbance, having regard to the reaction from the initial re-arrangement of the workings. The operating methods of the Netherlands Railways have already passed far beyond the situation in which the modern all-electric form of signalling control, with the push-button control panels, has superseded the older traditional form of mechanical lever interlockings. This, at a single stage, removed technical constraints and most of the physical effort; but it was felt that this was not quick enough, and that the most sophisticated aids to decision making were necessary.

Inevitably the word 'computer' comes to one's lips. But while a computer can be the fastest and most efficient decision-making device yet known it can function so only if it is fed with the fullest, most comprehensive, and most accurate information. To do this at a railway station of the size of Amsterdam Central would require a colossal amount of electronic equipment, and an even more colossal capital expenditure in order to meet what might be no more than ten or a dozen 'situations' in the course of an otherwise normal day's workings. In studying the problem and planning for the future the engineers of the Netherlands Railways came to the conclusion that the greatest measure of relief was likely to be most economically obtained if the operating staff could be relieved of their routine tasks, such as push button panel operation for signalling trains running punctually in their scheduled timetable paths, and free to concentrate on the more vital task of traffic regulation, when needed. It was considered that the control of the system as a whole should be on the principle of 'management by exception': with the situation normal, and train running to time the whole process of route setting and signalling should be automatic, on somewhat similar lines to those provided by the 'Programme Machines' that regulate the traffic on the Underground railways in London. If an exception to normal should occur, as in the case of an international train running late, the

35

system should alarm the operator concerned and provide him with full details of the current situation, so that the area likely to be disturbed can be minimised.

It is this principle that has governed the remarkable equipment that has been superimposed at Amsterdam Central upon an existing, and otherwise thoroughly modern installation of push button signalling control. Already its effectiveness has been found such that similar plans are being drawn up for its application at Utrecht, and it will no doubt be applied later to other crowded areas of this very busy railway system. Today the Netherlands Railways are indeed a veritable epitome of the changing aspect of all railway working. It is like the modern electric and diesel-electric locomotives; the ingenuity and success of their operation is concealed, not merely behind their sleek and largely 'faceless' exteriors, but in a wealth of electrical circuits and miniature electronic components. The railway enthusiasts of today have not been long either, if not exactly switching their love and allegiance from the steam locomotive, but in recognising the immense potentialities of the techniques of the new age, and in studying what lies behind the casings of the new locomotives, and on the floors beneath the panel rooms in the new signal boxes. But it is time we were leaving this splendid and forward-looking railway system: the hour of departure of the mid-morning express for Brussels and Paris is near, and our final experience of the Netherlands Railways is from a large and luxurious corridor carriage of the SNCF.

CHAPTER FOUR

Belgium — the first all-national railway system

The express for Paris leaves the new ultra-modern station of Rotterdam, swings round to the south, and is soon crossing the great bridge that gives so magnificent a prospect over the port area and all its manifold activities. We speed on over the level country of the Waal and Maas river deltas, through Dordrecht with a sight of its glorious cathedral, and on to the important junction of Roosendaal. Here the one-time Anglo-German mail route is intersected and it is also the frontier station for interchange with the Belgian railways. The actual border is some ten miles to the south, but until recently Roosendaal was the point of customs examination; it is still of course the station where locomotives are changed, and the system of electric traction changes from the Dutch 1500 volts to the Belgian 3000 volts. Since the setting up of the European Economic Community customs formalities for ordinary passengers have been waived. Engineering developments have also removed the necessity for engine changing with certain highly advanced types of locomotives; but I must not jump over the earlier part of the story, and motive power in Belgium had to pass through an extraordinarily varied 'line of succession' before arriving at the remarkable 'quadri-current' electric locomotives introduced in 1973.

Among the earlier railways of the world, those of Belgium are unique in being planned and sponsored by the State from the outset. By an Act of Parliament passed in 1834 the principle of State ownership was accepted, and thereafter the network was planned as a whole, to foster the industrial development of the country. In the stormy days of the seventeenth, eighteenth and nineteenth centuries Belgium was often referred to as 'the cockpit of Europe'; in the railway era it became a general cross-roads. Nevertheless in view of the unified origin and central planning that directed the network, it was remarkable that in technical matters its advance was less marked than in countries where there were many independent companies, each playing its own individual hand. Perhaps it was the very fact of national control from the start that hindered development! Hindrance or not, however, Belgian locomotive practice in the nineteenth century provides one of the most fascinating fields of research for the historian, and one cannot but regret that the many skilful photographers of the present day did not have their counterparts in the 'seventies' and 'eighties' of the last century, to capture in colour the fantastic machines that ran the rails in Belgium.

Just imagine the astonishment of a traveller from England entering Belgium for the first time, and climbing down from his carriage to watch the engine changing at Roosendaal; he would see the beautiful Beyer Peacock 2–4–0 of the State Railway, elegant in all its finery, uncouple and pull away, and then his gaze could well change into sheer disbelief that his eyes were seeing such things, as a Belgian 'Columbia' 2–4–2 came backing down. Was ever such an assemblage put on wheels? All angles and corners: a semblance of British style in its outside framing and coupling rods — but then that strange splayed out firebox, and above all the huge *square* funnel. The 'Columbias' were quite large engines for their day, but in outline they seemed to defy every canon of style, that demanded at least some balanced symmetry. They were nevertheless fascinating in their very oddity, though not very effective in their performance. The engineers of the Belgian State Railways seemed by the 1890s to have become excessively gadget minded, for these engines, like their predecessors, included a number of clever if unorthodox features.

It is interesting to recall that two truly great men in the locomotive history of the world were Belgians, and by a coincidence both were born in the same year, 1820. Alfred Jules Belpaire, inventor of the form of firebox that bears his name, was born at Ostend and became chief mechanical engineer of the State Railway in 1864. It was in that same year that his form of firebox, with its flat top and — in Belgium — wide sloping grate was first introduced. He later became Administrative President of the railway. His work as a locomotive

38

engineer won him international fame, and before his death in 1893 he had been accorded honours by France, Holland, Russia and Spain, in addition to his own country. But it may be no more than a coincidence that the wide adoption of his firebox in Great Britain and the U.S.A. did not come until after his death. Egide Walschaerts was born at Mechelen, and his career on the Belgian State Railways was throughout at a much humbler level. For a period of 40 years, from 1844 to 1885, he was mechanical foreman at the Schaerbeck Depot near Brussels, and the first form of his world-famous valve gear was patented as long ago as 1844. Although its first application was in 1848, it did not 'catch on', to use a colloquialism; it was largely forgotten until after his death in 1901, though its use began in France in the 1890s.

From one cause and another however, despite the influence and status of Belpaire, the Belgian State Railways gathered together an extraordinary assortment of locomotives, of which the 2–4–2 'Columbias' were in many ways the climax. They had been introduced in 1888, and after the death of Belpaire in 1893, the management seemed rather at a loss as to what to do for future motive power.

They did some 'shopping around', as the saying goes, looking at contemporary French, German and Austrian designs. Then some representatives went to Scotland in 1897, and saw the 'Dunalastair' 4–4–0s of the Caledonian Railway. To say that they were deeply impressed would be an understatement. The Belgian Government approached John F. McIntosh, the Locomotive Superintendent, and asked him to build five of the latest version of the 'Dunalastair' for service in Belgium. This of course he could not do because the Acts of Incorporation of the British railway companies forbade them to build locomotives except for their own use; but the Caledonian Railway Board were so delighted at this foreign recognition of the merits of their locomotives that they agreed to McIntosh acting as consultant and inspecting engineer if the contract was placed with a firm in Glasgow. The Caledonian Railway was on cordial terms with Neilson, Reid & Co.; the works of that company in the Springburn district of Glasgow was quite near to the railway works at St. Rollox, and liaison was easy. The Caledonian supplied a complete set of drawings and much expert advice, and apart from certain changes made to suit Belgian conditions, such as providing for the driver to be situated on the right hand side of the cab instead of on the left, the five locomotives were virtual duplicates of the Caledonian '766' class even to the details of painting, in the ever famous 'Caley Blue'.

When they arrived in Belgium they created something of a sensation. Even among the traditionally neat and artistically styled British locomotives of the nineteenth century the 'Dunalastairs' of the '766' series held a very high place; but alongside the strange chocolate brown Belgian 'Columbias' the contrast was quite extraordinary. Jack Hill has captured some of this effect in his picture of the boat trains at Ostend just about the turn of the century. In Belgium, if the first impressions created by the 'Dunalastairs' were those of surprise and outward admiration, their simplicity of mechanical design and splendid working efficiency led to the development of the type by Belgian engineers: larger 4–4–0s for passenger service, 0–6–0s for goods, and a 4–4–2 tank engine for shorter distance passenger duties. But before going on to describe the very interesting twentieth century development of the steam locomotive in Belgium something must be said about the railway network itself. For a network planned by direct Government supervision, the Belgian Railway system had some interesting and perhaps unexpected features. The capital city of Brussels was made the focal point of the entire system and the railway map of Belgium, in its most simplified form, could be likened to the 'spokes' of a wheel extending outwards from the central hub of Brussels.

Starting from the westward spoke, this was a line to the most historic city of Tournai, and continued over the French frontier to Lille and thence to Arras. The north-westward spoke went through Ghent and Bruges to Ostend, and the direct north line, including the very first railway in Belgium, ran via Malines to Antwerp. The main line running almost due east headed for Liege, and thence via Aachen into Germany and Cologne and next, the south-eastern line, passed through Namur and continued to the far south of the country into Luxembourg. The last of these main line spokes, running south-westwards from Brussels is the main line to Paris, passing through Mons, and entering France at Quevy-le-Petit. Although the general

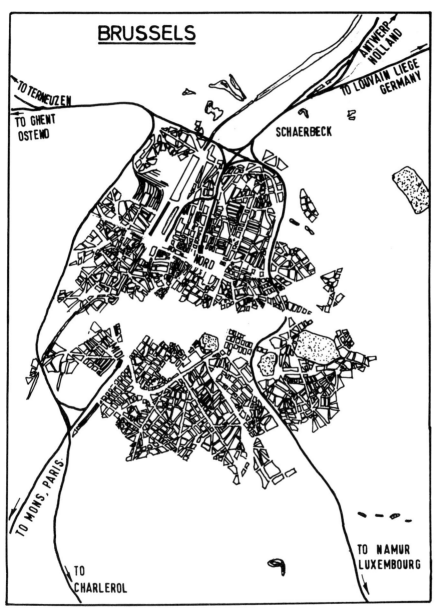

5. Railways in Brussels

layout of railways in Belgium was definitely Government inspired, not all of them were originally built with Government funds. One of the largest that was built by private enterprise, and afterwards taken over by the State was the Luxembourg line. It was actually built by an English company, and in the Continental Bradshaw of the 1870s was described as the 'Great Luxembourg Railway'. It also had a rather amusing subtitle; 'From London to the Baths of Germany, the Rhine, and Switzerland via Brussels, the Meuse and the Moselle'. At that time however when the railway was in private ownership one could not obtain a through ticket from England. It was necessary to re-book in Brussels.

This brings me to the railway geography of Brussels, which in some respects was similar to that of Paris — though for different reasons. Until quite recent years no railway penetrated into the city centre of Brussels. Originally, as shown on the accompanying sketch map the lines from Ostend, Antwerp, Liege, and even that from Luxembourg all came in at the Nord station through the elaborate system of junctions at Schaerbeck. On the other side of the city the lines from Tournai and Mons came in at the Midi station. As in Paris there were lines encircling the central area connecting the systems north and south of the city, and used by freight trains. The eastern link was also used by through express passenger trains from north to south, such as those running through from Holland to Paris, or to Luxembourg and Switzerland. But these trains had to enter Brussels Nord, a terminus, and then reverse direction before resuming their journeys to the south and south-west. It was the same in the case of through trains from Ostend to Liege and Germany.

The inconvenience of these reversals had been recognised from a very early date in Belgian railway history. A direct line from north to south through the very centre of Brussels had been proposed first in 1836. It became a major political issue, and for more than *seventy years* arguments ranged fierce and wide, with nothing in the way of a decision attained. Most of the controversy seems to have turned on the conservationist issue, for all the proposals seriously considered involved a surface line, and consequent demolition of property in the heart of the city along the proposed route. Shortly before the outbreak of the First World War however a scheme did actually receive approval, and work commenced on a viaduct leading north from the Midi station. The new central station was to have been sited almost exactly half way between the existing Midi and Nord stations, near the church of St. Gudule. But on the outbreak of war in August 1914 work was stopped; the construction partly completed was abandoned, and in the event work on this particular scheme was never resumed. In the 1930s there had been hopes that a resumption would be possible, but the outbreak of the Second World War finally sealed the fate of this long discussed scheme. How the idea of a central station eventually came to fruition must be told later.

Brussels was not the only Belgian city to have an inconvenient railway layout in the nineteenth century. An express train entering the country from the north soon comes to Antwerp, and there a complete half-circle to the west had to be negotiated to enter the magnificent terminal station. Originally this was the end of one of the 'spoke' lines from Brussels, and international trains had to reverse direction and proceed round the half-circle before continuing to the north. Nowadays, however, through trains call at the new East station on the direct line, and their passengers are denied the chance of seeing the spectacular front of the Central station. Those responsible for building some of the large city stations of Belgium seem to have had a taste for oriental adornment. The St. Pierre station in Ghent might be in the Middle East or India, while at Antwerp Central the outward end of the tremendous single arch train shed is flanked by a couple of magnificent minarets.

The nineteenth century aspect of most Belgian stations was equally distinguished by the signals. The English firm of Saxby and Farmer supplied much of the original equipment, using that highly distinctive mechanism by which two semaphore arms controlling traffic in opposite directions were mounted on the same spindle. Often the posts were mounted directly on the top of signal cabins themselves on gantries spanning the tracks, and made the approaches to Brussels, Verviers and elsewhere look like Charing Cross or London Bridge. By the end of the nineteenth century the Belgian State Railways had one of the most comprehensive systems of signalling anywhere on the continent of Europe. All the main line stations were fully interlocked mostly using the well-known 'rocker and grid' type of lever frame

43

manufactured by Saxby and Farmer, in England. This forward-looking attitude in Belgium was continued in the twentieth century, under the very distinguished signal engineer Louis Weissenbruch, who in 1903 designed and installed notable electric signalling for Antwerp Central station. But the historic and unfortunate situation of Belgium as 'the cockpit of Europe' repeated itself in 1914, and the occupation of most of the country by German forces for practically the entire period of the First World War not only stopped the normal order of railway progress, but led to expedients and improvisations which had to be removed before post-war development could begin.

The first weeks of war proved an exciting and desperate period for the Belgian Railways. While the fortress towns of Liege and Namur were holding out, bridges were destroyed, tunnels blocked, and in one case a *posse* of five unmanned locomotives was sent to meet a German troop train in head-on collision! A line of defence, and ultimate retreat was along a section of the Nord–Belge Railway between Liege and Namur. This was a line with a curious origin. Though forming part of the State approved network, it had been built by a British-owned company, incorporated in Belgium to which a concession had been granted in 1845. This was known as the 'Société de Chemins de fer de Namur à Liége et de Mons à Manage'. In 1854 however the British company ceased to work the line, and made it over to the Northern Railway of France, which under the name Nord–Belge worked it henceforth on payment of a fixed annual rental to the Belgian government. It became part of the main route from Paris to Cologne and the industrial districts of the lower Rhineland, which included another Nord–Belge section from the French frontier near Jeumont to Charleroi, separated from the original stretch by a section of purely Belgian State line between Charleroi and Namur.

Perhaps the most important international route of all, in Belgium, is that from Brussels southwards to the French frontier where another section of the Nord–Belge system extends from the complicated railway purlieus of Mons to the actual frontier at Quevy-le-Petit, and makes an end-on junction with the Northern Railway of France. It is a much industrialised area and it was here amid the coal tips, on that memorable Sunday of August 23, 1914, that the British

44

Expeditionary Force first met the armies of the Kaiser, and held them until forced by other circumstances into a long strategic retreat. The accompanying sketch map shows that the lines around Mons are only a little less complicated than those at Liege, Antwerp, or Brussels itself. For a railway system that was devised and subsequently empowered by the single authority of the central government these local complications may seem surprising, and more akin to those arising from the activities of individual companies as in Great Britain and in Holland, until one is reminded that Belgium has a greater railway mileage per head of population than any other country in the world.

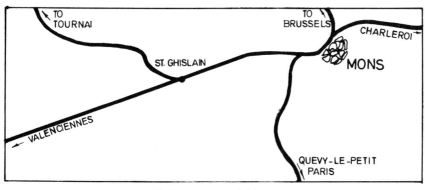

6. Railways around Mons

While the main lines running north and north-west of Brussels include no difficult gradients and could be operated effectively by the 'Dunalastair' type of 4–4–0, and their superheated Belgian-built developments, the lines running south and east were very different. On the important route to Liege, Verviers, and the German frontier there is much stiff climbing, while the Luxembourg line is very heavily graded. The Belgian State Railways began introducing six-coupled locomotives for passenger work as early as 1903, and in view of the existing association with the Caledonian Railway an affinity with the 4–6–0 'Oban bogies' of the latter railway was immediately claimed. So far as wheelbase was concerned there was a strong likeness but the Belgian engines had a much larger boiler. These powerful machines were put to work on the Luxembourg line, and

45

also on the through expresses between Brussels and Paris, working to the frontier station of Quevy-le-Petit. With coupled wheels no larger than 1600 mm. diameter they were hardly suitable for real express work, and it was only on the heaviest and slower trains north of Brussels that they displaced the 'Dunalastairs'.

At the end of 1904 some considerably more powerful locomotives were in hand: they were also 4–6–0s but with four cylinders. Machines of this type built by Maffei of Munich, had been introduced with success on the Bavarian railways and the Belgian State decided to try out the same layout of machinery, in which all four cylinders drove on to the leading coupled axle. The Bavarian engines were compounds, but of the two built for trial in Belgium by the La Meuse Company of Liege, one was a compound, and the other a 4-cylinder simple. Unlike the earlier 4–6–0s they were intended as real express engines and had 1981 mm. diameter coupled wheels. The four cylinders of the simple engine were 419 mm. diameter by 660 mm. stroke, and with a large boiler and pressure of 15 kg. per sq. cm. they were very powerful locomotives for that period. They were intended primarily for the international express trains running in connection with the packet service to and from Ostend, via Brussels and Liege to Cologne. The Belgian locomotives worked as far as Herbesthal, and over the eastern portion of the route there were severe gradients. The fastest of these trains, before the First World War, was the Ostend-Vienna Express, which had a total running time of 3 hr. 57 min. over the 260 kilometres from Ostend Quay to Herbesthal, an average speed of 65 km./h. The only intermediate stops were at Brussels (Nord), Ans, Liege, and Verviers. The start to stop average speeds on the longer stretches were around 72 to 77 km./h.

These large locomotives did not however meet requirements for very long and in 1910 the chief mechanical engineer, Monsieur J.B. Flamme, introduced one of the most extraordinary steam locomotives that had yet been seen in Europe up to that time. The 'Pacific' type was no longer a novelty, but not one of this shape! A first impression was that it looked all wrong, with the cylinders and most of the bogie far out in front of the smokebox door. Then a closer inspection revealed that the designer wished to keep the huge firebox, its steeply falling grate, and ashpan completely clear of the coupled wheels.

46

These latter had to go well forward, and as there was apparently no need or desire to have a very long boiler, the bogie, cylinders and running gear had to go still further forward. The result was very ugly. Because of the very high cylinder power of these engines it was thought desirable to divide the drive. The outside cylinders drove on to the middle pair of coupled wheels, and the inside cylinders on to the leading pair. The inside cylinders were indeed about 2.5 m. ahead of the centre line of the smokebox, which involved steam passages and the inevitable pressure drop between. They were reputed to develop over 1500 kilowatts, but the extent to which engines of this type were subsequently rebuilt suggests that their early success was somewhat illusory. They certainly had to do hard work over the heavy gradients of the Luxembourg line, but a quaintly worded description of them in *The Railway Magazine* of 1912 as 'the most powerful coal-consuming passenger engines in Europe' was truer by implication than in the way the phrase was intended!

Monsieur Flamme also designed a class of very powerful 2–10–0 freight engines, with a similar type of boiler and the same cylinder layout as the 'Pacifics'; but the large firebox was accommodated within the coupled wheelbase, and without the ugly forward positioning of the cylinders this freight engine looked much neater, and better balanced. Despite this close attention that was being given to locomotive design train speeds in Belgium were not very high in the period before the First World War. There were, in 1910, 62 runs made daily at a start to stop average speed of 75 km./h. or more and the fastest was 84.5 km./h. The distances run non-stop were however short by comparison with contemporary British and French runs, the longest being no more than the 121.5 kilometres between Brussels and Ostend Quay. One of the most praiseworthy Belgian services of the day was that provided by the hourly trains between Brussels and Antwerp, of which there was a total of 13 in each direction, covering the 44 kilometres in 34 minutes. This service was operated entirely by the 'Dunalastair' type 4–4–0 locomotives.

One of the few Belgian railways that originated outside the network planned by the State was the West Flanders, a line promoted with British capital that had its concession granted by the State as long ago as May 1845. Running south from Bruges to Roulers, it then made a circuit of towns in West Flanders, half circling to the west and then to the north linking up Menin, Comines and Ypres, and then heading due west for Poperinghe and the French frontier. It was one of the last in Belgium to be taken under direct State control, that event not taking place until January 1906; but in less than 10 years its western end became one of the most strategic lines in the entire history of the British Army. Those with memories of World War I will need no reminder of how Ypres, itself reduced in four terrible years to no more than so many heaps of rubble, formed the bastion of the Allied line in the north, the centre point of the great 'salient', the defence of which was all important, and which cost the armies of the British Empire hundreds of thousands of lives. Eight kilometres in rear but still within the salient area was Poperinghe, the railhead to which came munitions, food and reinforcements from that 'grand junction' of British military traffic, Hazebrouck, roughly 16 kilometres south-west of 'Pop', as every British soldier of those days knew it. From Hazebrouck lines of the French Northern railway ran to Dunkirk, Calais, and Arras. Today the one-time route of the West Flanders Railway is no longer a through route. Some of its sections are single tracked, and the section through Poperinghe to Ypres became the route of pilgrims to what still ranks as the world's greatest and most terribly costly battlefield.

PLATE 1

(a) A nineteenth century Dutch station scene, from a painting by Anton Pieck

(b) Nineteenth century Dutch station architecture — the handsome arched roof at The Hague

(a) One of the beautiful English-built 2–4–0s of the State Railway, by Beyer, Peacock & Co. 1880

PLATE 2 Dutch steam locomotives

(b) A later development to the 4–4–0 type, built by Beyer, Peacock & Co. 1899

(c) The important 4–6–0 type of 1910, for the State Railway, built with four cylinders all driving on to the leading coupled axle, to eliminate 'hammer blow' at speed

PLATE 3 Historic Dutch locomotives

(a) A scene at Hoorn, in 1936, with (on left), one of the 'Rhine-bogie' 4–4–0s, and a 'State' 4–4–4 tank on right

(b) A scale model, in the Netherlands Railway Museum at Utrecht, of one of the Netherlands Central Railway 4-cylinder 4–6–0s of 1911

(c) Scale model, also at Utrecht, of a North Brabant German Railway 4–6–0 of 1908 built by Beyer, Peacock & Co.

PLATE 4

The impressive arch of Antwerp Central station, Belgian State Railways, about 1900, with one of the Scottish-built 'Dunalastair' type 4–4–0s in the centre

PLATE 5 In the
Low Countries

a) A Dutch electric train,
leaving Delft

b) A Belgian 4-cylinder
de Glehn compound
4–6–0, of 1921
design, photographed
at Brussels Nord in
1929. This was a
design of which
75 were built, and all
survived the Second
World War

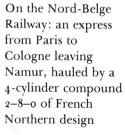

On the Nord-Belge
Railway: an express
from Paris to
Cologne leaving
Namur, hauled by a
4-cylinder compound
2–8–0 of French
Northern design

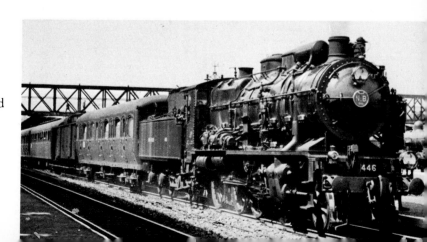

PLATE 6 Belgian Steam

(a) One of the compound 4–6–0s of 1921, as rebuilt and running in 1959, leaving Antwerp. Note modern colour light signals in contrast to those in Plate 4

(b) One of the extraordinary Flamme 'Pacifics', here specially turned out by Schaerbeck depot to work the Belgian Royal Train in 1953

(c) On the Brussels East West Junction line in 1953. Steam locomotives passing through the tunnels between the Midi and Nord stations were not allowed to emit any smoke or steam so they had to be hauled by electric locomotives

PLATE 7 Boat expresses on the Nord

(a) The 'Golden Arrow' at full speed near Orry-la-Ville, hauled by a Collin 'Super-Pacific'

(b) Arrival at Boulogne: boat train from Paris escorted by a man with a flag across the open quayside leading into the Maritime station

(a) A 4–4–0 de Glehn
4-cylinder of 1900

PLATE 8 Compound
express locomotives of
the Est

(b) The standard
4-cylinder 4–6–0 of
the pre-1914 period,
at La Villette, Paris,
1934

(c) Duchatel's huge
4-cylinder 4–8–2, also
at La Villette

PLATE 9

(a) The State Railway standard 4-cylinder compound 'Pacific': one of a batch built in Glasgow by the North British Locomotive Company during the First World War

(b) The same design as modernised in the 1930s, with improved exhaust arrangements, feed water heater and smoke deflecting shields, photographed at Batignolles, Paris, in 1934

PLATE 10 German electric trains

(a) A train from Freiburg on the Hollental line — the experimental 20,000 volt single phase system, that so impressed the French

(b) Electric locomotives at Heidelburg operating on the German standard 15,000 $16\frac{2}{3}$ cycles, traction system

PLATE 11

a) One of the Alsace-
Lorraine type of
de Glehn 4-cylinder
compound 'Pacifics'
leaving Arlon,
Belgium, in 1939,
with an express from
The Hague to Basle

) A German Diesel-
hydraulic locomotive,
passing the great
signal tower at
Frankfurt (Main),
with an international
express train

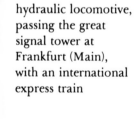

) Cologne: an express
for Frankfurt leaving
the main station, and
passing beside the
wonderful Gothic
cathedral. The
locomotive is one of
the standard 'light'
'Pacifics' of the '03'
class

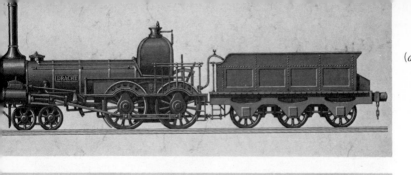

(a) The first locomotive built by the famous firm of Henschel, of Kassel: the 'Drache' for the Northern Railway of Hesse, 1848

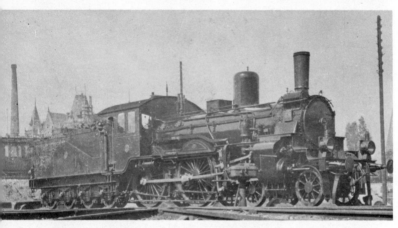

(b) Prussian State Railways — 4-cylinder compound 4-4-0 of 1895 era

PLATE 12 German steam locomotive development

(c) An early compound 4-4-0 fitted with the Schmidt superheater: the 'Angerapp' for the Elsass-Lothringen Imperial Railways

(d) One of the standard 'heavy' 'Pacifics' of the German Federal Railways, series '01'

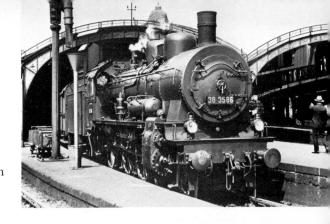

PLATE 13

(a) One of the numerous 'P8' class 4–6–0s of earlier Prussian design introduced in 1906, here seen at Cologne in 1929

(b) A Maffei 'Pacific' of Bavarian design also of 1906 photographed at Frankfurt in 1931

(c) One of the heavy standard 2–10–0 freight engines of the 3-cylinder '44' series, on the Bebra-Wurzburg line

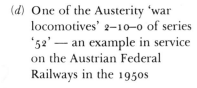

(d) One of the Austerity 'war locomotives' 2–10–0 of series '52' — an example in service on the Austrian Federal Railways in the 1950s

PLATE 14 Modern German
Signalling

(a) The control tower at
Munich main station

(b) A view in the control
room at Frankfurt,
showing the regu-
lators in the fore-
ground, and the
panel operators
ranged round the
windows

(c) Close-up of one of
the desk panels from
which points and
signals are operated
at Frankfurt

PLATE 15

(*) A truly ancient Austrian 0–6–0 built in 1860 for the Southern Railway. Until 1869 it was in active service on the Graz-Koflacher-Bahn, but is now scheduled for preservation

(*) A 4–4–0 of the Süd-bahn, of 1890 vintage, and at work on the Graz-Koflacher-Bahn until 1968

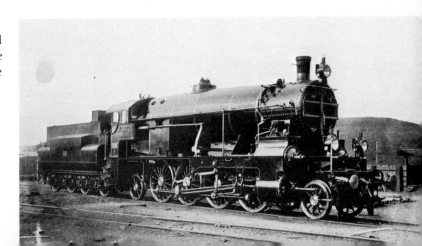

(*) One of the Gölsdorf 4-cylinder compound 2–8–2s of 1914 for the Amstetten-Seltzal line

PLATE 16

(*a*) The 'Orient Express' in the Tyrol, hauled by one of the Gölsdorf 2-cylinder compound 2–8–0 locomotives, circa 1900

(*b*) The electrically hauled 'Arlberg Express' at Landeck in the Tyrol

CHAPTER FIVE

Belgium — a momentous half-century

A traveller returning to Belgium after the four years of war and its immediate aftermath would have found many changes. It was not that direct destruction had been extensive, because except in the Ypres Salient and north of it, the battle line of the Western Front had lain outside Belgian territory. The railways of the country had been geared to military traffic feeding the German armies, and everything else became of secondary importance. Extensive removal of track facilities had taken place during the German occupation, to provide for military needs elsewhere, and a large number of bridges demolished; siding tracks had been removed. Although speed was of no consequence the lines that remained were for the most part kept in tolerably good shape, and the great battles that preceded the Armistice of November 1918 were fought on French rather than Belgian soil. Even so, nothing had been done in the years since August 1914 towards normal replacement of obsolescent rolling stock and fixed equipment and when the Belgian Government took over once again, in January 1919, it was to find that on a nationwide basis nearly one third of the pre-war track had been either destroyed, or removed; that 350 bridges needed replacement, and as many stations needed complete rebuilding.

One of the immediate after-effects of the war was the handing over by the Germans of much rolling stock, and many locomotives, by way of reparations. So in the early 1920s Prussian 4-cylinder compound 4–6–0s, and veteran German 'Atlantics' were to be seen working alongside Flamme 'Pacifics' and 2–10–0s, and the ubiquitous 'Dunalastairs'. Travelling on all but the international trains was a pretty miserable business in superannuated four-wheeled non-corridor stock, of the kind that the inimitable E.L. Ahrons once

49

referred to as dog-boxes. The international trains were for the most part made up of rolling stock from neighbouring countries, yet even so including all too many old timber framed vehicles. Rapid reconstruction works by the engineering divisions of the Allied armies, although of a temporary nature, was in fact not replaced by permanent structures until many years after the war, so urgent was the need for rehabilitation of railway facilities over the country as a whole.

Despite this extremely difficult situation plans for railway development in Belgium were notably advanced in the first ten years after the war. One of these was the construction of the direct line between Brussels and Ghent. The original railway network, with its system of 'spoke' lines from Brussels naturally tended to link up the principal centres of population, and while heading generally in the direction of Ostend, the line starting from the Nord station in Brussels made a somewhat roundabout route via Dilbeck, Alost, and Melle to reach Ghent; as far back as 1907 a scheme had been approved to build a new direct line running almost straight from a junction outside the Midi station. Work ceased on the outbreak of war in 1914, but enough had been done for the western half of this new line to be subsequently completed and brought into service in 1923. Connection with the old line was made at Denderleeuw, about 24 kilometres west of Brussels, though traffic still continued to run from the Nord station in Brussels itself. The new direct line from the Midi station was brought into service in 1933, and by-passed all intermediate towns. Part of the work however included a new connection to the important junction at Denderleeuw, which is the starting point of a number of subsidiary lines. The completion of the new direct line, together with the raising of the speed limit to 120 km./h., made possible a substantial acceleration of service with many trains covering the 42 kilometres between Brussels and Ghent at a start-to-stop average speed of 96.8 km./h.

One of the most striking features of postwar reconstruction in Belgium was a complete modernisation of the signalling system. As mentioned in the previous chapter the original signalling was very much according to British standards, and during the war this was altered to agree with German ideas and to a large extent operated by

German railwaymen. Not the least of the problems facing the Belgian State Railways on taking over control after the Armistice was to train their own signalmen in the working of the German equipment. The chief signal engineer of the Belgian State Railways, Louis Weissenbruch, was exiled in England during the war, and after making a study of many different signalling practices decided upon a new system for Belgium, when the time for reconstruction came. The extent to which earlier work had been altered and improvised during the German occupation made complete renewal essential. With the introduction of power signalling at the turn of the century, the upper quadrant type signal was used at certain large stations, though its application was not extensive and only provided two indications by each semaphore arm. Weissenbruch used three positions, with the arms actuated by the double-wire system, as then standard in Holland, Germany, Austria and Scandinavia. According to local conditions he used sometimes a single 'home' arm, and a single 'distant' arm, while elsewhere he installed two arm signals, which by different positions of the arms could provide four indications. The various aspects and their meanings are shown in the accompanying diagram. Progress with the re-signalling was rapid after the war, and by November 1919 the work on the busiest line of all, that between Brussels and Antwerp was completed. The Ostend line was re-equipped by March 1920 and the Luxembourg line by the summer of that same year.

At an early date after the war arrangements were made for the resumption of international express train services across Belgium, and to avoid the necessity of engine changing at frontier stations, certain trains from France were worked by locomotives of the Nord Railway from Quevy through to Brussels, while in the case of trains bound for Germany via Liege, French locomotives worked through from Jeumont. In this latter case the amount of purely Belgian mileage worked over was only that from Charleroi to Namur, as the rest of the route was owned by the Nord-Belge Company. Another interesting working developed towards the end of the period between the two world wars was that of Dutch locomotives working southwards from Roosendaal to Brussels on international express trains from Amsterdam.

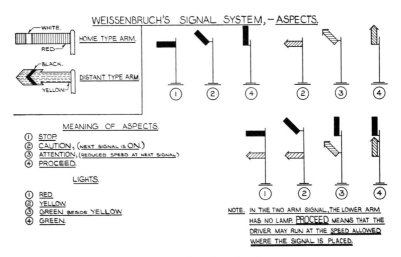

7. Weissenbruch's signals

The importance and intensity of traffic on the line between Brussels and Antwerp led to an early decision for its electrification. The interesting feature of this work, which was brought into service in April 1935, was that it was not the electrification of an existing very busy line, but the construction of an entirely new double-track electric railway alongside the existing steam lines. The initial service planned was that of a very fast inter-urban one, mostly of non-stop trains, though some called intermediately at Malines. The distance is 44.5 kilometres, and on their first introduction the non-stop trains made the journey in the level 30 minutes. Those stopping at Malines took 3 minutes longer. To lovers of the historic there was a little sadness that the new trains replaced the inter-city 'block' trains which were worked so efficiently for so many years by the 'Dunalastair' 4–4–0 locomotives. The new trains were built up of four-car multiple-unit sets, working on the 3000 volt direct current system with overhead wire supply. The choice of this system was curious in view of the prevailing tendencies in neighbouring countries. Both France and Holland had opted for 1500 volts direct current, and in Great Britain the historic Weir Report had recommended the same for all future electrification. The other country using 3000 volts d.c. was Italy, where new lines were being so electrified in preference to the three-phase alternating current system discussed in a later chapter of this book. It is true that the Brussels-Antwerp installation was introduced as a closely self-contained shuttle service, to the extent that commuter traffic out of the two cities was not provided for. At the same time it was well known that the Belgian authorities envisaged a general extension of electric traction on their main lines. As originally introduced there were three electric trains an hour, each way, between Brussels and Antwerp, with an increase to one every ten minutes in the morning and evening peak hours. The purely suburban trains out of both cities at first remained steam hauled.

In the meantime some interesting developments in main line steam power were continuing. It was generally known that the huge, misshapen Flamme 'Pacifics' had not proved very successful, and since the end of the war had been subjected to a considerable amount of rebuilding. The number of 4-cylinder 4–6–0s of various designs formed the backbone of the passenger locomotive stud. At about the same time as the 4–6–0s referred to in the previous chapter were introduced, with all four cylinders driving on to the leading coupled axle in the Maffei style, a class of 4-cylinder compound 4–6–0s of the de Glehn type was also put to work. In the period of reconstruction after the end of the war, this design in a modernised superheated form, was chosen as a standard and orders for 75 of them were placed with various Belgian firms. These engines had all the qualities of reliability and efficient performance for which the de Glehn type is renowned. From 1934 onwards six of them became guinea pigs for trials of a different form of drive. Originally of course they all had the traditional de Glehn arrangement, with the high pressure cylinders outside and driving the second pair of coupled wheels, and the low pressure inside, and driving the leading pair. The three experiments — two engines of each kind — were:

1. Compound   — all four cylinders in line.
2. 4-cylinder simple   — all four cylinders in line.
3. 4-cylinder simple   — divided drive, as per de Glehn.

The other 69 engines of the original class remained as built, except for the addition of modern refinements such as multiple-jet exhaust, feed water heaters, and such like. Except for one, which was destroyed in military action, all of them survived the *Second* World War.

It could be inferred, but with what justification I am not prepared to guess, that the results of the experimental rebuilding of those six engines was reflected in the fifteen new 'Pacifics' put into service in 1935. In outward appearance they provided a very striking contrast to the Flamme type, and in their distinctive front-end screening they were likened to Sir Nigel Gresley's celebrated 2–8–2 'Cock o' the North', which had been completed at Doncaster just a year earlier. The dimensional differences between the Flamme and the new design of 'Pacific' were interesting, both being 4-cylinder simples.

Belgian Pacifics

	Flamme	1935 Design
Cylinders (four)		
dia. mm.	500	420
stroke mm.	660	720
Coupled wheels mm.	1980	1980
Heating surfaces		
evaporative sq.m.	234	229.5
superheater sq.m.	62.8	109.3
Grate area sq.m.	4.9	4.9
Boiler pressure kg./sq.cm.	14	18
Nominal tractive effort (85% boiler pressure) kg.	19,750	19,550

The tractive effort of the Flamme engine was of course enormous for the period, but it turned out to be nominal only. The strange feature of the 1935 design however was that while all the cylinders were in line the drive was divided. The photograph (Plate 66) of one of these engines shows how the coupled wheels are set back from the bogie, to avoid having too short a connecting rod for the inside cylinders, driving on to the leading pair of coupled wheels, while the outside running gear reveals the rather inordinate length of piston rod, again to avoid having too long and heavy a connecting rod. It was an arrangement that had been used in England on the Great Central Railway 4-cylinder 4–6–0s of the 'Lord Faringdon' class,

54

first introduced in 1918. The new Belgian engines proved very successful, and were mainly responsible for operating the much accelerated passenger services put on in the last years before the Second World War.

The new main line from Brussels Midi to Ghent was certainly put to good purpose in those years, and the average speed of the fastest trains running non-stop to and from Ostend Quay was increased to 106.2 km./h. This was all the more creditable because at that time the speed had to be reduced considerably in passing over the curve and junctions in the middle of Bruges. In keeping with the general spirit of enterprise which animated the Belgian Railway in the years between the two wars the situation was first improved by the construction of a finely graded and aligned avoiding track, whereby non-stopping trains passed entirely clear of the old station, its junctions and level crossings, and this was followed by the building of an entirely new station with all modern facilities, adjacent to the new line. By the summer of 1937 start-to-stop average speeds of more than 100 km./h. were the rule rather than the exception over such relatively short distances as Brussels to Ghent, 54.5 kilometres, and Ghent to Bruges, 48.5 kilometres. By contrast the electric service between Brussels Nord and Antwerp, over its somewhat secluded track, 44.2 kilometres in 29 minutes, showed an average of only 91.5 km./h. There were however no fewer than fifty trains each day making the latter run.

It was in 1939 that Belgium snatched the honour of having the fastest steam run in the whole world from the far-famed 'Hiawatha' express of the Milwaukee railroad in the U.S.A., by scheduling a light-weight special *rapide* over the 93 kilometres from Brussels Midi to Bruges in 46 minutes — a start-to-stop average of 121.25 km./h. To run these trains the Belgian State Railways had to some extent emulated the Milwaukee example, by designing a special high-speed 'Atlantic' locomotive for the job. Though effective enough aerodynamically, the new locomotives introduced in 1939 were striking, rather than handsome. Their tractive effort was little more than half that of the 1935 'Pacifics', but the trains provided accommodation in three coaches for no more than 12 first class, and 100 second class passengers, and weighed in all only about 168 tonnes. These very fast trains which made the journey of 114 kilometres between Brussels and Ostend Quay in the even hour, inclusive of the stop at Bruges, were taken off after the outbreak of war in September 1939; but with Belgium not originally involved, and the 'phoney' period developing, they were re-instated in March 1940. With these trains the permissible maximum speed between Brussels and Ghent was 125 km./h. increased to 145 km./h. onwards to Bruges. Over these same stretches of line the big 'Pacifics' showed themselves capable of maintaining start-to-stop average speeds of 100 km./h. and slightly over with loads up to 500 tonnes.

The decision to build special 'Atlantic' engines for the high speed trains of 1939 may well have originated in the satisfactory experience the Belgian State Railway had with some of the 4-cylinder compound 'Atlantics' of the Prussian State Railways taken over as war reparations. This was a standard design of which large numbers had been in service in Germany from 1907 onwards. They had the four cylinders in line, and all driving on the leading coupled axle; furthermore, with a very large firebox set behind the rearward coupled axles, the trailing wheels were located at the extreme rear end, making in all a very long wheelbase. The Belgians used these engines on the Calais-Brussels Pullman express, with much success. The new Belgian streamlined 'Atlantics' of 1939 while having the drive on to the leading coupled axle were of more orthodox wheelbase spacing, with the trailing wheels beneath instead of behind the firebox. They were 2-cylinder simples, with 480 mm. by 720 mm. cylinders, 2100 mm. coupled wheels, and a boiler pressure of 18 kg. per sq. cm.

The very fast 'Atlantic'-hauled trains between Brussels and Ostend could have been regarded as something of a 'stunt', but there was nothing of this nature about some of the other accelerated services operated in Belgium during the last years of peace. The Luxembourg line with its long gradients of 1 in 62 in the Ardennes was not exactly a speedway, but the 'Edelweiss' Pullman express was booked at an average speed of 84 km./h. on its non-stop run from Namur to Luxembourg City. Reference has already been made to the Flamme 2–10–0 freight engines, which were used in pairs on the heaviest goods trains over that route; but in 1930 some enormous

2–8–2s were built specially for passenger working on the Luxembourg line, that had the distinction of being the heaviest passenger engines in Europe. Without their tenders they weighed 130 tonnes. Unlike other Belgian passenger locomotives they had only two cylinders, but 720 mm. diameter by 720 mm. stroke. The coupled wheels were 1700 mm. diameter, and the boiler pressure 14 kg. per sq. cm. The nominal tractive effort at 85 per cent. boiler pressure was 29,000 kg. — an exceptionally high value for a European passenger locomotive.

There seemed no limit to Belgian railway enterprise in the 1930s and in addition to the electrification, introduction of notable new steam locomotives and accelerated train service, the long standing problem of communication between the Nord and Midi stations in Brussels was successfully tackled, though administratively in a rather unusual way. In the previous Chapter I told how the earlier proposals for a surface line through the heart of the city were halted by the outbreak of the First World War, and how the unfinished works were subsequently abandoned. In 1930 a new plan was launched by the Government for an underground line, built on the cut-and-cover principle. For purposes of financing however, although the new line was to be worked by the Belgian National Railways, a separate body was created by an Act of Parliament in July 1935 to carry out all the work, including such things as acquisition of land, placing constructional contracts and so on. It was named the 'Office National pour L'Achèvement de la Jonction Nord-Midi'. One of the conditions imposed was that while the railway would charge fares in proportion to the mileage run over the new line, they would be subject to an additional tax or toll to help defray the cost of construction.

At the time construction was started there seemed no little doubt as to how the connection would be used, and the railway press of the day was full of gratuitous advice! But the provision of six tracks throughout showed that it was to be no mere 'link', but a main artery of through north to south traffic. I did not have occasion to use the line personally until after the Second World War. Little detail as to its completion had been published in the meantime, and travelling to the new Central station in the Brussels portion of the Night Ferry from

London gave me something of a surprise. The building of the junction line was accompanied by extensive reconstruction of both the Nord and Midi stations. The former was converted into a through station, with 12 platforms. The Midi station was made the base for all originating traffic, and where remarshalling of through trains took place. Of the 22 platform roads, 12 were equipped for through trains. The junction line itself has three intermediate stations, though two of these originally had platforms only on the eastern pair of tracks, used by the Antwerp trains. The new Central station has platforms on all six tracks, and it was in arriving here on the 'Sleeper' from London that I had such a surprise. Platform-wise Brussels Central is no more than a glorified 'underground' station as found on the Inner Circle in London, and it is only on reaching the upper levels that more extensive station facilities are discovered. It is at the Midi station that all the shops, cafes and such like of a large Continental railway station are to be found.

The adoption of the cut-and-cover system of excavation for so wide a tunnel involved some interesting work, because the channel had to be no less than 35 metres wide, through the very heart of Brussels. The eastern and western sides were bounded by sheet steel piling, and steel shoring was erected in such a way that it formed the framework for the reinforced concrete of the completed tunnel. On account of the width of the tunnel five supporting columns for the shoring had to be provided at intervals. The accompanying diagram shows this interesting work. Today, through expresses such as those from the Dutch cities to Paris, or to Switzerland, call at the Nord station and then usually pass over the junction line without stopping to arrive at the Midi to change locomotives, add extra coaches and so on. It is the more 'local' of the passenger trains, or those terminating in Brussels that call at the Central additionally. There are, in all, upwards of 1000 trains now passing over the junction line daily.

For the second time in this century the railways of Belgium suffered immense damage and disruption following the Nazi invasion of May 1940; but as in the 1920s the recovery afterwards was extraordinarily swift and purposeful. A remarkable feature of this recovery was the readiness of Belgian engineers to profit, even by the destruction. In the early stages of the war when some 350 bridges

NORD   MIDI

8. Brussels East-West link line

were destroyed to hinder the enemy invasion, no help or advice was given towards their rebuilding; but when the same process was repeated in reverse, ahead of the victorious Allied advance in 1944, opportunity was taken after the liberation of the country to make detailed metallurgical inspections of the way bridge girders had withstood or collapsed under the effects of high explosive, and a scientific paper of immense interest was subsequently published. Reconstruction was such that Belgium was the first country in Europe to be able to schedule runs at a start-to-stop average speed of more than 100 km./h. From April 1946 three trains in each direction daily made the run of 44.2 kilometres between Brussels and Antwerp in 25 minutes. These trains were two-car electric units.

While the conversion of main lines to electric traction was a major point in the longer term plan of post-war recovery, new locomotives were urgently needed, and 300 2–8–0s were built in North America by the Montreal Locomotive Works, by the Canadian Locomotive Works of Kingston, Ontario, and by the American Locomotive Company. They were received in 1945-1947 and proved of great value in getting things moving once again. Apart from such expedients, the twenty years that followed the liberation in 1945 were a time of complete modernisation. The last steam train was run in 1963, and by that time the entire country was served by a network of fast multiple-unit electric trains, with powerful electric locomotives working the freights and the international expresses. As in the 1920s there was a complete revision of signalling practice, with the introduction of techniques that were becoming normal in Great Britain, France and elsewhere, and the application of modern science to automatic train control. Prior to the war colour light signals,

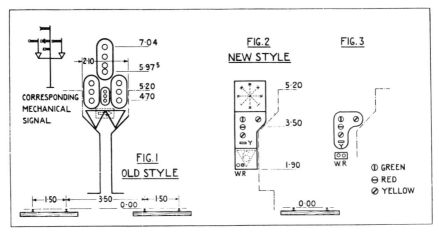

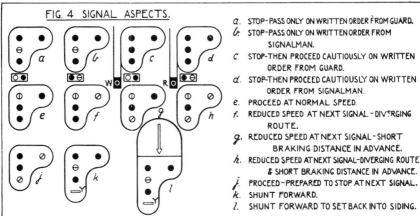

9. Belgian colour-light signals

somewhat in the British style, had been installed on the Brussels-Antwerp and on the Charleroi-Namur lines: but realising that very extensive replacement would have to be made after the war, an entirely new system was worked out. The Belgians set themselves the task of designing one universal type of colour light signal capable, if required, of presenting the entire series of indications required in Belgian railway operating practice, namely: 'stop', 'proceed',

60

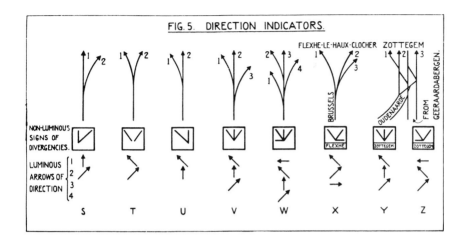

FIG. 5. DIRECTION INDICATORS.

'direction set up', 'speed', 'wrong road movement', 'shunt forward', 'set back into siding', 'caution', or 'attention'.

The new signal in its most complete form is shown in the accompanying diagrams, and is made up of three parts. The centre one gives the main indications, by means of the colour light units and the shunt indications; the upper part gives the direction signs for junctions, by means of illuminated arrows, while the lower part gives subsidiary indications, speed limits, and so on. The code of aspects, as shown in the second diagram may at first sight seem complicated, but they are elaborations of the basic indications of red for stop; yellow for caution; and green for proceed at normal speed. The complete code is an ingenious and well thought out contribution to modern railway practice, and continues the fine traditions that have been characteristic of the Belgian National system since its inception. The fifty years from 1913 to the end of steam traction did indeed constitute a period of upheaval, storm and stress, and, withal, striking technological advance, that would be hard to parallel by any other railway administrations.

CHAPTER SIX

Brussels to Paris non-stop,
past and present

I have taken the running of the high-prestige inter-city expresses as the centrepiece of this Chapter, though it does in fact gather in certain other international express services that converge upon the historic routes into Paris of the Northern Railway of France. That from the Channel Ports of Boulogne and Calais is nowadays not so well known to British travellers as it used to be. The speed and frequency of air travel has robbed it of its one time supremacy in London–Paris communications, while the Night Ferry service, via Dunkirk, and travelling southwards through Lille and Arras, is not very conducive to sight-seeing, railway or otherwise. It is the crack international rail routes from Paris to Holland and North Germany with which I am now particularly concerned, the first through Brussels and the second through Liege, which join a few miles inside French territory at Hautmont Junction, 1.8 kilometres west of Maubeuge.

It was in June 1923 that the first non-stop express trains between Paris and Brussels were put on. This was really a remarkable piece of international railway enterprise and co-operation, because the Belgian system had by no means recovered from the effects of the war, and speed north of Quevy was limited to 75 km./h. throughout. In those years however the enterprise of the Northern Railway of France knew no bounds, and although their part of the route lay through country that had seen some of the most sustained and severe fighting of the entire four years of war the track had been restored to such condition as to permit of average speeds of over 100 km./h. between Paris and Aulnoye. Because of the severe restrictions in Belgium the overall time between the two capital cities was $3^3/_4$

hours, for 310 kilometres, an average of 83 km./h. The route lay over historic ground. At Hal, not many miles to the east is the battlefield of Waterloo, while 60.5 kilometres from Brussels the non-stopping trains slow down for the curve through Mons. Up to this point the gradients have been no more than slight; but immediately after Mons there begins a stiff climb on a gradient of 1 in 100 towards the Franco-Belgian frontier. It was on the high ground south of the town that on Sunday August 23, 1914, the German army came almost unexpectedly against the strength of the British Expeditionary Force. The German commander thought our army was at Tournai, 40 kilometres to the west, and hoped to outflank them in his drive towards Paris. As it was, in this battle among the coal tips he was held up for ten desperate hours.

The railway geography of Mons is complicated. Lines from Tournai, Valenciennes and Manage converge upon the Paris–Brussels main line in its vicinity, not to mention a complex of local mineral lines. The trunk line to the south, formerly part of the Nord-Belge system, reaches the frontier in 14 kilometres from Mons, at Quevy-le-Petit, where today the change of traction system takes place. When the non-stop expresses between Paris and Brussels were first put on in June 1923, making an overall average speed of 82.8 km./h., the locomotives used were those of the first series of Nord 'Pacifics', purchased in 1912 under somewhat strange circumstances. Until 1911 Monsieur du Bousquet had been chief mechanical engineer of the Northern Railway, and in close co-operation with Alfred de Glehn, of the Société Alsacienne, in Belfort, he had developed the 4-cylinder compound system to a degree of high efficiency. After the great success of the Nord 'Atlantics', to which reference is made subsequently, du Bousquet designed two huge 4-cylinder compounds of the 4–6–4 type for experimental purposes; but he died two months before the completion of the first of the two locomotives, and his successor, Georges Asselin, was almost immediately presented with a situation that precluded the long-sustained development work necessary on so large and novel a design of new locomotive. In short, certain international incidents in which the German Kaiser was involved revealed the risk of a major war, even as early as the year 1912.

Nevertheless the Nord needed new and more powerful locomotives, and the management turned once again to Alfred de Glehn. It was a rather anomalous position, that in face of a threat of war a French railway should have turned to a manufacturer so near to German territory! But although most of the French province of Alsace had been annexed by Germany after the war of 1870–1871, the Société Alsacienne was in the territory of Belfort, which remained French, and de Glehn himself was ready enough to continue co-operation with the Nord, as wholeheartedly with Asselin as he had done with du Bousquet. De Glehn had a 'Pacific' design 'ready-made' for the Nord to adopt. In 1909 he had built some 'Pacifics' for the then Prussian controlled Alsace-Lorraine Railways, and with no more than minor alterations in detail this design was accepted by the Nord, and delivery taken in 1912 for 20 locomotives. They were good, hard-working machines though they had not much opportunity for displaying their prowess as fast express engines when war came in 1914, and all train services on the Nord was subjugated to the needs of military traffic. In the years from 1920 however they came into their own, and were the first engines to work the Paris-Brussels non-stops.

When first introduced these trains were of no more than light formation, around 220 tonnes, and they proved so much within the capacity of the 'Pacifics' that they were soon turned over to the du Bousquet-de Glehn 'Atlantics', then about 25 years old, and changed from their original condition only by the addition of superheating. These engines had been pace-setters to the last degree. Immediately upon their introduction they attracted what was virtually world-wide attention by their performances on the English boat trains from Calais and Boulogne to Paris; in 1903 the Great Western Railway of England bought one for trial, and the Egyptian State Railways had some for the Cairo-Luxor expresses. The Paris-Orleans Railway had some slightly larger ones, and the du Bousquet-de Glehn system of compounding was used in Germany, Switzerland, Spain, and India on locomotives of varying types and sizes. On the Nord itself, the International trains heading for Brussels, or Liege were considerably lighter in formation than the English boat trains, and they proved an ideal field of activity for the 'Atlantics'. In their earliest days before

64

the First World War their superlative performance between Paris and Calais was frequently used by some commentators as a rod to scourge the backs of British locomotive engineers, who, it was alleged, could well have taken lessons in engine designing from the Nord.

It is perhaps inevitable that one becomes hotly engaged in discussions about locomotives immediately upon entering on Nord metals, at Feignies, because in the first thirty years of the twentieth century the company followed the most enterprising, individual, and successful mechanical engineering policy of any in France. It is true that the setting aside of du Bousquet's great 4–6–4s was a pity, and the acceptance of the Alsace-Lorraine 'Pacific' design no more than an expedient in the face of an impending national emergency; but du Bousquet had produced another design in 1907, the immense significance of which has perhaps never been fully appreciated outside French locomotive engineering circles. Despite the excellent work of the 'Atlantics' there were times when increased loads on the Calais trains needed a six-coupled engine; the difficulty then was that the permanent way department would permit no greater axle load than $16\frac{1}{2}$ tonnes, when loads of up to 20 tonnes per axle were being used on the largest British engines. On the Nord, in planning a new design of 4–6–0, the wheel diameter was fixed at 1740 mm. against 2040 mm. on the 'Atlantics' to save weight; then to make up for the reduction in wheel diameter the cross-sectional area of the steam passages was made 25 per cent. greater, so that for the same speed of steam through the steam passages the piston speed could be increased by 25 per cent. The boiler was the same as the 'Atlantics', and despite their smaller coupled wheels the new 4–6–0s ran just as freely, and exerted a greater tractive effort. When the time came to develop new locomotives for post-war traffic, it was to the design of these du Bousquet 4–6–0s rather than to the Alsace-Lorraine type 'Pacifics' that the men of the Nord turned for inspiration.

The situation in France towards the end of the First World War was extremely difficult in motive power. The Government, looking forward to the time — not then far distant — when the concessions to the individual railway companies would end, and they would all be State owned, made an attempt to standardise locomotive power. At that time there was only one group of lines in France directly owned by the State, with a main line running southwestwards from a junction on the Western Railway main line at Chartres, and continuing south to termini at La Rochelle and Bordeaux. The rest of France was neatly parcelled out between the Western, Northern, Eastern, the Paris, Lyons and Mediterranean, the Orleans, and south of Bordeaux, the Midi. The Etat system was originally much the smallest of all, but before the war the Western had been brought under State control, and amalgamated with the original 'Etat'. It so happened that just before the war the Etat had developed a fine new design of 4-cylinder compound 'Pacific', and to further the cause of standardisation, the Government placed orders for no fewer than 400 of these locomotives from 1916 onwards with various firms. Because of wartime difficulties in France, with some of the largest manufactures in enemy hands, an order for 45 of these engines was placed with the North British Locomotive Company, and given war munitions priority.

While the majority of these fine locomotives were allocated to the Etat itself, in 1921 a batch of 40 went to the Est, and in the following year another 40 were allocated to the Alsace-Lorraine, then happily in French territory once more. The Orleans also had 40, but that company, like the Nord and the PLM had very definite ideas of their own about locomotive design, and those 40 Etat Pacifics eventually found their way to the Alsace-Lorraine, after 20 of them had had a brief sojourn on the Nord. In the meantime the Nord, far from entertaining any ideas about national standardisation, was busy designing its own post-war 'Super-Pacific'. The lesson of the du Bousquet mixed traffic 4-6-0s had been fully absorbed, and the new engines were given exceptionally large steam passages. Every single feature of the design was most carefully worked out, and these engines were soon performing positively Herculean feats with the English boat trains, which frequently loaded to over 500 tonnes. In the mid-1920s it would not have been too much to claim that the finest locomotive performance in the whole world was being put up between Paris and Calais. By contrast, the loads on the principal expresses running on the routes towards Belgium rarely exceeded 350 tonnes at that time, and could be handled comfortably by the older engines.

This brings me back, rather belatedly I fear, to the line from the Belgian frontier, which is joined at Hautmont Junction by that from Liege and North Germany. The actual frontiers are 6.8 kilometres to the north on the Brussels line, and 13.4 kilometres to the east, at Erquelines on the line to Liege. Actually however the engine-changing point on this latter route was at Jeumont, 1.8 kilometres on the French side of the frontier, and 239 kilometres from Paris. Although the purely Belgian line from Brussels to Liege traversed by the international expresses from Ostend, is severely graded, and includes the precipitous descent from Ans into Liege on a gradient of 1 in 30, the line from Jeumont is little removed from level throughout. It is not however a high speed route, for in following the valley of the Sambre as far as Namur, and that of the Meuse onwards there is almost continuous and often severe curvature, that precludes fast running. Resuming the journey towards Paris, from Hautmont Junction, the station names bring poignant memories of the early weeks of the First World War: Landrecies, scene of a sharp night action in the town streets during the Retreat from Mons; and then Le Cateau, where the hotly-contested delaying action by the British Second Army played so important a part in disrupting the famous Schlieffen Plan of the German High Command.

By the time Le Cateau is passed French expresses, whether steam as of old or electric today, are really 'flying'; but before then most of the *rapides* will have stopped briefly at Aulnoye 8.7 kilometres from Hautmont Junction, and an intersecting point of major importance. Here the line towards Belgium crosses the great north to south artery that runs just inside the French frontier through Hazebrouck, Lille, Valenciennes, Sedan, and Thionville to Metz. It is primarily a freight route, and saw the first major application of the 25,000 volt alternating current system of traction, about which so much will be written before this book is completed. This frontier route is also used by international express trains from Calais to Switzerland, continuing south from Metz down the Alsace-Lorraine main line through Strasbourg and Mulhouse to Basle. There is also yet another north to south express route avoiding Paris, from Amiens eastwards, and crossing our present route at Tergnier, which continues by Laon and Rheims to join one of the Est main lines at Chaumont-sur-Marne. At

Tergnier the line to Paris enters the valley of the Oise, and we can enjoy a spell of sustained fast running, until slowing down slightly at Creil, where the line from Amiens and Calais is joined. We are now only 51 kilometres short of Paris, and on to one of the busiest sections of main line in all France.

Before ending the steam saga of this historic group of lines, the developments of the 1930s must be described. It was in the summer of 1932 that non-stop running was first introduced between Paris and Liege, 366 kilometres and providing, so far as distance was concerned, a striking counterpart to the time-honoured run of 364 kilometres of the Cornish Riviera Express between Paddington and Plymouth. There was similarity also in that high speed could not be made over the latter part of the journey. In the French case the booked average speed from Paris to Liege was 95 km./h. and this meant covering the 239 kilometres to passing Jeumont in 134 minutes, at an average speed of 106.3 km./h. — much the fastest run in Europe over so long a distance. In the same summer the times of the non-stop Pullman expresses between Paris and Brussels had been brought down to 3 hr. 25 min., though with faster running then possible over the Belgian part of the journey this overall average of 90.7 km./h. did not require a higher average than 96.8 km./h. between Paris and Feignies. By the summer of 1939 however the time between Paris and Brussels had been brought down to the level three hours — a splendid average of 103 km./h., although it had been necessary to ease the time of the Liege non-stops down to 3 hr. 59 min. — an average of 91.8 km./h. compared with the ambitious 95 km./h. of 1932.

The Second World War played havoc with train services, but it was rather remarkable that despite the war and the German occupation from May 1940 onwards that seven large 4–6–4 express locomotives of a new design should have been built. They were one of the first products of the central office of studies and designs set up by the French National Railways, after the general amalgamation of 1938. These new locomotives were the work of De Caso, but although produced by the central authority they were used only in the Northern Region, and on the Belgian lines particularly. They were originally designed as ultra-high speed locomotives to haul trains of 200 tonnes at 170 km./h. on level track; but in the post-war

68

recovery period, and until the electrification of the lines in question, they worked in the ordinary express service to and from Jeumont, turn and about with rebuilt Chapelon 'Pacifics' of the Paris-Orleans design. Although these latter engines came to be used in many parts of France, the story of their inception and outstanding success belongs so essentially to the Orleans road that it must be deferred until a later chapter of this book. Both varieties of the De Caso engines were very successful. Three were 3-cylinder simples, and the other five were 4-cylinder compounds, though of these latter one, No. 232 U1, differed in detail from the rest. Tests on the road and on the stationary testing plant at Vitry-sur-Seine showed without any doubt that locomotives of outstanding capability had been produced; but the post-war decision to terminate the use of steam as soon as possible on French railways prevented the further development and general introduction of these engines on the Northern Region. A run made in 1943 when the 130.8 kilometres from Amiens to Paris were covered in 85 min. with a gross trailing load of 845 tonnes was considered normal rather than exceptional work with the De Caso 4–6–4s.

When the decision to terminate steam traction on French railways was taken, it was generally considered that the 1500 volt direct current traction system already installed over a lengthy mileage of the Orleans line would be used. This system was indeed adopted for the electrification of the main line of the Paris, Lyons and Mediterranean, and for the southward extension of the Orleans electrified network; but in the zone of Western Germany that was occupied by French forces after the war there was a short electric line that connected the Rhine valley with a tourist region in the Black Forest that had been equipped experimentally at 20,000 volts alternating current at the commercial frequency of 50 cycles per second. French railway engineers became intensely interested in this line, because the fixed equipment could be designed so much more cheaply, even though the locomotives were likely to be more expensive. But the preliminary investigations were so favourable that the French railways decided to make a main line trial, and a 77.5 kilometre stretch on the Geneva-Chamonix line was equipped. It was determined that the cost of installing the system would be no more than two thirds of that of the 1500 volt d.c. system.

Although extensions to the latter were being rapidly made in France, the savings possible with 25,000 volts a.c. at 50 cycles were such that a major installation was decided on; and the line chosen was the heavily used north to south route between Valenciennes and Thionville. A stretch of 304 kilometres was involved, and traffic studies showed that 105 new electric locomotives could replace 304 ageing steam locomotives. So the notable project went ahead, with the definite intention that if it proved successful this would be the system of electrification for all future conversions in France. It was not a decision to be taken lightly, because in all surrounding countries, not to mention the extensive installations of 1500 volts d.c. in France itself, the systems of electrification were different. Belgium was adopting 3000 volts d.c; so also was Italy. Germany, Austria and Switzerland used 15,000 volts a.c. at $16^2/_3$ cycles, for reasons that will be discussed later. While in the great majority of cases locomotives were changed at the international frontiers, there was the case of the Paris-Brussels non-stop expresses, and in the 1950s a degree of international co-operation in Europe was beginning that was to have deep repercussions from the railway point of view. It was in this atmosphere that French electrical engineers designed locomotives that could operate on more than one traction system.

Outstanding among these are the high power quadri-current type of French National Railways, which have been designed to operate on any of the standard gauge electrified lines in Europe. The traction motors operate on 1500 volts d.c. but the electrical equipment is such that by appropriate switching they can receive power from any of the four different overhead line systems now prevailing. These locomotives are fitted with four pantographs, but these do not correspond exactly to the four traction systems, as might be imagined, but to the physical details of the different overhead line construction. For example although the traction system is the same in Germany, Austria and Switzerland, the same pantograph cannot be used in all three, because of the differences in the construction of the overhead line and the clearance provided. Actually the four pantographs are used as follows:

Pantograph	Used on	
	Country	Overhead Supply
No. 1	France	1,500 v d.c.
	Holland	1,500 v.d.c.
	Belgium	3,000 v d.c.
	Luxembourg	3,000 v d.c.
No. 2	France	25,000 v a.c.
	Luxembourg	25,000 v a.c.
	Italy	3,000 v d.c.
No. 3	Switzerland	15,000 v a.c.
No. 4	Austria	15,000 v a.c.
	West Germany	

On the French quadri-current locomotives, which have a maximum continuous rate of 4450 kilowatts, arrangements are included that make it possible to change from one traction system to another *without stopping*. And this brings me back to the run from Brussels to Paris, and the change from the 3000 volts d.c. of Belgium, to the 25,000 volts a.c. at 50 cycles of the Northern Region of the French railways, near Quevy-le-Petit.

Nine years ago I had the privilege of riding one of the big quadri-current locomotives at the head of the Pullman express, 'Etoile du Nord', and not only saw how a very fast and heavy train was successfully timed, but watched how the change over of traction system was carried out, at a speed of about 100 km./h. The Brussels-Paris non-stop expresses are very much faster now than when they were first introduced in 1923, when the time was $3^3/_4$ hours. Now the 310 kilometres are covered in 2 hr. 22 min., at an overall average speed of 130 km./h. Also while the original load was no more than six coaches, with a total weight to be hauled of about 220 tonnes, on this trip of mine we took ten of the 'grand-confort' coaches, scaling

71

up to a full 500 tonnes. Through Belgium the maximum speed permitted was then 140 km./h., and we took $29^1/_4$ minutes to cover the initial 60.5 kilometres from Brussels to Mons, easing there to 85 km./h. through the station, with its curves. We approached the Franco-Belgian frontier at 126 km./h. and then came the interesting change of traction system.

Power was shut off the motors, and then the driver changed the selector index on his instrument panel in the cab, from the Belgian-Luxembourg 3000 volt d.c. position to the French 25,000 volt a.c position. This defined automatically the new pantograph to be raised, and interlocked simultaneously the group of electrical controls corresponding to the traction system being approached. At that stage none of the circuits were energised, but when all was proved correct, the appropriate pantograph was raised, and contact was made with the overhead line. Automatic checking then took place to ensure that the current being received in the pantograph was in accordance with the group of electrical controls selected by the driver's positioning of the index pointer. In other words the whole system was electrically proved. Once all was found correct the driver could restore power to the motors. It sounds elaborate, and takes a little time to describe; but it all took place in a matter of seconds, and we actually ran the 4.2 kilometres from Quevy to Feignies in a few seconds over two minutes, at an average speed of 120 km./h. including the changeover.

So we continued in dashing elegant style to the outskirts of Paris, often running up to the maximum speed permitted on this French main line, 160 km./h., with the great locomotive riding with surpassing smoothness and ease. There were four slight checks to our sustained high speed; but the 210 kilometres from the intersection with the pioneer 25,000 volt line at Aulnoye, to Saint Denis, were covered in $88^3/_4$ minutes, at an average of 142 km./h., and so we came in towards journey's end. I always think the Nord has the most impressive entry into Paris, running so near to the hill of Montmartre, crowned by the exquisite 'Sacré Coeur', while for the railway enthusiast in steam days there was a sight of the big locomotive running sheds of La Chapelle, which was always such a fascinating parade ground of Nord express locomotives. On the east side of the line a little before reaching La Chapelle are the yards and connections to the Petite Ceinture Line, which makes an easterly circuit of the city to reach the Gare de Lyon, and Austerlitz station. Many a time I have travelled in trains having through portions from Calais to the Riviera, and after the usual fast run up to the Ceinture junctions we had then been drawn with great deliberation round the connecting line, pausing at the occasional adverse signal, almost brushing the sides of lofty tenement houses, and crossing one or more of the minor boulevards.

This time however we are going into the Gare du Nord, under those noisy viaducts where the Metro trains go clattering across the main line, and into the great terminus and the maelstrom of arrival, where all the atmosphere of any big station greetings, reunions, frustrations of porters, luggage and all else, is intensified by the top-speed animation of Paris herself. Just now our stay is of the briefest; the Gare de l'Est is next door, and we shall soon be out again on the route of the Orient Express.

CHAPTER SEVEN

Paris eastbound —
route of the 'Orient Express'

Paris is fortunate in the architecture of her large terminal stations. The Nord has a massive solidarity that grows upon one. The Gare de Lyon, less encompassed by other buildings than most of them, is distinguished by its tremendous clock tower, but the Est, in the decoration of its great central arch is perhaps the finest of all. Even so, railway enthusiasts from far and wide, sparing hardly a glance for the architecture, could scarcely wait to get inside; for there, on the spacious concourse, was enthroned a magnificent example of a Crampton locomotive: 'Le Continent'. This priceless relic, a classic of industrial archaeology is no longer there, and one has to travel the length of the Est system, and most of that of the Alsace-Lorraine, to see her now in the French railway museum at Mulhouse. Thomas Russell Crampton, an English engineer and once at Swindon under Daniel Gooch, found the French railways much more receptive to his spectacular invention of a locomotive with a single pair of huge driving wheels at the extreme rear end. Many of them worked on the Nord, on the PLM and on the Orleans; but on the Est they were the standard express passenger engine down to the year 1878. Indeed 'prendre le Crampton' was colloquial French for 'going by train'.

What became the Chemin de Fer de l'Est, and is now the Eastern Region of the French National Railways, had as a major component the Paris and Strasbourg Railway, which name is carried in full on the preserved Crampton engine; and so settled was the locomotive department of the Est in its affection for the Crampton type that when engines, with greater tractive power than a single pair of driving wheels could provide, were at last needed, they designed in 1878 what were virtually four-coupled Cramptons. They were remarkable engines, having coupled wheels of no less than 2308 mm. diameter, a large boiler and excellent valve gear. They ran easily up to 120 km./h. on suitable sections of the line. There were however not many trains on which such standards of performance were needed, and no more than ten were built. A much larger number was built of a similar type with smaller wheels, for general passenger and mixed traffic service. The 2308 mm. engines of the '501' class had, however, been well proved in service when the famous 'Orient Express' was first put on in 1883, and for a period of about 14 years they had that train to themselves between Paris and Strasbourg.

There can have been few trains anywhere in the world that have surpassed the 'Orient Express' for pure glamour; but it did not hurry, and in the 1880s the morning express leaving the Gare de l'Est at 9.45 was the best train from Paris into the Rhineland of Germany. Even so, whatever the Crampton locomotives or their four-coupled derivatives could do in the way of maximum speed the averages from start to stop were barely above 65 km./h. This morning express took 6 hr. 10 min. to do the 354 kilometres from Paris to Nancy, an average of only $57^1/_4$ km./h. The run included seven intermediate stops of which that at Epernay was for half an hour, presumably for refreshments at lunch time. The Est line to Nancy is one of the most level of any radiating from Paris. It follows the valley of the Marne for the first 210 kilometres and then successively those of its tributaries, the Saulx and the Ornain until more than 260 kilometres out. It is only then, in crossing the watershed, and in descending into the valley of the Meuse near Commercy that any appreciable gradients are encountered. The one-time Paris and Strasbourg Railway, which is recalled on the preserved Crampton, was cut short after the war of 1870–1871, and the German frontier was reached at Igney Avricourt, 410 kilometres from Paris. Although no longer a stopping place this one-time frontier post is still significantly marked on the railway today. During the time that most of Alsace and part of Lorraine were part of Germany the railways were changed over from left hand running on double track to the right hand, favoured in Germany and Austria, and German type signalling installed. After the restoration of these territories to France, in 1919, the railway layouts were left as they were, and flying junctions put in at

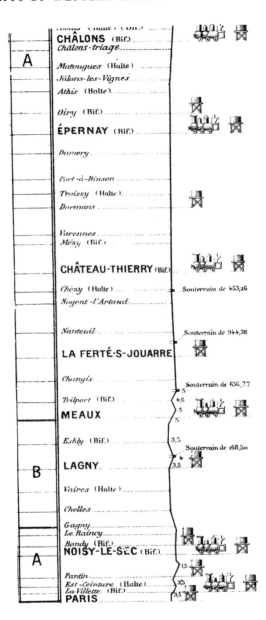

10. Portion of an old Est working timetable, showing features of the line, where locomotives were stabled, and where water was available

Igney Avricourt to effect the changeover from left hand to right hand running, without the inconvenience of surface intersections.

Although Professor Foxwell and Lord Farrer were not very complimentary to the Est, in their classic work of 1889, *Express Trains English and Foreign*, it was perhaps just as well that the trains did not run too fast, because most of the rolling stock was four-wheeled and entirely without corridors. Not only that, but the Crampton type of locomotives however favoured they might have been in France, rode distinctly 'hard', and at any kind of speed were severe in their treatment of the track. It is on this account that they found so little favour on English lines like the London and North Western, on which there was a general urge to speed up as early as the 1850s. Although all the stops on the Est line were quite brief, the fastest train, the 9.45 out of Paris, stopped for 6 minutes at Chalons, 5 minutes at Bar le Duc, 4 minutes at Toul, and 17 minutes at Nancy, in addition to the half-hour refreshment stop at Epernay.

While the original Paris and Strasbourg line is the principal subject of the present itinerary, the Est had a second main line, through Troyes and Chaumont to Belfort, and Switzerland over which the running, in the latter part of the nineteenth century, was somewhat faster. In this case there was the stimulus of competition, with the PLM via Dijon, and with the non-French route from Ostend, over the Belgian State Railways to Luxembourg, and then over the Prussian-controlled Alsace-Lorraine line to Basle. However my most abiding memory of the Est line to Belfort en route for Berne, was when our engine succeeded somehow in derailing its tender when leaving Vesoul, and of the interminable delay waiting for another engine to come from Belfort and draw the carriages clear, once the delicate job of uncoupling had been done between two vehicles strongly linked but out of line. We were very late for an evening engagement in Berne! The line was then steam worked, and I must hasten on to the interesting locomotive developments on the Est from 1900 onwards. By that time, of course, the fame of the du Bousquet-de Glehn 4-cylinder compounds on the Nord was attracting worldwide attention, though the Est, in adopting the compound principle, never used the 'Atlantic' type.

In 1900 a class of big, rather ugly compound 4-4-0s was

introduced. They had a squashed up appearance, having the bogie centre set back some distance in rear of the chimney. Apparently they had a good deal of teething troubles with them, not least with coupling rods. These engines had the usual de Glehn arrangement of cylinders, but coming to ride one of them on the morning express from Paris, as far as Chaumont, the late Lord Monkswell was surprised to notice that the coupling rods had been removed, and that the engine was running as a 'double single', in the style of the Webb 3-cylinder compounds on the London and North Western Railway. Apparently they had had an extraordinary failure with one of these engines, the aftermath of which he saw in the sheds at Chaumont. It can best be described in his own words:

It appears this machine had her wheels keyed on the axles by means of round instead of the usual square keys, and these round keys had allowed the wheel to shift a little on its seat, so that the coupling rods were twisted up into the most extraordinary shapes. We went to have a look at these coupling rods, and it was one of the most wonderful things I have ever seen — they were simply twisted up like pieces of wire; in one of them there was almost a perfect right angle, and yet so good was the metal they were made of that there was not a crack anywhere. In consequence of this incident many of the engines of this class were having their coupling rods taken down to see how they got on without them. From what I saw of the work of No. 2423, I should say the experiment was a success, as with a heavy train on steep adverse gradients the engine did not skid at all.

For the record I may add that with a load of 260 tonnes, the 167 kilometres from Paris to Troyes were covered in $126^3/_4$ minutes, exactly to time and the 95.5 very hilly kilometres on to Chaumont took 2 minutes less than the 79 minutes allowed. This was good work for the year 1900, and Lord Monkswell noted particularly that despite the absence of coupling rods the engine did not slip at all when starting away, or when pulling hard on the heavy gradients beyond Troyes. The Est railway did not however develop the 4–4–0 type for fast passenger working, and unlike the other French railways favoured the 4–6–0 type. Although rather festooned with all the accessories that Continental engineers hang on their locomotives, the Est 4–6–0s were a fine job, and at a time when all the other French railways were using 'Pacifics', they held the work down admirably, until after the First World War. Then, as previously mentioned, they took 40 of the Government-ordered Etat type 'Pacifics'. The Est locomotive department however, did not attempt to develop the 'Pacific' in the same way that the Nord, PLM and Orleans did. The ideas of Monsieur Duchatel, who was chief mechanical engineer in the late 1920s were running in quite a different direction.

About this time a friend and I received his permission to visit the running sheds at La Villette just outside Paris, and to take photographs, and I remember how the voluble little supervisor who took us round so enthusiastically almost hustled us past one of the Etat 'Pacifics' to give us a glowing picture of the merits of one of the old 4–6–0s. But at that time the pride and joy of the Est were the gigantic 4–8–2s of Duchatel's own design. Shortly before I went to La Villette there had been an editorial article in *The Railway Engineer* entitled 'A Great Locomotive', and great these 4–8–2s certainly were, to stand beside. They were designed particularly to work over the difficul gradients of the Belfort line, rather than the 'Orient Express' route; but after the prototype built at the Epernay Works of the Est had been fully tested orders for another 43 were placed with outside manufacturers, and they came into general use on both main routes out of Paris. The locomotive authorities of the Etat were also interested, and the prototype No. 241,001 was tested on the Paris-Cherbourg line, giving excellent results. In all essentials these huge 4–8–2s were de Glehn compounds; they weighed 115 tonnes in working order, without their tenders, and had the high nominal tractive effort of 29,000 kg. One feature remarked upon by connoisseurs of locomotive design outside France was the very high boiler pressure of 23.2 kg. per sq. cm. Hitherto, 20 kg. per sq. cm. had been about the maximum, though in later years boilers pressed to 24 kg. per sq. cm. became quite common in the U.S.A.

It has unfortunately to be told that these great locomotives were not entirely successful. In ordinary service because of riding characteristics and of their effect upon the track, they had to be limited to a maximum speed of 110 km./h., but worse than this were defects in the frame design. Because of the amount of curvature on the main lines resulting from following the courses of large rivers in order to secure good gradients, the Est, and also the PLM, built their locomotives with plate frames of reduced thickness to impart a degree of flexibility, and to accord with a theory that the locomotive and the track were two parts of a single entity, one having to fit in with the other. The Nord and the Orleans on the other hand built their locomotives on massive frames. The former policy envisaged the development of a high output of power, but not to put forth any excess over normal, as when there was, for example, lost time to be recovered. The engines of the Nord and the Orleans were expected to withstand hard thrashing, when accelerating or climbing heavy gradients.

The weakness of the Est design, as applied to the 4–8–2s was dramatically revealed in a series of comparative tests conducted over the Nord main line in 1933 between Paris and Calais. These tests were undertaken at the instigation of the Nord, and the competing engines were set some very hard tasks. Naturally each of the competitors was out to uphold the honour of their own railway, and the Est 4–8–2 had to be worked extremely hard to keep time. The first of the class to be tested fractured a frame in the very first group of runs. Another engine was substituted, and did the same after running 970 kilometres. Finally a *third* was produced and this managed to finish the tests. While it was a distinctly black mark against the design, the failures occurred through doing work beyond what it had been designed to do. Although so large and nominally powerful a locomotive the proportions had to be determined to enable it to work at a certain medium rate of power output. Of course one of the oft-quoted attributes of the steam locomotive, as compared with the diesel, is that a skilful crew could coax an inordinately big effort from it for a limited period, by mortgaging the supply of steam in the boiler; in these French tests, while the Nord and Orleans engines could stand this treatment with impunity, the big Est 4–8–2s while giving the power were not structurally strong enough to withstand the extra forces that had to be transmitted through their frames.

The Strasbourg main line of the Est certainly includes a great deal of curvature. I have travelled its length in the cab of one of the latest electric locomotives, which was of course an ideal place from which to see the line and enjoy the beautiful scenery. The river Marne makes a course that is a great deal more winding than the railway, and in many places the hillsides are pierced with tunnels to keep a reasonably good alignment. It is a delightfully pastoral countryside, and on my last journey over the line in the summer of 1974 I was struck by the complete absence of modern urban development. The old-world villages with their picturesque red roofed houses remained as they had been for decades past. One saw the cathedrals in country towns like Meaux, and Chalons-sur-Marne, while Chalons, as a military centre and a major railway junction also had extensive marshalling yards. On this route Chalons is not the only intermediate point to have a dual personality. To vintners, epicures and their kind Epernay is famed as a centre of the champagne trade, where the wines known as the *Vins de la Riviere* are made; but to the railwayman Epernay is the site of the principal locomotive works of the Est where, among other celebrities, the first of the giant 4–8–2 locomotives was built.

Yet railway-minded as I am, — exclusively so as I am alleged to be by some of my womenfolk! — I cannot somehow place Epernay in the same category as Crewe or Altoona. Set in so fair a countryside, in a community dedicated to champagne, the making of locomotives would seem to the outsider as some 'under the counter' activity, whereas in fact Epernay had as fine a tradition as any locomotive building establishment on the railways of France. This main line of the Est has for me a certain air of tranquillity, which my most recent journeys on, when we covered much of the route at 160 km./h., did very little to dispel. I think of earlier journeys, including one when we were westward bound on the 'Orient Express', and had slept well through the night from Munich. I raised the shutters of our sleeper soon after daybreak, and just lay watching the countryside of the Marne valley roll by. There are thrills to be sure, when one is riding in the cab of a modern electric locomotive. The French have excelled in the way they have rebuilt the trackwork at complicated junctions, where to the passenger the speed in earlier days was hair-raising. There used to be an old joke among hardened travellers that French trains always put on their biggest spurts when they were approaching a bad curve, or a junction with an alignment like a dog's hind leg. Nowadays the passenger would scarcely be aware of places like Epernay or Chalons-sur-Marne, which are swept through at a steady

150 km./h. It is the visitor in the cab seeing the curves and network of lines ahead who momentarily holds his breath till the locomotive glides through with scarcely a tremor.

It is at Chalons that the route of one of the important north to south lines is intersected. From Amiens it has come south by Laon and Rheims, and uses our own line for 20 kilometres or so, before following the valley of the Marne to the south, and heading for Chaumont, Vesoul, and Belfort. Before the nationalisation of the French railways the international service over this line was operated jointly by the Est and the Nord, with change of locomotives at Laon where the two railways joined. This is another French route of which I have pleasant memories of early morning travel from the south towards Calais. One took the avoiding line outside Rheims soon after dawn, with a distant view of the reconstructed cathedral, and then came the stop for engine changing almost in the shadow of one of the loveliest cathedrals in all France, with the welcome addition to the train of the dining car.

The transition from the Marne valley to that of the Meuse, over steep gradients about which I shall have more to say when discussing the most modern electric locomotives, brings a significant change in the scenery; for we enter a chalk countryside, and at Sorcy there is one of the most colossal cement works I have ever seen. Apart from this however the landscape after we enter the valley of the Moselle remains very pretty, right up to the outskirts of Nancy. The fastest electric trains of today cover the 354 kilometres from Paris to Nancy in 160 minutes, at an overall average of 132 km./h., and in this neighbourhood there will probably come a first sight of an unusual and very functional form of electric locomotive. It will be one of a numerous class, the initial working of which had a profound influence on the development of electric traction on railways, not only in France but all over the world, — one of the pioneer 25,000 volt a.c. 50 cycles freight locomotives put on to the Valenciennes-Thionville line. There was certainly little in the way of external styling in the design of these locomotives. They have a prominent 'nose' extending front and rear from a central cab, in which the controls like the external shape were functional to the last degree. No sophisticated driving console was provided, and in a rather crowded ensemble the

82

driver stood sideways, so that he could see fore and aft from the cab, with equal facility.

When the success of the 25,000 volt a.c. system was assured, by the efficient working of these pioneer freight locomotives, the design of express passenger and mixed traffic units followed the style of the latest 1500 volt d.c. locomotives on the Orleans and PLM lines, so far as body work and wheel arrangements were concerned. These in turn were derived from the very successful introduction, on the Bern-Lötschberg-Simplon Railway in Switzerland, of the all-adhesion type of electric locomotive, just at the end of the Second World War. Arising no doubt from long experience with steam locomotives it had previously been considered that electric locomotives intended for high speed running should have a leading bogie, or at least a two-wheel truck, and in Switzerland, and in the earliest French main line electrification schemes the locomotives were designed in this way. The earliest British main line diesel-electric locomotives were similarly equipped. But Swiss engineers and those of the Lötschberg line in particular, faced with the haulage of heavy loads on their steeply graded routes, sought to make the entire weight of the locomotive available for adhesion. By a scientific re-appraisal of bogie design a very efficient and excellent riding locomotive on two four-wheel bogies was produced, which has formed the virtual prototype of later Swiss designs; of a variety of French ones; and of the British high speed electric locomotives operating between London and Glasgow.

The electric locomotives first used on the 25,000 volt a.c. line between Paris and Strasbourg were of the same design as those on the first stage of the Nord electrification, between Paris and Amiens. They were capable of developing 3730 kilowatts continuously, and were of course able to master easily any task initially put to them on the easy gradients existing over most of the line. Externally they could be described as 'neat boxes', finished in a pastel shade of blue. The maximum speeds were at first limited to 140 km./h. and this the locomotives used to attain very quickly from rest, and sustain it wherever track conditions permitted.

From Nancy it is no more than 40 kilometres directly north to Metz, but the principal express trains southward from Belgium, through Luxembourg to Switzerland, take the former Alsace-Lorraine main line south east from Metz and join our present route at Reding, just to the east of Sarrebourg. Metz itself is a major junction and is the first stopping place from Paris on some of the Trans-Europe-Express trains heading into Germany via Saarbrücken. As the principal city in the annexed German province of Lothringen, after 1870–1871, Metz came in for some special treatment by the new owners. In his book *The Land of France*, Ralph Dutton writes:

The traveller who arrives at Metz by train will find himself in one of the most hideous and grandiose stations in Europe. It was built under the Germans in 1908 in what was supposed to be the Romanesque style. Grey sandstone was used, and this fantastic erection was capped by a spinach-green roof.

The Kaiser was well known for his interest in railways, and it is believed that he had a hand in the design.

Fifty-six kilometres east of Nancy the Est main line comes to Igney Avricourt, and the one-time Franco-German frontier. Here the eastbound and westbound tracks change positions to permit of right hand running on the former Alsace-Lorraine lines. Instead of the stop at the old frontier post the crack trains now execute the changeover at 160 km./h. via the 'flyover'. After the return of this territory to French sovereignty in 1919, it would have been easy enough to change the tracks themselves back to left hand running had it not been for the signalling. The Alsace-Lorraine line had been fully equipped in the German style, which in the days before colour light signalling was vastly different from the French. While there were numerous local differences in practice on the railways of France, the basic stop signal was the red and white chessboard, or *carré*, presented broadside on to the driver when a stop was required, but turned edge on, to be virtually invisible, for all clear. There were various discs, the block semaphore, and chessboards with different colours, some presented diamond fashion. The basic German code was quite different, and much simpler. It consisted essentially of a two-arm semaphore for junctions, and nothing more than a single upper quadrant semaphore for a stop signal on plain line. The great

84

difference between the French and German systems will be apparent from the diagrams on pages 86 and 87.

By the time the old frontier is crossed the Vosges mountains are piling up to south of the line, and for the next 50 kilometres the railway is making its way round their northern flanks, amid splendid scenery. The curves and gradients are more severe, and in the 22.5 kilometres between Reding and Saverne speed is limited to a maximum of 120 km./h. From the latter station however the line emerges into the Plain of Alsace, and it is straight and level going to the outskirts of Strasbourg, with the station names predominantly German in style: Schwindratzheim, Mommenheim, Vendenheim, Mundolsheim, and finally the big marshalling yards of Hausbergen. At Strasbourg itself the old city is surrounded entirely by a chain of canals, and the railway does not penetrate at all. The passenger station lies on the western side, and forms a junction between the north to south main line of the Alsace-Lorraine system, and the connecting line which swings round eastward to the south of the city, to cross the Rhine and enter Germany at Kehl. The principal goods station lies to the northwest and the goods lines, connecting in all major directions, run completely clear of the passenger station complex.

Railway meals, other than those taken in full dining cars, are apt to be hurried and indigestible. The bun served in English railway refreshment rooms was a long standing music hall joke. But eating is a serious business anywhere in France and I shall always recall the pleasure of meals enjoyed at station restaurants in Alsace. There is — and the present tense still emphatically applies! — nothing hurried or slipshod there. The table linen and cutlery are immaculate; the service both in its attitude and attention is faultless. The only trouble is that they always seem to imagine that one has as much time as if spending the whole night dining out. One night a French engineer and I were taking the 20.45 express from Strasbourg to Mulhouse. We sat down to dinner soon after 18.30, but the meal was served with such dignity and deliberation that we had to run to catch the train!

No mention of the Strasbourg line would be complete without reference to the latest electric locomotives. The French National Railways have greatly developed the external styling of their electric and diesel electric locomotives, which with their distinctive colouring

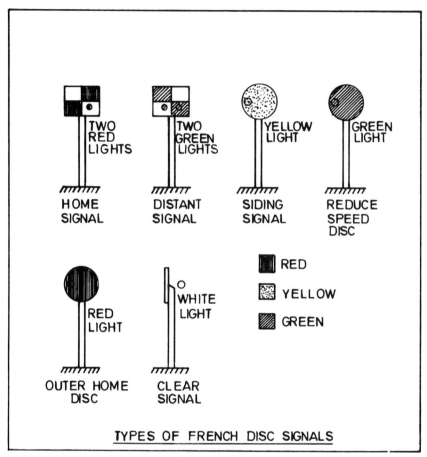

TYPES OF FRENCH DISC SIGNALS

11. Diagrams of French (above) and German (opposite) signalling

makes them among the most striking modern locomotives to be found anywhere. But it is in the electrical controls that the 'BB 15000' class on the Strasbourg line are outstanding. The French set considerable store upon the precision of their train running, and the exact observance of the line maximum speeds. In Great Britain, whereas the nominal maximum speed on the principal routes is now 160 km./h., the man with a stop watch can often clock 170, 175 or sometimes as much as 180 km./h. in favourable circumstances. It is not so in France. Where the limit is 160 km./h. it *is* 160 km./h., and

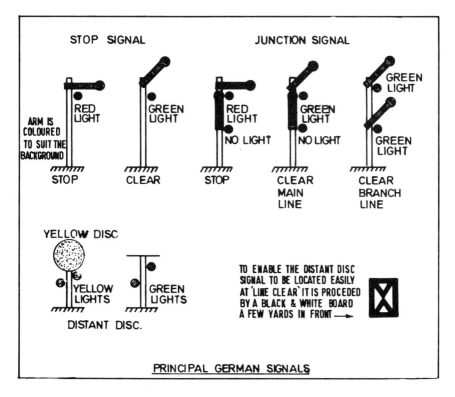

STOP SIGNAL   JUNCTION SIGNAL

RED LIGHT   GREEN LIGHT   RED LIGHT   GREEN LIGHT   GREEN LIGHT

ARM IS COLOURED TO SUIT THE BACKGROUND

NO LIGHT   NO LIGHT   GREEN LIGHT

STOP   CLEAR   STOP   CLEAR MAIN LINE   CLEAR BRANCH LINE

YELLOW DISC

YELLOW LIGHTS   GREEN LIGHTS

DISTANT DISC.

TO ENABLE THE DISTANT DISC SIGNAL TO BE LOCATED EASILY AT 'LINE CLEAR' IT IS PROCEDED BY A BLACK & WHITE BOARD A FEW YARDS IN FRONT ➝

PRINCIPAL GERMAN SIGNALS

no more. This requires considerable skill on the driver's part, especially where a very powerful locomotive has a load well within its powers. On these latest locomotives the electrical controls are such that the driver can pre-select the speed at which he requires to run; the locomotive will then rapidly accelerate or decelerate to that figure, irrespective of the load, or gradient, and remain there until the driver makes another adjustment.

One evening I was riding in the cab of one of these locomotives on the 'Stanislas' express, which is booked to run the 354 kilometres from Nancy to Paris in 160 minutes. We had a very heavy train for such a sharp timing, of 660 tonnes, and were running first at the line maximum speed of 140 km./h. between Toul and Commercy, beside the river Meuse. Then we came to that difficult 24 kilometres where the line crosses the watershed between the Meuse and Marne valleys.

The gradient is rising at 1 in 125 from Leronville, and then after passing the summit at Ernecourt it descends at 1 in 125 to Nancois. The speed limit is 140 km./h. through Leronville station, and then 150 km./h. up the bank and down the far side to Nancois. To maintain the maximum line speed here required a mighty big effort with a train of 660 tonnes, but in response to the driver's setting of the pre-selector the locomotive duly responded, and we topped the bank at exactly 150 km./h. But then, with the driver taking no action at all that speed was also maintained precisely *down* the ensuing descent. The electrical controls applied the brakes to prevent the speed rising even a fraction over the limit. It was a wonderful demonstration of modern locomotive engineering.

CHAPTER EIGHT

Into the Rhineland — the old German state systems

Entering Germany from the west there are now six major express routes, of which no less than three originate in Holland. The situation was rather different at the turn of the century, when except for the connection at Igney Avricourt traffic into the Prussian controlled states of Elsass and Lothringen from the west was definitely discouraged. In this Chapter I am concerned with the lines leading from the main line of the Eastern Region of the French railways through Epernay and Chalons, though the whole complex of railways in the Rhineland is fascinating in its historical aspects. The entire course of the Rhine from Mannheim to the cities of the Ruhr is one of the most densely populated regions on the Continent of Europe, and the railway network that developed in the nineteenth century was appropriately extensive. By the time of the Franco-Prussian war of 1870–1871 most of the one-time independent railways in Germany had been brought under the control of Prussia. Indeed, Bismarck tried to secure the absorption of all the railways under one Imperial direction. But the states of the south and south-west stood out resolutely against this plan, and they were not eventually joined into a fully co-ordinated national system until the end of the First World War.

In the years between there were a number of local administrations, all part of the Prussian State Railways, but exercising a certain degree of autonomy in their own areas. The exception was the unfortunate Alsace-Lorraine, taken over from France, directly controlled in every respect from Berlin, and renamed the *Imperial* Elsass-Lothringen. The accompanying map shows the various administrations as they were operating in the Rhineland just prior to the turn of the century, and it

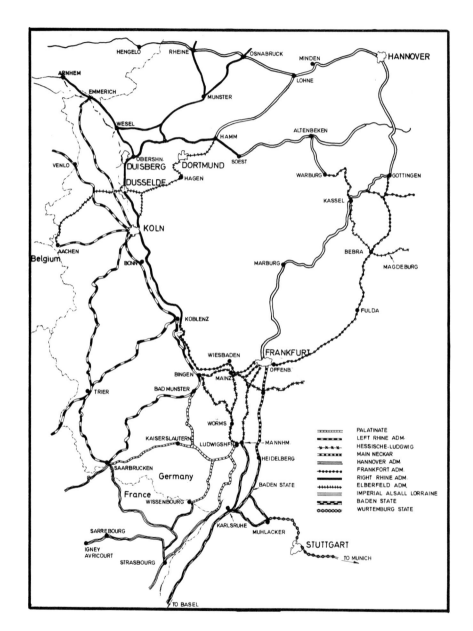

12. West Germany — railway systems about 1890

will be appreciated that the situation was complicated. The lines delineated by the codes on the map are those over which the so-called German express trains of the day were run. The single thin lines show the subsidiary lines, some of which have subsequently been elevated to more important roles. The map shows clearly how the location of the Alsace-Lorraine main line was used parallel to the new frontier of 1871, with only the two westerly connections. Prussia took very little interest in the running of the 'Orient Express', and but for the influence of Austria the express service between Saarburg and Igney-Avricourt could also have been severed.

Enough of preliminaries, however; we are now entering this interesting region over the route of the present TEE, the 'Goethe', which after running the 355 kilometres from Paris to Metz non-stop in 160 minutes crosses the frontier in Germany just after Forbach and reaches Saarbrücken in $3^3/_4$ hours from Paris. The 'Goethe' continues to Frankfurt but Saarbrücken itself, junction of six main routes, is a railway centre of no mean interest. Here I may be falling a prey to the accusation once levelled against me by an irate, ultra-modern young reader of *The Railway Magazine*, who weighed in heavily against what he called my preoccupation over the surviving pockets of steam. When I was there last, in 1972, there was certainly plenty of steam around Saarbrücken, though actually it was not my interest in locomotives that was the prime cause of my visit. It was here in earlier days that the Left Rhine Administration made contact with the Alsace-Lorraine, and it was over a fascinating route of the former that I came to Saarbrücken. It is a corner of Germany that is well off the track of the average tourist, and reached by an exceedingly picturesque line from Cologne. In the map relating to the year 1900 Saarbrücken features on only a single route, that from Metz to the Mainz-Frankfurt area; but today it is a busy enough traffic centre to be the scene of one of the most sophisticated examples of modern automated train control in Western Europe.

At the moment I am more concerned with an earlier epoch in German railway working. Even the steam locomotives that are still so much in evidence around Saarbrücken are of the Second World War period, and later. The through express passenger trains, and the TEE flyers were electric; but the '052' class 2–10–0 freight engines were to be seen everywhere. This class provides an all-time object lesson in specialist engine designing. Before the war the Reichsbahn, as it was then, had a very powerful series of 2–10–0s designated series '44'. A lighter version, series '50', was produced in 1939 that would have a higher route availability, and bring the advantage of a 2–10–0 to lines where the '44' class had been prohibited, on account of weight. Even in its lightweight form the series '50' was a big engine, with a tractive effort of 22700 kg. for an all-up engine weight of $86^1/_2$ tonnes. As the war developed, and large additional quantities of locomotives were needed — against the acute shortages of raw materials that were then prevalent — a new austerity version of the series '50' was designed, to effect a maximum saving in materials and production time. Everything that could be dispensed with was discarded; every part that could be made lighter or more economically was redesigned, but in saying this it must not be imagined that weight was saved by using high grade alloys, or aluminium. None but the basest of materials were permitted, and so emerged the series '52'. Whereas the '50' with its tender weighed 146 tonnes, the '52' was no more than 119. Eventually more than 10,000 of these locomotives were built — *ten thousand*! It is not surprising that many of them are to be seen when travelling in Germany.

Another modern steam locomotive class actively engaged in Saarbrücken, and elsewhere in West Germany is the '23' class of 2–6–2, first introduced as recently as 1953. Between the two World Wars the Prussian 'P8' class of mixed traffic 4–6–0s had been one of the most popular 'maids of all work' on the Reichsbahn. There had originally been no fewer than 3850 of them, and on the complete amalgamation of all the German railways into the national system in 1924, a total of 2975 were still active. By the end of the Second World War the still numerous survivors of this class were at the end of their tether, and replacement was needed in the form of a medium mixed traffic unit with a high route availability. The outcome was the striking '23' class. I shall never forget my first sight of one of these engines when it backed on to an international express at Venlo, in succession to the Dutch electric locomotive that had hauled our train from the Hook of Holland. It was the immense height — seeming positively to tower over the large air-conditioned coaches of our train. They are powerful locomotives, but absolute heavyweights compared to the war series '52'. The tractive effort of the class '23' is 15370 kg., and with their tenders they weigh as much as 145.5 tonnes. There is a tank engine version of them, with the 2–8–4 wheel arrangement.

The line northward from Saarbrücken to Cologne, is one of sustained railway interest and great natural beauty. Following the valley of the Saar at first, through Saarlautern, Merzig, and Saarburg the line is working its way round the southern flanks of the Schwarzwalder Hochwald, with a summit rising to nearly 915 m. Then at Trier comes the confluence of the Saar with the Moselle, and our railway route intersects the main line in the Moselle valley running from Thionville north eastwards to Koblenz. There is a gem of railway topography on this line. At Cochem where the river is making a series of tremendous convolutions among hills clothed with vineyards the railway takes a short cut in tunnel — the Kaiser Wilhelm tunnel, the imposing entrance facade of which is surmounted by a huge sculptured representation of the Imperial eagle. Trier is a considerable railway centre where many series '52' 2–10–0s could be seen grouped around the roundhouse turntable. Our own route strikes off northward at Ehrang, where there was another parade of steam locomotives at the roundhouse, and enters the region of the Eifel uplands. It is an extremely pretty countryside, with villages of half-timbered houses, richly wooded hillsides, and small towns obviously dependent on the timber trade. The line abounds in sharp curves most of which were taken very fast, but nevertheless quite smoothly. At Euskirchen one is down to level country once more, though still finely wooded until nearing the outskirts of Cologne. At the moment however I am retracing steps to Saarbrücken, so as to approach Cologne, instead, up the famous reaches of the Rhine valley from Mainz.

The eastward run from Saarbrücken takes the train through beautiful mountain country to enter the territory of the former Palatinate Railway, a privately owned concern. This line participated in the working of a through service between Rotterdam and Basle. In Germany the Left Rhine Administration ran this service as far south as Bingerbruck, where the Palatinate took over, for the run through

Bad Kreuznach, Neustadt, and Landau to the end-on junction with the Alsace-Lorraine system at Weissenburg. As will be seen from the map on page 90, the Palatinate had a parallel main line running directly south from Mannheim, also to link up with the Alsace-Lorraine. The Palatinate made locomotive history in 1898 by being first on the continent of Europe to introduce the simple 'Atlantic' type. They were neat, distinctive looking engines, with inside cylinders and a conical fronted smokebox. The performance required of them was modest, namely a speed of 100 km./h. on level track with a train load of 220 tonnes. They were painted an orange-brown, with nothing in the way of lining, and like some other Continental locomotives of the day this colour was continued forward to include the smokebox and chimney. They could not be claimed as the first 'Atlantics' in all Europe, because in 1894 Karl Gölsdorf had introduced a 2-cylinder compound on the Kaiser Ferdinand Northern Railway in Austria.

Mannheim was the meeting point of three different railways that were all outside the Prussian influence and control. The principal international route from the south was that of the Baden State Railway, from Basle, passing through Freiburg, Appenwein and Karlsruhe. Between the last two stations this line formed part of the route of the 'Orient Express', before it turned east once again towards Stuttgart. The Baden State Railway had some of the fastest trains in Germany at the turn of the century, one of which covered the 262 kilometres from Mannheim to Basle in 4 hr. 50 min. inclusive of seven intermediate stops. The average speed exclusive of the time spent at stations was $60^1/_2$ km./h., which was reasonably good considering that the section between Mannheim and Karlsruhe was then single line. A glance at the map is enough to show how severely this independent line was in competition with the Alsace-Lorraine. North of Mannheim was a triangle of country served by the Hessische-Ludwig Company, with Frankfurt and Bingen at the northern points, and before reaching Mainz the line from the south, running on the left bank of the Rhine, is drawing near to the remarkable complex of railway connections, by which the cities on the left and right banks are linked before the river itself enters upon its most spectacular reaches.

Countless travellers in varying degrees of descriptive and exotic prose have tried to convey something of the unique scenic attractions of this great river in the 189 kilometres between Mainz and Cologne. The fact that there is a main line of railway on both banks in close proximity to the river for the whole distance makes it a familiar place for tourists travelling far beyond Germany itself. At the time with which I am now mainly concerned, the Hessische-Ludwig line on the left bank ended at Bingerbrück, where the Left Rhine railway from the north turned up the valley of the Nahe, to head for Saarbrücken. From Bingerbrück onwards it was 'Left Rhine' for the international trains throughout to the Dutch frontier just short of Arnhem. Opposite to Mainz the line on the right bank is at first that of the Frankfurt Administration, and this continues to Niederlahnstein, opposite Koblenz, where junction is made with the tracks of the Right Rhine Administration. We are now fairly into the network of lines that were controlled by the Prussian State Railways, and can turn from old time administrative matters to the pleasures of travel by these truly beautiful routes.

If one has the time there is no doubt that the ideal way to see this section of railway is from one of the river steamers. Even with the privilege of a cab-pass on an electric locomotive one is inevitably concerned with the purely railway aspects of the journey: the speed, the incessant curvature, the frequency of other trains. And although this is necessarily not the fastest stretch of the Bundesbahn of today, the curves give the impression of a more breathless haste than 200 km./h. on a straight, open line. From one of the splendid new river craft one can see it all at leisure. The numerous trains on both banks can be conveniently noted; the type of locomotive can easily be identified, and the load seen, and all the time one can be enjoying the magnificent scenery, and the succession of mediaeval castles, monuments and other points of interest that crowd the course. To try and absorb anything of the passing scene from a fast train is exhausting to the point of frustration. The most lasting impression could well be of the feature the guides say little or nothing about — the extraordinary volume of freight traffic on the river, conveyed for the most part in barges so heavily loaded that their decks are nearly awash.

All the same the railway journey between Mainz and Cologne can be a delightful interlude on a long journey up from Switzerland, providing one is prepared to eschew all attempts at detailed notetaking. Several times when travelling on the 'Rheingold express' — in one case through from Lugano to the Hook of Holland — I have enjoyed dinner on this stretch. Although one can be very conscious of the curves the modern coaching stock rides superbly, and the way the smart young waitresses keep their feet and render immaculate service, curves or no curves, is not the least impressive feature of the run. It was not however until I made a leisurely journey down stream from Wiesbaden that the great beauty of the river, and the intensity of the rail traffic on both banks, was fully brought home to me.

Not the least interesting feature of the present railway network is the wealth of connections from one bank to the other. Including the two bridges at Mainz itself there are no fewer than eight bridges across the Rhine, culminating in the celebrated Hohenzollern bridge leading across into Cologne main station. The cross connecting lines are finely engineered, with flying junctions to avoid any conflicting route intersections on the level. The section between Mainz is the most intricate, and a schematic diagram of the lines involved is shown in the accompanying sketch. For simplicity the river has been shown as straight, whereas it is actually making a continuously serpentine course. The railway traffic is far from all electric. There seem no inhibitions on the Bundesbahn over letting steam locomotives operate under the electric wires, and many freight trains hauled by one or another of the various types of 2–10–0 can be seen nipping smartly along, and around Koblenz the heavy traffic from the Saarbrücken direction, along the Moselle valley, joins in. The journey by river craft does not need to be taken in its entirety. There are many stops, at charming villages, particularly on the right bank, with cafes providing all kinds of sustenance, and many points of vantage to photograph the passing trains. One can see from the river the junction at Bingerbrück, where the one time Hessische-Ludwig Railway ended, and the Left Rhine route began, and at Koblenz the bridge leading to the intricate junctions on both banks.

In their celebrated book of 1889 Foxwell and Farrer took a poor

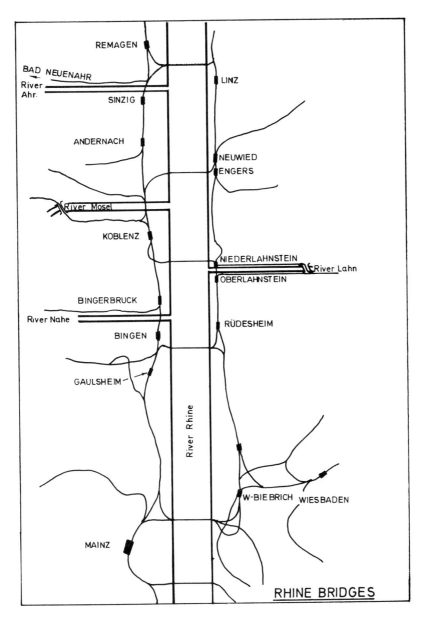

13. Diagram of lines on both banks of the Rhine below Mainz

view of the assumption of control by Prussia of so many hitherto independent German railways, and quoted the 'best express' of the Left Rhine Administration as taking 3 hr. 5 min. to cover the 155 kilometres from Cologne to Bingerbrück with five intermediate stops. Its intermediate speeds, start-to-stop, were pedestrian in the extreme, such as 53.25 km./h. from Cologne to Bonn, 50.75 km./h. on to Remagen, 53.25 km./h. on to Koblenz, nearly 58 on to Boppard, and a final spurt at 60.5 km./h. over the last $43^1/_2$ kilometres into Bingerbrück. Today the fast electric trains cover the full 191 kilometres from Cologne to Mainz in about two hours, with stops at Bonn and Koblenz. The 97 kilometres from Koblenz to Mainz are run in 52 minutes, start-to-stop, at an average of 111.5 km./h. One might imagine that the restaurant car staffs have special training in keeping their feet on the curves before allocation to these trains! Although there are such comprehensive facilities for crossing from one bank to the other, all the fast trains are routed along the left bank.

In the first years of the present century there was much improvement in German train speeds generally, though nothing compared to what was achieved in France at the same time. The Left Rhine had a run over the 61.5 kilometres from Bingerbrück to Koblenz at an average speed of 72.5 km./h.; but this might be a concession to passenger comfort on a line having so many curves, the 'Eilzug' trains of the Left Rhine — that is those that 'hurried' — seemed to hurry very slowly. It is only fair to add that great improvements had taken place further south, and that the enterprising Baden State Railways had, by 1907, a run at 88 km./h. over the 105 kilometres from Freiburg to Baden Oos. This train, the 9.49 up from Basle also made start-to-stop average speeds of 73.5 km./h. to Freiburg, 80.75 km./h. from Oos to Karlsruhe, and 85.5 km./h. from Karlsruhe to Mannheim. Today the speeds of the TEE trains over the four successive sections are 109.5, 138.5, 121 and 109.5 km./h. More of this however in a later Chapter of this book. In the early 1900s the Baden State Railways were relying upon 'Atlantic' engines very similar to those in use on the Prussian State Railways for maintenance of the fast express schedules.

The railway geography of the Rhineland, from Cologne to where the great river enters Holland, is complicated. At Cologne itself the main station, beside the stupendous Gothic cathedral, is on a site dating from the 1850s, when the first bridge to the right bank of the Rhine was built. The spectacular Hohenzollern bridge, with its neo-mediaeval watch towers at each end, was built in 1911, and increased the carrying capacity at that location from two to four tracks. The situation of Cologne Hauptbahnhof on the bank of the river is slightly reminiscent of Newcastle-on-Tyne, as it was before the construction of the King Edward Bridge. Left Rhine passenger trains from the south have to make a complete circuit west of the city, and then enter the station heading in a direction not far removed from due south. Freight trains bound for the Ruhr avoid this by taking the right hand spur in the triangle junction at Köln-Bayerthal and crossing the South Bridge into Köln-Dentz. Passenger trains bound for Belgium, or the route into Holland through Venlo must reverse their direction in Köln-Hauptbahnhof, but the 'Rheingold' express, having arrived in Cologne from the South continues over the Hohenzollern bridge and then turns north to pass through Dusseldorf, Duisberg and Wesel, before reaching the Dutch frontier beyond Emmerich.

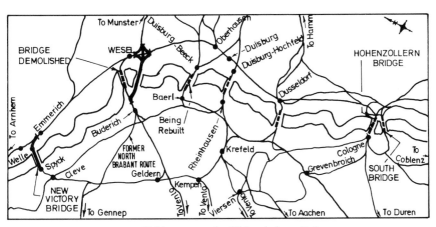

14. Bridges over the Rhine below Cologne

Before the final campaigns in the Second World War there were six bridges over the Rhine between Cologne and the frontier, located as shown in the accompanying map, carrying between them sixteen tracks. All were destroyed in 1944–1945, and in the subsequent rebuilding, the bridge at Wesel was replaced on a new site that enabled improved connections with the main line on the right bank of the Rhine to be made. At the Hohenzollern Bridge the ornamental towers at each end were so severely damaged by bombing that they were not rebuilt. One of the most remarkable and gratifying things about the war damage in Cologne was that although the magnificent cathedral was so near to the station and the western end of the Hohenzollern Bridge, such was the precision of the bombing of the railway targets that the cathedral escaped all but superficial damage. The story of the reconstruction of the Rhine bridges, under the supervision of engineering units of the British Army, would make a book in itself.

The network of railways north and west of Cologne does not witness the fastest passenger train running in Germany. Foxwell and Farrer had a good deal to say about it in 1889. It was the section between Cologne and the Belgian frontier station of Herbesthal that came particularly in for their scorn. This section formed part of two important international services; from London, via Calais, to Berlin and the 'Nord' express service from Paris. The 'express' that left Berlin at 11.37 gave the following startling average speeds:

Country	Journey	Railway administration	Average speed km./h.
Germany	Berlin–Herbesthal	Prussian State	50
Belgium	Herbesthal–Blandain	Belgian State	26
France	Blandain–Calais	Nord	40$^1/_2$
Sea passage	Calais–Dover	London, Chatham & Dover ship	27$^1/_2$
England	Dover–Victoria	London, Chatham & Dover Railway	70

The total distance of 1203 kilometres took 29 hr. 13 min. an average of 41.25 km./h., with the Channel crossing done at faster speed than the run across Belgium!

A writer in *The Railway Magazine* of 1907 has this to say:

On either side of the Rhine international trains between England, Holland, Belgium and South Germany, Austria, Switzerland and Italy seem unable to attain a higher speed than 42 or 43 m.p.h. (67–69 km./h.), whilst the ruling average seems to be 37 and 38 (59–61). The Railway, which follows closely the course of the river, must necessarily be fairly level, and if there are some fairly sharp curves, they should not be sufficient to bring the speed down to such a disappointing figure. The important service between Herbesthal and Cologne is terribly poor. The splendid 1.50 p.m. express of the *Nord* company, which achieves its first 95 miles out of Paris at over 60 m.p.h. (100 km./h.) is brought into Cologne in the following leisurely fashion:

Distance Miles	Section	Time, point to point min.	Speed m.p.h.
$9^3/_4$	Herbesthal–Aachen	19	31
6	Aachen–Stolberg	10	36
$13^3/_4$	Stolberg–Düren	24*	35
$24^1/_4$	Düren–Cologne	36	$40^1/_2$

* Inclusive of brief intermediate stop at Eschweiler

Why the principal expresses from Belgium and France cannot pass by the mighty and magnificent cities of Stolberg, Eschweiler and Düren without stopping at them is a secret locked up in the impenetratable bosoms of the officials of the Prussian Eisenbahnverwaltung.

Today the 'Nord Express' maintains an average of just 97 km./h. between Aachen and Cologne, which is still in some contrast to its 124 km./h. run from Paris to St. Quentin. For my own part I have always found the entry into Germany from Venlo rather tedious. The Rheingold express used to travel that way, and even though there was some interest in getting the services of one of the new 2–6–2 tender engines of class '23' the pace always seemed to be singularly unhurried. Nowadays the Rheingold travels via Arnhem, and takes the route down the right bank of the Rhine as far as Cologne; but the

Hook of Holland express to Munich and Innsbruck, now known as the Rhein Express travels via Venlo, and makes rather brisker running than of old. Even so, the 89 kilometres from Venlo take 74 minutes, with one intermediate stop at München Gladbach. The Rheingold itself takes 86 minutes over the 132 kilometres from Emmerich to Cologne, with intermediate stops at Duisberg and Dusseldorf.

The lines running east from the Right Rhine main line lead through the heavily industrial Ruhr, and out beyond head for Berlin and the northern cities of Germany. In Chapter Two I have told how, in 1892, the mail services for north and central Germany came to be routed via Flushing and the North Brabant line, and how in 1897 the mails for south Germany too were switched to this route. The Dutch locomotives of the North Brabant company worked through from Boxtel to Wesel, covering the last half of the journey in German territory. Wesel thenceforward became a general junction point for the Anglo-German mail traffic, which went thereafter east to Berlin; north-east to Bremen, Hamburg and the Baltic; and southward via Cologne. Reference to these mail trains has taken us into an area where the railways of Imperial Germany made some of their best running, and it is now time to look at the locomotives of the Prussian State Railways in some detail.

CHAPTER NINE

Prussia — locomotives to 1914

In studying the design of the steam locomotive it is interesting to reflect upon the major contributions made in the course of its history by engineers in different European countries, after the fundamentals had been established by the early pioneers in England. France, for example, in the person of Anatole Mallet, gave us the compound locomotive, later developed in that country to such remarkable success by du Bousquet, and de Glehn. Belgium gave us the Belpaire firebox and the Walschaerts valve gear, while in Holland the vital link between the machinery layout and the track was first openly enunciated. Then, in the 1890s the researches of a Prussian physicist, Dr. Wilhelm Schmidt, opened the way to the application of superheating. The principle then was far from new; it went back to the days of Dionysius Papin in the very dawn of steam engineering, and to Richard Trevithick (who had rather passed from the railway scene since the early runs in South Wales and Euston Square), who told Davies Gilbert in a letter dated 1828 that he was building a small locomotive containing what was undoubtedly an early form of superheater. McConnell of the London and North Western Railway, two French engineers, and a certain Mr. Ingram of the Baltimore and Ohio Railway all devised forms of superheaters; but by the year 1870 all were being discarded, and it was not until Dr. Schmidt's work was noticed and taken up by Herr Geheimiath Garbe of the Prussian State Railways that the modern development began.

Helped and encouraged by the practical tests made on the line by Garbe, Schmidt began to apply his designing skill, and experience of steam engineering generally, to locomotives and by 1897 he had produced the first version of the Schmidt superheater. The theory was sound and the stakes were high. In the conventional Stephensonian type of locomotive steam was used at its natural temperature of formation in the boiler. This varied according to the working pressure used. In the ordinary domestic kettle steam is formed when the water reaches 100° C., but if the pressure in the boiler is 10.5 kg. per sq. cm. steam is formed at 181° C., and at 14 kg. per sq. cm. the temperature of formation is 195° C. Its nature is then known as 'saturated', and in using it thus there is always the problem of condensation. If however the steam is further heated after its formation — superheated — two important attributes are realised: its volume is much increased, and it becomes more fluid. The first means that its capacity for doing work is greater, and the second means that it flows more freely through the valves and the steam passages and contributes to a freer running engine. On the debit side there is the difficulty of lubrication. Saturated steam, containing innumerable particles of water is a natural lubricant, whereas hot, dry superheated steam is just the reverse. Knowledge of this debit side deterred many engineers from the immediate adoption of superheated steam in locomotives.

Schmidt's early experiments were not entirely successful. There was trouble with overheating of the tubes, and consequent leakage, and several versions of the superheater were tried before he produced the form that, with various detail modifications, has been used in steam locomotives ever since. This epoch-marking development took place in 1902, and represented the biggest step forward in steam locomotive history since the early pioneer days. The honour of it rests entirely with Schmidt, and the Prussian State Railways. At that time the express passenger work on the Magdeburg and Altona divisions of the railway was being done by a variety of 4–4–0s of moderate capacity. Some were 2-cylinder compounds on the von Borries system, which having outside cylinders and Walschaerts valve gear looked very odd when viewed from the front. The running on the Magdeburg line to and from Berlin was not very fast, but some good speed was run on the express trains between Hamburg and Berlin. In 1901 Lord Monkswell clocked one of the compound 4–4–0s to cover the 127 kilometres from Berlin Lehrter to Wittenberge in $94\frac{1}{4}$ minutes, and then to continue over the 65.75 kilometres to Hagenow in $46^1/_2$ minutes, respective start-to-stop average speeds of 80.75 and 84.75 km./h., and much above the level of performance currently in vogue in the Rhineland. The load was about 200 tonnes.

Running conditions on this important main line were rather strange at that time. The track was lightly laid, with rails weighing no more than 27.8 kg. to the metre, and speed was officially limited to 90 km./h.; but despite this the 12.51 express from Hamburg to Berlin was booked to cover the first $159^1/_2$ kilometres to Wittenberge in 113 minutes, and the remaining 127 kilometres in 91 minutes, giving start-to-stop averages of 84.75 and 83.75 km./h. These were manifestly impossible to observe without exceeding the speed limit, and this was regularly done. On a journey when Lord Monkswell rode on the footplate of one of the 2-cylinder compound 4–4–0s, with a load of 197 tonnes, the speed actually reached a maximum of 100 km./h. The firing was very carefully done, with about seven shovelfuls of coal every five minutes, keeping the fire very thick at the back of the box. The coal was a mixture of large lumps and slack, with a certain proportion of briquettes. Seeing that this fast schedule was being kept with a load heavy for that period, over a gentle undulating road the working was certainly economical in fuel consumption.

It was to an engine of this same general type, but as a 2-cylinder simple, that one of the earliest forms of the Schmidt superheater was applied, in 1900. Externally it appeared as a kind of saddle around the upper part of the smokebox, and one of these engines was displayed at the Paris Exhibition of 1900. They had cylinders 500 mm. diameter, 600 mm. stroke and 1980 mm. coupled wheels. The boiler pressure was 12.5 kg. per sq. cm. At that time however the Prussian State Railways seemed rather to have over-reached themselves in the way of service accelerations on the Berlin-Hamburg line, for when Lord Monkswell made his footplate journeys the Altona division had not got an express engine available for the continuation of the journey east of Wittenberge, and a 1750 mm. mixed traffic 4–4–0 was put on. Nevertheless this engine ran well, averaging precisely the line maximum speed for a measured 80 kilometres, covered in $53^1/_4$ minutes. Speed several times mounted to over 100 km./h., and the engine although steaming freely, gave its distinguished visitor a distinctly rough ride. The fast schedule was exactly kept, so that he had no complaints, except that of the severe vibration.

Before leaving the non-superheated engines of the Prussian State Railways, the working of the English mail trains from Flushing provides further interesting examples of contemporary performance, in this case between Hanover and Minden in 1901. On one occasion a brand new 2-cylinder compound 4–4–0 was provided to work a heavy train of 310 tonnes, and ran the 64.5 kilometres westbound in two minutes less than the 54 minutes allowed — an actual start-to-stop average of 74.3 km./h. Lord Monkswell records that the firing was heavy throughout, with six shovelfuls of a mixture of small coal and briquettes put on every two minutes; but the engine responded well and made a good run. When loads were heavy these Prussian trains were often double-headed. A picturesque class of 2–4–0 2-cylinder compounds was available for assisting when necessary. Like the later 4–4–0s they had outside Walschaerts gear and the von Borries system of compounding. They had 1750 mm. diameter coupled wheels, and with their tall, strongly tapered stove-pipe chimneys and large cabs they looked every inch the progenitors of the 4–4–0s. The design dated from 1887, and over 100 of them were at one time in service.

As so often happens when one is making spot checks on locomotive performance the service requirements of the day do not make the maximum demands upon the power available, and this was certainly the case when Lord Monkswell returned from Minden to Hanover on the Flushing mail train, and the load turned out to be no more than five corridor coaches and a luggage van, only 175 tonnes. To work this they had one of the very latest Prussian locomotives of the day, a 4-cylinder compound 4–4–0, that had been shown at the Paris Exhibition in 1900. It was a very easy job to run the 64.5 kilometres in 51 minutes start-to-stop, and Lord Monkswell wrote:

The run had been remarkable only for the wonderful smoothness of motion of the engine. The faster she ran the smoother she went and at 100 km./h. her behaviour was admirable. It was possible to throw all one's weight on to one's heels without feeling any discomfort.

In 1902 Lord Monkswell records in his travelling diary:

As experiments carried out with trial engines using superheated steam appeared satisfactory, Herr Geheimiath Garbe succeeded in persuading the Minister of Public Works to allow him to design and have built some others slightly different, and containing certain improvements.

Garbe was not the only distinguished engineer who had to go with cap in hand to higher authority before he built superheated locomotives. They were more expensive, and those who held the purse strings just would not believe the economies in fuel consumption that were promised. In England nine years later, on the London and North Western Railway, C.J. Bowen Cooke, on the threshold of the most spectacular advance in British locomotive history, had to plead similarly with his general manager. In Germany Lord Monkswell was invited to witness the trials of the first 4–4–0 fitted with the later form of the Schmidt superheater, and in February 1902 rode a locomotive called 'Angerapp' and destined for the Alsace-Lorraine Railway. The trial took place with a train of empty coaches from the Grunewald Station, Berlin to Gusten, the first section of the line to Frankfurt (Main) and a run of about 160 kilometres. The engine was a 2-cylinder simple fitted with indicator shelters at the front for test purposes (on which many men were engaged), while in addition there were *nine* men in the cab — as Lord Monkswell pointedly remarks: 'an awful crush'! No doubt that was why he recorded no details whatever of the running, and commented merely: 'No difficulty was experienced anywhere, but the speed was not high and I did not consider the work done anything extraordinary'.

These early Prussian superheater locomotives certainly blazed the trail, and Schmidt soon became a household name in railway engineering circles. Not for the first time however the excellence and abundance of steam coal in Great Britain induced a time lag of almost a decade before the general adoption began, and then, emphasised by the results on the London and North Western, the impact was little short of sensational. In Germany the broad results of superheating that justified Herr Garbe's proposals for further development, were shown in the working of the 4–4–0 locomotive No. 74, which had been exhibited in Paris in 1901. It was in use on the line running southeast of Berlin towards Breslau, in competition with 2-cylinder von Borries compounds of similar general proportions. The schedules on that line were not very fast. One of the best trains was allowed 72 minutes for the 81.5 kilometres from the Schleschen station to Frankfurt-on-Oder, and then 40 minutes for the next 48.5 kilometres on to Guben. This required a sustained speed of about 80 km./h. on level track, with train loads of around 300 tonnes. On a number of trials it was found that the non-superheated compound engines used 12 per cent. more coal and 30 per cent. more water than the superheated No. 74.

From these beginnings the Prussian locomotives fitted with Schmidt superheater developed rapidly. Although having to provide for a diversity of routes and administrations a marked degree of standardisation was achieved, as in quantity-production of a design of mixed traffic locomotive of the 2–6–0 type. For general purposes it seemed that the Prussian State Railways were veering away from the compound, at a time when it was enjoying such popularity in France and Austria. The simplicity of mechanical design in a single expansion locomotive, with no more than two outside cylinders and the Walschaerts valve gear to make all the working parts readily accessible, was an attraction in a general service engine intended for both passenger and goods working; while the results quoted in the previous paragraph had suggested that greater economy in fuel and water consumption could be effected with the Schmidt superheater than by compound expansion. The Prussian 2–6–0s of 1902 were powerful units having cylinders 520 mm. diameter by 660 mm. stroke, and coupled wheels 1520 mm. in diameter. Many of them were built for service all over the Prussian State controlled lines.

At the same time however for the highest class of express passenger service locomotives of considerably more sophisticated design were being introduced, and in them compounding was combined with superheating. In 1903 a class of 4-cylinder compound engines of the 'Atlantic' type was introduced in the Hanover Division. All four cylinders were placed in line, driving on to the leading coupled axle. The high pressure cylinders were inside, with inside Walschaerts valve gear and the low pressure cylinders outside, with valves

108

actuated by linkage from the inside Walschaerts valve gear. The boiler, including the superheater, was a large one and the firebox spreading out across the frames behind the rearward pair of coupled wheels, had a grate area of 2.7 sq. m. These engines were specified as for 'high speeds', and one of them created much interest at the St. Louis Exposition of 1904, in the U.S.A. Little however is known of their actual performance, and it is probable that the rather complicated arrangement of the valve gear restricted the free flow of steam, and precluded the attainment of the high speeds desired.

After the annexing of the department of Haut-Rhin, and Bas-Rhin by Imperial Germany in 1871 — almost the whole of Alsace except for a small pocket of territory round Belfort — the Société Alsacienne de Constructions Mecaniques was acutely aware of the chill that had followed the lowering of the curtain along the new Franco-German frontier, and they set up a new works at Graffenstaden, near Strasbourg, where locomotives could be built in Germany. In 1903 the Prussian State Railways, anxious to try alternative methods of compounding, ordered six de Glehn compound 'Atlantics' for the Magdeburg and Cologne division. These engines were virtual duplicates of the famous compounds already doing such excellent work on the Nord, and Midi railways in France, and of the well-known 'La France' on the Great Western Railway of England. There were one or two external differences, such as the type of cab, safety valve and sandbox, but in every essential they were entirely of the de Glehn standard design of the day. They were nevertheless not the first French compounds put to work on the Prussian State Railways; for between 1899 and 1902 a number of mixed traffic 4–6–os had been built at Graffenstaden, generally similar to locomotives currently in use on the Northern Railway of France.

While this Chapter is primarily concerned with Prussia, and the application of superheating that had such a worldwide influence, the independent railways in other parts of Germany were also showing much enterprise in the development of locomotive design. This was especially the case in Bavaria, where the firm of Maffei, in Munich, was playing a very prominent part. In 1904 a very powerful 4-cylinder compound 4–6–0 was introduced, notable among other things in *not* having a superheater. This was generally in accordance with contemporary French and British practice, and typical also of the independent attitude towards Prussia then taken by the states of South Germany. Although all four cylinders drove on to the leading coupled axle, the layout of the machinery was the reverse of that on the Prussian high speed 'Atlantics' of the previous year. The high pressure cylinders of the Bavarian 4–6–0s were outside the frames, together with the Walschaerts valve gear, while the low pressure cylinders were inside. These 4–6–0s were the forerunners of a long and distinguished series of Maffei express passenger locomotives.

The experience of the Prussian State Railways with the de Glehn compound mixed traffic 4–6–0s had been so generally favourable that in 1906 the 4–6–0 type, but in a much simplified form, was adopted as the future standard mixed traffic unit. This followed the pattern of the 2–6–0 engines of 1902 in having two cylinders only, outside Walschaerts valve gear, and Schmidt superheater. The cylinders were 575 mm. diameter by 630 mm. stroke; coupled wheels 1750 mm. diameter and boiler pressure 12 kg. per sq. cm. Externally they looked extremely functional, with all auxiliary equipment hung on outside for ease of maintenance, and a stove-pipe chimney extended upwards in characteristically German fashion, to the maximum height of the loading gauge — far above the level of all the other boiler mountings. They were well designed, solid, reliable engines, and eventually several thousand of them were built, classified 'P8' on the Prussian State Railways. One fears however that the rapturous enthusiasm of another English writer, one who once apostrophised them as 'the world's most famous 4–6–0', would be challenged by many whose technical judgment, not to say sentiments, lay elsewhere. They were undoubtedly very sound and dependable engines, the very longevity of which is a tribute; but as hard, slogging work-horses, rather than the refinement of the highest class of express passenger units.

The first of them were built by Schwartzkopff of Berlin, and between 1906 and 1921 no fewer than 3370 of them were purchased by the Prussian State Railways, the distinctive initials of which, KPEV, stood for Königlich Preussiche Eisenbahn Verwaltung. Many more were built for other German states after 1914, and also for Rumania, Latvia, and Lithuania. Some were handed over to Belgium as war reparations. Construction continued, to a virtually unchanged design, from 1906 to 1925, until a total of 3950 had eventually been reached. As a further tribute to the soundness of the original design, the engines, whether imported by other countries or furnished as war reparations, were well appreciated everywhere. Nevertheless the outstanding success of this extremely simple and straightforward design, following the numerous and more complicated adventures of the KPEV into more elaborate channels did not stay the progress; and while for mixed traffic and secondary express duties such large scale reliance was placed upon one of the simplest of Continental locomotive designs, for top grade express passenger work the KPEV still indulged in compounds, and like machines of greater complexity.

The 'Atlantic' phase in Germany had definitely begun to wane by the year 1911. Until then it was only Bavaria that had introduced big 4–6–os for the most important express passenger work. But so far as Prussia and the rest of Imperial Germany was concerned Bavaria and the famous locomotive manufactory of J.A. Maffei lay rather outside the pale. The KPEV bought its locomotives from firms like Borsig, Schwartzkopff, and Henschel, with the addition of the Graffenstadt works of the Société Alsacienne. Maffei had advanced from the 4–6–o to the 'Pacific' type in 1908, with a first batch of twenty 4-cylinder superheated compounds for the Bavarian State Railways, but the KPEV remained faithful to the 4–6–o; and in 1911 embarked upon an interesting programme of development with locomotives having coupled wheels 1980 mm. diameter. To an onlooker it might have seemed that having established a solid second line of motive power with the 'P8' mixed traffic 4–6–o — locomotives indeed that could handle the principal express passenger trains if necessary on the moderate speed timings then operating — the KPEV could afford to experiment a little with their top line power.

They were currently using passenger or fast mixed traffic engines having between them five different types of drive, three compound and two simple. Of the former there were many of the 2-cylinder von Borries type, with outside cylinders; there were various de Glehn 4-cylinder locomotives with the drive divided between two axles, and also the 'high speed' 4-cylinder 'Atlantics' with all four cylinders driving on the leading coupled axle. The simples were of the 2-cylinder type, with Walschaerts valve gear, and the 4-cylinder

4–4–0s with all four cylinders driving on to the leading coupled axle. For the new express passenger 4–6–0s only one thing seemed certain — that they must have more than two cylinders. They were also to be considerably larger than the 'P8' mixed traffic class. The interesting outcome was that in the space of six years, 1911–1916, no fewer than 530 new express passenger 4–6–0s were supplied to KPEV. That there should have been four different varieties could have been understandable if those varieties had at first been represented by a few locomotives of each; but bulk deliveries of all four were taken.

The most numerous were 202 engines of class 'S10' 4-cylinder simples, superheated, with all four cylinders in line and driving on the leading pair of coupled axles, in the Maffei style, but in this case built by Schwartzkopff. Concurrently, delivery began of a series of 4-cylinder compounds in the de Glehn style, with the high pressure cylinders outside and driving the middle pair of coupled wheels, and the low pressure inside and driving the leading pair. One important feature of the de Glehn system was absent, and that was the use of independent valve gears for the high and low pressure cylinders. I think it would be agreed by anyone with running experience that the de Glehn compounds in general were difficult engines to drive. The multiplicity of controls needed experience and skill, and when this was given, as with the highly trained express drivers in France, the results were superlatively good. But they were certainly not engines for common user service, and it is probably this that weighed heavily in the Prussian decision to provide only one set of valve gear. The divided drive had the advantage of equalising the loads on axles and axleboxes between two axles, and to apply the driving thrust at two points in each frame. On the other hand one lost the advantage of an accurate dynamic balance, which the Maffei arrangement of drive provided. Both the simple and the compound 4–6–0s had an adhesion weight of only 50 tonnes, which was light in comparison to that of large British 4–6–0s of the same period.

There were some curious differences between the two designs, apart from the arrangement of the drive, and the disposition of the cylinders. The total evaporative heating surface and the superheating surface was roughly the same, 154 and 149 sq. m.; 53 and 52 sq. m., but the simples had a grate area of only 2.1 sq. m. against 2.97 sq. m.

in the compounds, while the respective boiler pressures were 12 and 15 kg. per sq. cm. The compounds were thus theoretically the more powerful. There were eventually two varieties of 4-cylinder compound, the second having all four cylinders in line but the drive divided as previously. This involved abnormally long connecting rods for the outside cylinders and relatively short ones for the inside, with a still greater disturbance of the dynamic balance. There were in all 232 4-cylinder compounds, classified 'S10[1]' — this covering both varieties of cylinder disposition.

The fourth variety of Prussian superheater 4–6–0 express locomotive was a 3-cylinder simple of which 96 were built between 1914 and 1916. Because of the outbreak of war in August 1914 little was at first known of these interesting engines, and when the news of them did eventually reach Great Britain they became a point of some controversy. Three-cylinder simple locomotives had been gaining in popularity in England since the introduction of J.G. Robinson's large 0–8–4 tank engines for hump shunting in Wath marshalling yard; but in them, and in the subsequent development of the drive by Vincent L. Raven on the North Eastern Railway, three separate sets of valve gear had been used, in each case the Stephenson's link motion. The Prussian engines of 1914 had only two sets of Walschaerts gear outside, and the motion of the valves for the middle cylinder was derived by a conjugated gear working off the two sets of outside valve gear. The news of this Prussian valve gear 'broke' just about the time when the first Gresley 3-cylinder locomotive, also with conjugated valve gear, was creating much interest in British engineering circles. Although there were considerable differences in detail the principles of the conjugated motion were the same. Gresley's first patent was dated 1915, and the first locomotive was completed at Doncaster works in 1918, so that it seemed that the Germans could claim priority. In the controversy that developed, however, it was revealed that while working in the drawing office of the Great Western Railway at Swindon, H. Holcroft had devised a conjugated valve gear in 1909, which had been patented on the instructions of G.J. Churchward, but not at that time taken up. It eventuated therefore that while the first design was British the first application to a locomotive was undoubtedly German.

These 3-cylinder simple 4–6–0s, which were classified 'S10²', proved to be the last express passenger engines to be built for the Prussian State Railways, though some were built new for Poland after the end of the First World War. Although the Prussian administrations had devoted a great deal of time and energy towards the development of their locomotive fleet, and were rewarded by good reliable service, the timetables of the years before the war did not give a great deal of opportunity for sustained fast and hard running such as that required in France, and on English railways like the Great Western and the London and North Western. Nevertheless a press report of 1913 relating to the 4-cylinder compound 4–6–0s with in-line cylinders created something of a flutter in British railway circles. It read:

The new engines are reported to be doing excellent service on hilly as well as level sections; for example, on the Grunewald-Mansfeld line, taking a car load of 470 tons up continuous inclines of 1 in 100 at the remarkable speeds of 34 and 38 miles per hour without forcing the boiler. On level lines car loads of 593 tons, or total loads of 736 tons, have been run at 59.4 miles an hour.

The nominal tractive effort of these German compounds was greater than that of any contemporary British locomotive, and if indeed the speeds of 55 to 61.5 km./h. on the 1 in 100 inclines were actually sustained, rather than averages over the whole length, the effort involved would have been very high. On the other hand the maintenance of a speed of 96 km./h. on level track with a load of 600 tonnes would not have required much more than 746 kilowatts in the cylinders, of which many contemporary British passenger locomotives would have been capable. Kilowatts output or not, however, the saga of Prussian locomotive development in the twenty years leading up to the fatal year of 1914 is a fascinating one.

CHAPTER TEN

German Railways mainly since 1920

It would be impossible to condense even a brief chronology of so eventful a half-century of German railways affairs into a single Chapter, let alone anything in the way of a connected history; but my task in writing about the German railways since the fall of the Hohenzollerns is made easier by the marked epochs into which that history falls. Of the period between 1920 and 1950 I have little to say. That it was a period of intense resurgence from the aftermath of war is well enough known; that in the 1930s the Reichsbahn made some highly spectacular advances in speed was amply documented in the railway press of the day. Nevertheless, in common with many others, I felt the statistics were something of a facade: yet another medium for projecting the image of the party that had swept so dramatically and ruthlessly into power. In a different way it was an echo of the arrogance of the old Imperial days: 'Deutschland über alles' once again. One could not help taking note of the prowess of the new streamlined diesel railcar trains. The performance of the 'Flying Hamburger' was real enough, and the neophytes in England chorused loud and long that once more we had been left behind, in the race for railway development.

But had we? Sir Nigel Gresley, chief mechanical engineer of the London and North Eastern Railway, and one of the foremost British advocates of speeding up, went to Germany, travelled on the 'Flying Hamburger' and was impressed to the extent of inviting the manufacturers to submit proposals for a similar train, to give the fastest possible service between London and Newcastle, while complying with all prevalent speed restrictions, curves and gradients of the line. The result was surprising. The Germans put forward a train of three articulated vehicles providing seating for 140 passengers, and having regard to all the running conditions the times they offered were 4 hr. 17 min. on the southbound journey, and 4 hr. 15$^1/_2$ min. going north. Over the distance of 433 kilometres the latter time represented an average speed of 101.5 km./h. against the 124.8 km./h. average of the 'Flying Hamburger' in Germany. Why such a disparity? Early in 1935 the LNER made some trial runs, and found that with an ordinary 'Pacific' engine and a load of six standard coaches the London–Newcastle run could be made in less than four hours. Moreover, while the German train proposed by the makers of the 'Flying Hamburger' provided seating for 140 passengers in considerably more cramped conditions than ordinary third class passengers enjoyed in Great Britain, the LNER test train had seating equivalent to 204 *first* class passengers, and full restaurant facilities into the bargain.

It was obvious that the main line between Berlin and Hamburg was more favourable to sustained high speed than that between London and Newcastle, and that given equal conditions a standard British locomotive could make equal or better times than the German diesel railcar. While the intrinsic merit of the performance of the 'Flying Hamburger' and of the trains subsequently introduced did not show the superiority that had first been imagined, the speed of service provided certainly hit the headlines in the railway press. It can also be appreciated today that a new standard of passenger travel was being introduced in the more cramped conditions of the railcars. It was the style of the modern airliners, in which the time of transit is so relatively short, that the spaciousness and facility for moving about in an old-style restaurant, corridor train are not called for.

Railway enthusiasts, both professional and amateur, went to Germany to see for themselves, and of these one at least had a very disagreeable experience that showed, even as early as 1935, that the situation was 'jumpy'. A retired British railway officer, a *littérateur* and statistician of high reputation, taking what was thought to be abnormal interest in certain railway activities at Frankfurt-on-Main was arrested, taken to Berlin, and imprisoned for some time while his case was considered by the German Public Prosecutor. The fact that he was ultimately released without trial did not lessen the uneasy

116

thoughts left by this affair, nor the discouragement it gave to any serious student of railway matters who had desires to visit Germany, and see things for himself. So I must be forgiven for quickly turning over the pages of history to the early 1950s, where in the State of Western Germany the Federal Railways were making swift recovery from the shattering impact of the Second World War. Two Chapters earlier in this book I have mentioned the new steam locomotives built to tide over the intervening period before full modernisation, and it is of the splendid developments in electric traction, signalling, and traffic controls that I now have to write.

In 1966 my book *Britain's New Railway* was published. It dealt with the construction over the tracks of the old London and North Western of the new high speed all-electric railway from London to Liverpool and Manchester. In the 1950s the West Germans were also building a new railway. One of the most difficult situations arising from the war was the partition of the old Germany, and the lowering of the economic and political barrier of the Iron Curtain from north to south. This caused great changes in the railway strategy of the country. Previously there had been a striking resemblance to that of England, with a number of fast running main lines radiating from the capital city of Berlin, as with London, and the heavily trafficked industrial area of the Ruhr and the Rhineland providing a strong likeness to our own Lancashire-Yorkshire complex. But in the post-war years all was changed. The flow of commerce, industry and tourism in West Germany was primarily between north and south, and the modern railway, the Bundesbahn, was newly equipped to suit this, together with a much freer interchange of traffic with the west.

The situation was epitomised in 1957 by the inauguration of the network of Trans-Europe-Expresses, a new conception of fast inter-city trains, providing comfortable and congenial accommodation for business men and others who travel regularly between the cities of Western Europe. The network was conceived on an international basis, and was quickly developed to include all the countries forming the original European Economic Community and Switzerland as well. The underlying idea was to combat the loss of railway traffic to the air services, and to make possible out-and-home journeys on the same day, with sufficient time for business at destination. How the 'new' railway system of West Germany was built up is graphically displayed on the accompanying sketch map showing how the TEE routes had been developed by the year 1967, and how the country had become an intensely used artery of north-south traffic.

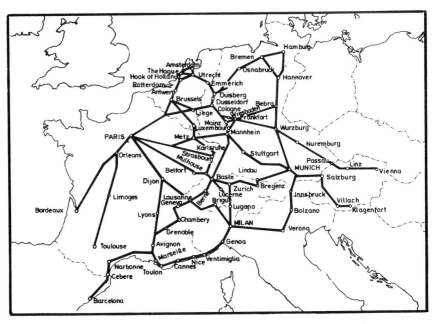

15. Trans-Europe-Express routes — in 1967

While the aim was to have this network entirely electrified as soon as possible, using the 15,000 volt alternating current system at $16^2/_3$ cycles per second, many areas had necessarily to remain steam worked for many years. I have already referred to the operations centred upon Saarbrücken. Considerable steam activity still remained at Osnabrück and Hamburg; from the latter city, indeed, the international express trains running north through Schleswig-Holstein into Denmark provided the last remaining example of heavy express passenger working with the large 'Pacific' engines introduced by the Reichsbahn between the two World Wars. Before going on to the modern developments in West Germany more than a passing mention is deserved by this family of notable steam locomotives. In

118

the design of these engines the influence of the former Prussian State Railways was strong. The 'Pacific' series '01' introduced in 1925, a simple 2-cylinder job, was the backbone of the German express passenger service in 1925–1939, though they were restricted to a maximum speed of 130 km./h. A total of 231 was built. To provide power for faster running a revised version with three cylinders was introduced in 1939, with slightly greater tractive power. It was these latter engines, classified '012' that were doing such good work in Schleswig-Holstein until quite recently. With seven coach trains of 300 tonnes speeds up to 145 km./h. on level track were customary, while with heavier loads of around 500 tonnes one could record speeds up to about 127 or 128 km./h.

In turning to more modern systems of traction, despite the spectacular performances of the diesel railcar trains German industry at first had little success with diesel locomotives. After the war, however, the situation changed markedly and the success achieved with hydraulic transmission, particularly with the 1641 kilowatts B-B type locomotives built for the Federal railways, created much interest abroad. At the time the modernisation plan of British Railways was launched in the 1950s, the engineers and management of the Western Region were so impressed with the performance of the German locomotives, that authority was obtained to depart from the general policy of British Railways in introducing diesel-electric locomotives, and what became well known on the West of England route as the 'Warship' class were built to the same design and specifications as the Bundesbahn locomotives of the same weight and tractive power. In their striking red livery the German diesel-hydraulics undertook many important services, before the extension of electrification.

The standard electric express passenger locomotive of today is the 'E10' of which nearly 400 are in service. These have a rating of 2699 kilowatts, and a maximum speed of 150 km./h. For the fastest expresses this latter was not eventually enough, and a selected group of these general service passenger locomotives were re-geared to permit of running up to 160 km./h. I had a very interesting run in the cab of one of them working the northbound 'Rheingold' express, from Basle to Karlsruhe. What impressed me particularly were the various aids to timekeeping provided for the driver. The schedule, particularly that between Freiburg and Karlsruhe, is very fast. When I made my run in 1967 only 58 minutes, start-to-stop, were allowed for this distance of 136.5 kilometres. The locomotives are of high power in relation to the loads hauled, and insistence is placed on the strictest observance of all speed restrictions. At the same time there would equally be the risk of a driver losing time if he did not run up to the high standards required. A continuous speed graph of the journey is mounted on a bracket just in front of the driver. It is in the form of an oblong book, the pages of which are turned over as the journey proceeds. It shows not only a continuous graph of the speed required for timekeeping with the particular train, but superimposed on this graph is a second one showing the maximum speed permitted over every mile of the line. Thus the driver has always before him a reminder of the speed at which he must run to keep time but also, if he were running late, the maximum at which he could run for recovery of lost time.

Actually I found there was not a great deal in hand with these fast trains. Because of delays in marshalling at Basle we were 14 minutes late, and by running up to the maximum permitted, we regained only one minute to Karlsruhe, covering the 136.5 kilometres from Freiburg in 57 minutes, an average of 143.7 km./h. We had plenty of running at 160 km./h., and the locomotive rode very smoothly. The line is virtually level throughout and in the broad level plain of the upper Rhine valley one quickly lost all impression of high speed. There was certainly more 'movement' when I transferred from the locomotive to the 'dome' observation car of the train, and noted that we ran the 61.2 kilometres from Karlsruhe to Mannheim in $27^3/_4$ minutes, at an average of 132.2 km./h. The dome car is a delightful viewpoint for enjoying the scenery, and at a maximum height above rail level one is certainly conscious of the speed on such a fast train as the 'Rheingold'.

At Mannheim the line is approaching the very heavily trafficked area of the Rhine, that extends in such beautiful scenery practically to Cologne; but the big station there will always remain in my memory for an incident that occurred during the visit of the Institution of Railway Signal Engineers in West Germany in 1966. Our party was travelling by a rather roundabout route from Munich to Wiesbaden, and the members' itinerary included a stop to inspect the then-new signalling installation at Mühlacker. The ladies of the party meanwhile proceeded on a road tour to the northern fringes of the Black Forest. Motor coaches were to bring both parties to Mannheim, to connect with a northbound express train to which three additional coaches had been added for our party. Something went wrong with the calculations, and although both parties began their northbound road journeys on time, it soon became apparent that working to the speed limit imposed upon these luxurious vehicles there was not a hope of our reaching Mannheim in time to catch the train. The coach with the ladies arrived first, and they encountered the full fury of the station master, whose rage apparently was not that our party had missed the train, but that three coaches had been added unnecessarily. However a Swiss lady matched his spleen with her own indignation in his own language, and by the time the male party arrived tempers had subsided somewhat, and a more helpful attitude was evident.

Mühlacker, where we had seen a new signalling installation, is an important junction on the route of the 'Orient Express'. It lies roughly halfway between Karlsruhe and Stuttgart, and from the main east-west line there diverges to the north a line leading to Brucksal and Heidelberg. But though incorporating some interesting technical details Mühlacker is a relatively small plant compared to modern German practice, and to see the full flowering of Bundesbahn ideas in the way of concentrated control, and central regulation of traffic, one must journey to Frankfurt-on-Main, or Munich. Into the gigantic towers that architecturally alone lend such distinction to the rail approaches to these cities is, in each case, packed a positive symposium of modern railway operating practice in the German style. The over-riding conception has been to bring the overall surveillance of traffic movement within a perimeter circling some distance out from the main station to bear upon the inner workings, and stage by stage the supervision of actual running is delegated, right down to the details of shunting in and out of the station platforms. The entire control is carried out on the topmost operating floor of the tower. Frankfurt was the first of the large city stations to be equipped in this way; but after several years of operational experience, when

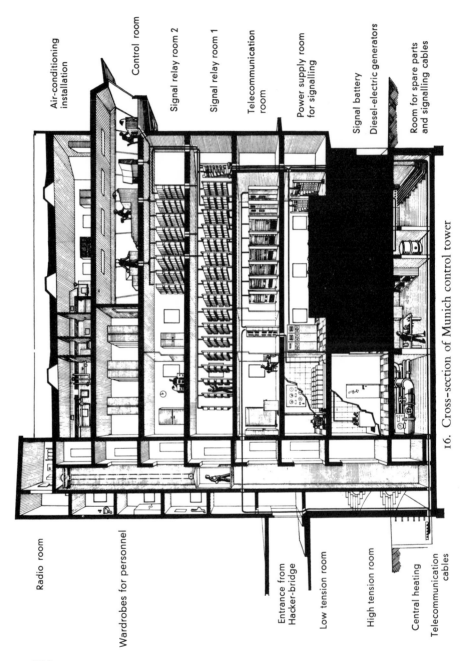

Air-conditioning
installation

Control room

Signal relay room 2

Signal relay room 1

Telecommunication
room

Power supply room
for signalling

Signal battery

Diesel-electric generators

Room for spare parts
and signalling cables

Radio room

Wardrobes for personnel

Entrance from
Hacker-bridge

Low tension room

High tension room

Central heating

Telecommunication
cables

16. Cross-section of Munich control tower

122

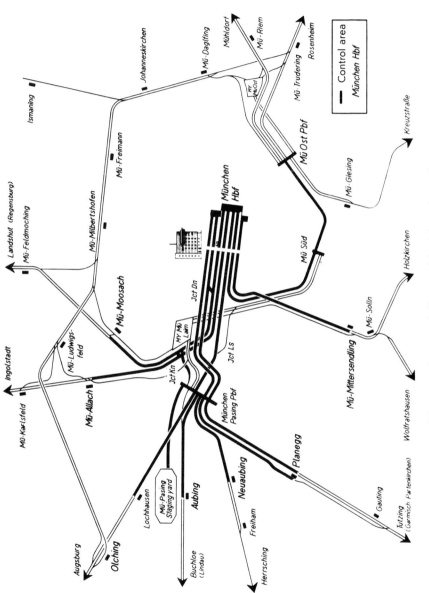

Ismaning

Landshut (Regensburg)

Johanneskirchen

Mü-Feldmoching

Mü-Milbertshofen

Mü-Freimann

Mü-Dagtfing

Mühldorf

Mü-Riem

Ingolstadt

Mü-Moosach

Mü-Ludwigs-feld

Rosenheim

Mü Trudering

MY Mü Nord

München
Hbf

Mü-Karlsfeld

Jct Dn

MY Mü
Lam

Mü Ost Pbf

Mü Süd

Jct Ls

Mü-Giesing

Augsburg

Olching

Jct Kn

Mü-Allach

Lochhausen

Mü-Pasing
Staging yard

Aubing

München
Pasing Pbf

Neuaubing

Mü-Mittersending

Mü-Solln

Holzkirchen

Kreuzstraße

Buchloe
(Lindau)

Freiham

Planegg

Wolfratshausen

Herrsching

Gauting

Tutzing
(Garmisch-Partenkirchen)

━━━ Control area

München Hbf

17. Diagram of approach lines to Munich main station

123

the time came to modernise Munich the same principles were applied.

The technique has been developed to make maximum use of the typical major station layout in West Germany, which is a terminus. One can see the same general layout at Stuttgart, at Zürich and Lucerne in Switzerland, and at Tours, Marseilles and Orleans in France. None of these latter stations, except perhaps Zürich, deals with such heavy traffic as is handled daily at Frankfurt and Munich. At these two stations the chain of delegation is in three stages. There are first of all two overall supervisors, whose chief concern is the running in the outer approaches to the area. The signalling and point setting is normally automatic, but the supervisors are able to intervene if necessary to alter priorities according to the needs of the moment. Next in the chain of control are two station supervisors, who between them regulate all train working in the station and its immediate approaches. They keep a watching brief over the operators at five desk-type panels, from which the signals and points are operated. The station areas are divided into five sections at Frankfurt, and four at Munich. The operators at these panels are in effect, local signalmen, and the station supervisors, who have a large illuminated diagram of their own, co-ordinate the work of the individual men.

I mentioned earlier that the point setting on the approach lines is normally automatic. The trains carry their timetable reporting numbers in a prominent position, and at certain key positions in the approach to the various junctions these numbers are read by a photo-electric scanner, and fed into a computer. The reporting number is not merely a *number*; it is also a code which gives the destination of the train. On receiving the number the computer determines the route to be followed at junctions, and sets the points accordingly. The overall supervisors in the control tower have the reporting numbers of trains displayed on their illuminated diagram as soon as such trains enter the control area. If everything is running according to plan the trains are routed according to their numbers, and it is only in case of emergency, or some irregularity or undue lateness that the supervisors intervene. Then they can over-ride the automatic system, and initiate special procedures. The operating floor in the control towers at Frankfurt and Munich is a remarkable place. The section in which the local panel operators are ranged round in the arc of a circle is contained in a platform extending a little beyond the general line of the tower building, so as to give a completely uninterrupted view of the tracks below. These panel operators are the only ones who need to see any of the actual train movements. The station supervisors and the overall controllers work entirely from their respective illuminated diagrams.

At Frankfurt and Munich, as at the other large European stations previously mentioned, through trains have to enter, and reverse direction on leaving. This of course means the addition of a fresh locomotive at what was previously the rear end of the train, and involves light engine movements that would not be necessary if the train was continuing straight through. In the case of two of the French stations mentioned, at Tours and Orleans, the terminal stations are now by-passed by all through trains, as is also the station at Antwerp; but the German stations involve reversal, with the additional traffic movements in consequence. So far as the signals themselves are concerned, the German code of aspects is based on the fundamental use of the colours red, yellow and green, with elaborations derived from the upper quadrant semaphore signalling practice, still in extensive use on some main, and many subsidiary lines.

The Deutsche Bundesbahn was one of the first railways in the world to begin active development towards regular running at more than 160 km./h., and while the commercial departments of the railway urged the case for acceleration to attract more business, and provide more effective competition with internal airlines, the operating men had to do some urgent rethinking on the actual philosophy of train running. The existence, on the same line, of trains scheduled at widely differing point-to-point speeds is a worldwide problem. It is not only a question of line capacity — of fitting in the different trains so as to make maximum use of the line, and minimising the chances of a slow train delaying a faster one; there is the vital matter of providing adequate signalling for all classes of train. The signals must be so spaced, and their aspects so displayed, that if a stop is required because of another train ahead or the setting up of a crossover movement at a junction, there is adequate distance for a train to be stopped from its maximum speed in the distance between the first warning signal and the obstruction. On the fast running main lines in West Germany, such as that of the 'Rheingold', the signalling is designed to suit the TEE trains travelling at 160 km./h.

Commercial needs demanded speeds of at least 200 km./h. for certain prestige trains, while it was envisaged that some of the lesser expresses would be upgraded to the 160 km./h. standard. At other times during the day there would also be stopping passenger trains, and express freights, which would also require the signalling as already designed and installed. Using technical terms for one or two sentences, in stopping a train it is its kinetic energy — the energy due to its speed — that must be destroyed; and kinetic energy is proportional to the *square* of the speed. So that in the case of locomotives and trains of the same weight, the one travelling at 200 km./h. would take more stopping, to use a colloquialism, than one at 160 km./h. by the ratio of the squares of 200 to 160 — 1.55, or one and a half times more. Thus signalling that provided safe stopping distance for 160 km./h. would not be good enough for 200 km./h. Re-arrangement of the signalling to suit one or two very fast trains would have been a very expensive matter, and would have restricted the capacity of the line at other times by preventing slower trains from following so close behind each other as previously. So, special provision has been made for the very fast trains, while retaining the existing signalling.

Choice of a route for the application of the new principles fell upon that between Augsburg and Munich, and this involved even greater divergence from the existing signalling arrangements. The authorised maximum speed on that line is 140 km./h., and provision for 200 km./h. meant taking into account a *doubling* of the kinetic energy of the train. A special form of cab signalling was devised which gives the driver advance warning of signals before he can actually see them. This is fitted only to the locomotives working the 200 km./h. trains, and it is actuated by a system of inductive pick-up from apparatus located in the track. It is a fine example of modern electrical engineering, though the interpretation needs a little experience from the driver. If there is a signal displaying a warning indication some distance ahead advance notice of this is received in the cab and the

126

brakes are applied in readiness, even though the signals along the line which can be seen may be displaying the 'all-clear' indication. The warning aspect is yet out of sight, ahead. On the Augsburg–Munich line the braking distance for 200 km./h. has been established as two and a half times as great as for 140 km./h. and the cab signalling apparatus gives advance warning accordingly.

It is not only in respect of signalling that the preparations for 200 km./h. running have extended. The 'E10' type electric locomotives used on the 'Rheingold' were not considered to have adequate power, and for haulage of seven-car trains of about 310 tonnes the 'E03' class was introduced having no less than 6527 kilowatts. The West German railways do however make a practice of piling on the power, to a far greater extent than is currently practised in France, as will be apparent from the concluding Chapters of this book. Many of the TEE trains are of comparatively light formation, though provided with powerful electric locomotives. A few years ago I travelled from Frankfurt to Munich by the 'Hans Sachs' and this conveyed a load of only five coaches as far as Nuremberg, and four thereafter. This is a picturesque way to the south, and with the lightness of the load making any detailed study of the locomotive work pointless, I was able to enjoy the scenery to the full. We ran the 136 kilometres from Frankfurt to Wurzburg in 85 minutes, start-to-stop; took exactly the 65 minutes for the 103 kilometres on to Nuremberg, and at that time the train made a non-stop run onwards to Munich, via Ingolstadt, just 200 kilometres in 111 minutes. The train now runs via Augsburg, and makes the final 61.5 kilometres run into Munich in 32 minutes. The TEE train 'Blauer Enzian' (the Blue Gentian) used to do this run in 28 minutes, but at the time of writing the time is 31 minutes.

On this occasion we were on our way into Austria, but no railway enthusiast can leave this part of Germany without paying a visit to the Deutsches Museum, claimed to be the largest technical museum in the world. Among an almost bewildering variety of exhibits, in Bavaria, it is an opportunity to pay tribute to a steam locomotive design that has so far escaped mention, and yet is one of the truly great designs of the world. I have referred to the prowess of J.A. Maffei in building 4-cylinder compound 4–6–0s that had no small influence in countries far from Bavaria. This type was developed into the excellent class '18' 'Pacific', which a fellow enthusiast has described as the very symbol of Bavarian and German steam power. In Munich it is remembered with pride that among pre-Reichsbahn locomotive designs the Class '18' far outlasted any of the Prussian express types. There are two of these locomotives preserved in Munich, one that has been restored to original condition and is in the museum, while the second is on display outside the head office of Krauss-Maffei.

A connoisseur of locomotive performance naturally wants to know how the working of these engines compares with that of contemporary designs elsewhere; but generally speaking such comparisons were difficult to make. The West German policy of steam locomotive utilisation was to arrange workings that required no more than moderate rates of steaming in the boiler. Express trains were for the most part lightly loaded and the tasks of haulage well within the capacity of the locomotives concerned. There was no regular running *a l'outrance*, as in France, or in the positively murderous style meted out to American locomotives. The Germans by gentle treatment sought to obtain very long mileages between visits to works for overhaul, and no more than moderate consumption of the rather poor coal habitually fired in West Germany. So, one regards the Bavarian Class '18' 'Pacifics' with respect, but without any real data on which to make comparison with a Collin 4–6–2 on the Northern Railway of France, or with a Gresley 'Pacific' or a 'Royal Scot'.

PLATE 17 Austrian viaducts

(a) The spectacular Trisanna bridge on the eastern ascent to the Arlberg
Tunnel, with the picturesque Wiesberg Castle alongside

(b) The Kalte Rinne viaduct on the Semmering line, photographed from the
foot-plate a few seconds after the train had passed over it

PLATE 18 The Schneeberg rack
railway

(*a*) A picturesque winter scene
with a train descending. The
plume of steam comes from
the counter-pressure brake.
The tower on the skyline
marks the summit of the line

(*b*) One of the smart little steam tank engines, modernised with Giesl oblong
ejector at the summit — Hochschneeberg

(a) 2–6–2 passenger tank engine for local traffic: of 1911

PLATE 19 Swiss steam locomotives

(b) Two generations of mountain power on the Gotthard line: a Maffei 2–8–0, piloting one of the de Glehn 4-cylinder compound 4–6–0s

(c) One of the standard 4-cylinder compound 4–6–0s on the Jura-Simplon line, dating from 1902

PLATE 20

(a) Swiss Federal Railways: international express train near the southern end of the Gotthard line passing through Capulago, hauled by one of the powerful 'Ae6/6' electric locomotives

(b) Bern-Lötschberg Simplon Railway railcar train crossing the Luegelkinn viaduct on the steep descent into the Rhone valley

PLATE 21 Swiss mountain routes

(a) Kleine Schiedegg on the Jungfrau Railway, with the great peaks Eiger and Mönch as a majestic background

(b) Zermatt station, terminus of the Big-Visp-Zermatt Railway, with the famous peak of the Matterhorn showing over the mountain slope

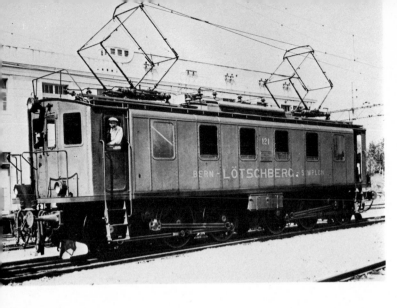

PLATE 22 Locomotives of
the BLS

(a) The first electric
locomotive 'Ce6/6'
of 1910

(b) The great 3357 kilo-
watts 'Be6/8' of 1926

(c) The latest model: the
'Re4/4' of 1964, of
5068 kilowatts

PLATE 23 Italian signalling

(a) Old style mechanical block post on a station platform, with the station-master giving the 'right away' for departure of a train

(b) A modern panel box, with all-electric control, at Piacenza

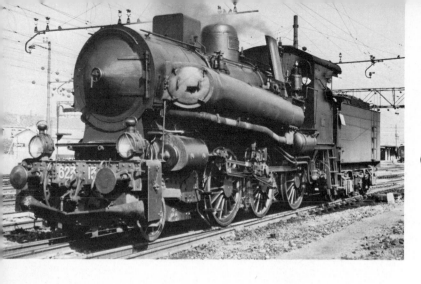

PLATE 24 Italian
locomotive variety

(a) 2–6–0 steam loco-
motive with Franco
Crosti boiler, at
Venice

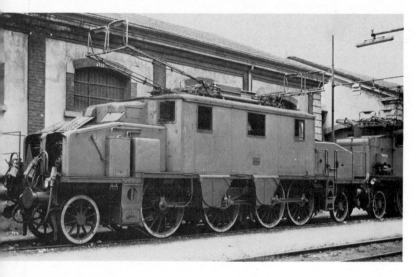

(b) Three-phase electric
locomotive at
Ventimiglia

(c) 2–6–0, with inside
cylinders and outside
valve gear, leaving
Milan (Porta Genova)
for Alessandria

PLATE 25 Modern Italian trains

(a) Electric railcar at Chiusi, on the Florence-Rome main line

(b) The high-speed 'Settebello' electric train — Milan and Rome service

PLATE 26 On the French Riviera

(a) Monte-Carlo, the old station about 1900

(b) Paris, Lyons and Mediterranean Railway: one of the coup-vent ('wind-cutter') 4-cylinder compound 4–4–0 locomotives

PLATE 27 French
locomotive development

(a) Paris-Orleans
Railway: one of the
Forquenot 2–4–2
express locomotives
dating from 1873

(b) Chapelon rebuild in
1934, as 4–8–0, of the
very first type of
'Pacific' in Europe,
the Paris-Orleans
'4500' class of 1907

(c) The impressive post-
war '241P' class of
4–8–2 on the SNCF
— 4-cylinder com-
pound, here seen at
Marseilles (La Blan-
card shed)

(a) The passenger station in 1910, showing the picturesque arched roof over the platforms

PLATE 28 Dijon — historic pictures

(b) The locomotive running shed about 1860, with Stephenson type long-boilered 2–2–2 engines outside

One of the 4-cylinder compound 4–6–0s of the du Bousquet '3500' class, as modernised with Lemaitre exhaust arrangements, leaving Paris with an express for Compiegne

A Chapelon rebuilt 'Pacific' of the Orleans type on northbound express approaching the Lamorlaye viaduct

One of the de Caso 4-cylinder compound 4–6–4s on a Lille express leaving Paris

PLATE 30

(a) A view, about 1865, inside the round-house at Nevers, Paris, Lyons and Mediterranean Railway

(b) Orleans Railway: the Austerlitz station, Paris, showing in centre the through electrified lines to the Quai d'Orsay

PLATE 31

Express from Hendaye to Rome leaving Menton, hauled by one of the American-built '141R' class 2–8–2 (oil fired)

(*a*) Western Region: passenger train near Lisieux, hauled by a diesel-electric locomotive of the '68000' series

PLATE 32 Modern French power

(*b*) Orleans line: two 200 km./h. Flyers at the Austerlitz station, Paris: on the left the 'Capitole', for Toulouse; on right the 'Etendard' for Bordeaux. These trains leave within 5 minutes of each other, at 7.45 and 7.50

(*c*) One of the latest thyristor controlled a.c. electric locomotives on the Paris-Strasbourg line, here seen after working the 'Stanislas Express' from Paris

CHAPTER ELEVEN

Into Austria — history and locomotives

Leaving Münich for Salzburg we were on the route of the 'Orient Express', but by an intermediate 'fast' that made a number of intermediate stops. We were in no hurry that afternoon, and could enjoy the beautiful scenery, especially where the line is making its way round the picturesque lake, the Chiem See. But before reaching this pleasant spot we had stopped at the important junction of Rosenheim, from which an international route leads southward through the Inn valley to Kufstein and the Tyrol, and thence to Innsbruck. In the earlier days of Austrian railroading the principal route from Vienna to Innsbruck, and by the Arlberg Tunnel into Switzerland ran for part of its way through Bavaria. The direct line crossed from Austrian territory soon after leaving Salzburg, followed the Bavarian main line to Rosenheim, and then turned down the Inn valley to Kufstein. By this route the distance between Salzburg and Innsbruck is 194 kilometres. The famous and long-lived Emperor Franz Josef strongly disapproved of such an important Austrian lifeline running through a section of German territory, and at his command an all Austrian route was surveyed and ultimately built.

The railway set-up in Austria was in any case rather complicated, with some lines privately owned and others owned by the State. Except in the area north and north-west of Vienna there was virtually no competition. One of the most extensive of the private companies was the Südbahn, which consisted of two separate and physically unconnected systems. It was enterprised in the days of the old Austro-Hungarian Empire, and its eastern complex provided a main line, then entirely in Austrian territory, from Vienna to Trieste, with a second major route running north-eastwards from Pragerhof to Budapest. The second section began with a junction with the Bavarian system at Kufstein, followed the Inn valley to Innsbruck, and thence over the Brenner Pass to the Italian frontier, which was then near Ala, and only 40 kilometres short of Verona. One can imagine the proud Emperor's concern, when the original main route from Vienna to Switzerland consisted of four sections:

1.	Vienna-Salzburg	:	Kaiserin-Elisabeth
2.	Salzburg-Kufstein	:	Bavarian State
3.	Kufstein-Innsbruck	:	Südbahn
4.	Innsbruck-Buchs	:	Austrian State

This route became of extreme importance after the Franco-Prussian war of 1870–1871, because it provided a route from Vienna to Paris that was independent of the Prussian control of the lines through Alsace and Lorraine. It was to obtain a route outside *all* German territory that the new route from Salzburg to a junction with the Südbahn at Worgl in the Inn valley was constructed. This was built by the Kaiserin-Elisabeth Railway, which in 1882 was taken over by the State, the full title of which was the Kaiserlich Königlich Oesterreichische Staatsbahn.

The State Railway had two distinct problems in providing its motive power. The line eastwards from Salzburg is essentially an express route, as was also the main line northwards from Vienna to Prague. In contrast the detached western route from Innsbruck, through the heart of the Tyrol, and the Arlberg Tunnel to Switzerland involved almost continuous heavy hill-climbing and no opportunity for fast running. In the Austria of Imperial days one name transcends all others in the field of locomotive engineering, that of Gölsdorf, over a period of more than fifty years. A succeeding Chapter relates the story of how the principal main line of the Südbahn was carried so dramatically over the Semmering Pass, on its way to Trieste, and from an early date in the operation of that difficult route, the locomotive superintendent was Louis Gölsdorf. In 1861 his son Karl was born, and from an early age he began to gain experience of locomotives in his father's office. He won high academic distinction, and after seven years work on the State Railway he was appointed Chief Mechanical Engineer, at the early age of thirty. From that time onwards, to those who took more interest in travelling than merely getting to journey's end, it can be said that Karl Gölsdorf and his locomotives were synonymous with the Austrian railways themselves. Wherever the visitor entered Austria, at Buchs, Salzburg, Trieste, or Prague, there was one of the tremendously arrestive Gölsdorf locomotives waiting to haul his train. To be sure of seeing one today a visit to the museum in Vienna is necessary, though I saw some of them still working at Graz in Styria, in 1966.

Karl Gölsdorf built few locomotives other than compounds, and at the very beginning of his career he solved the problem of starting that led so many other distinguished engineers into complications, and unsatisfactory performance. His early engines all had two cylinders, like those of von Borries in Germany, and these being outside gave the 'front-view' an unbalanced look. Unbalanced or not, however, his starting valve enabled locomotives to get away from rest without any elaborate procedures from the driver, and apart from Austria and Hungary it was used on locomotives in America, Germany, Greece, Italy, Russia, Servia, and Turkey. The internals of the starting valve were of course hidden from the gaze of the onlooker from a station platform, or from the lineside; but what was so very apparent — almost aggresively so! — in the early Gölsdorf locomotives was the arrangement of double domes. On large American locomotives what was often taken for a second dome was the container for the sand used for applying to the rails, when adhesion was bad; but on Gölsdorf's locomotives there really were two domes. Steam was collected in the rearward one and then passed forward in a large pipe to the forward one, which contained the regulator.

At the turn of the century expresses from Salzburg would be taken eastwards to Vienna by a 4–4–0 type of Gölsdorf compound. In Austria, as in Germany however, it seemed that the policy of the railway managements in Imperial days was to run at the slowest speeds that could be 'got away with'. Professor Foxwell commented that the 'Orient Express' ran faster in Rumania than in Austria, and made an average speed of only 52.5 km./h. between Munich and Vienna. As in Germany the technical skill of locomotive engineers was exercised in production of devices that would reduce coal consumption, and give long trouble-free service between successive visits to shops for overhaul. That prodigious note-taker, and author of a three-volume, 2000 page work *Railways and Scenery*, Mr J.P. Pearson, records details of what he calls a fast train on the main line to Vienna. He joined the train at Attnang-Puchheim, after having travelled by local trains from Salzburg through the beautiful Salzkammergut district, and this 'fast train' hauled by a compound 4–4–0, took 5 hours 6 minutes to do the 243 kilometres to Vienna, an exciting average of 47.6 km./h. There were, it is true, fourteen intermediate stops; the longest start-to-stop run was over the final 38 kilometres from Neulengbach into Vienna, covered in 49 minutes, or 77.6 km./h.

The Salzkammergut is a region of rare charm of high mountains, lakes as lovely as any I have ever seen, and villages like Hallstadt and St. Wolfgang that are positively theatrical in their beauty. It used to be served by a railway that was closed in 1957, but is still remembered with much affection in the district. It was one of those little railways that seem to blend so perfectly with the countryside. One could not imagine going storming out to St. Gilgen, or to the far end of the line at Bad Ischl in a 160 km./h. diesel railcar; the old 760 mm. gauge railway with superannuated steam locomotives was much more to the point. At one time also this Lokalbahn provided something of a prestige run. Bad Ischl was a favourite country resort of the Emperor, and he had his own special saloon on the railway to convey his guests from Salzburg. Although Attnang-Puchheim was the nearest point of the main line to Bad Ischl, with a standard gauge rail connection, the Imperial way was to go via Salzburg and the Lokalbahn. It is recorded that Brahms, Johann Strauss, and other celebrities from the Vienna Opera, when commanded to Bad Ischl, travelled that way. His villa will be less happily remembered as the place where he signed the ill-fated declaration of war on Servia on July 28, 1914, and so precipitated the First World War and the eventual disintegration of his own empire. I was too late to see the Lokalbahn in action; but I did see steam in the Salzkammergut, on the spectacular mountain railway to the summit of the Scharfberg. Seen from any angle this is a most striking mountain, but when I was at St. Wolfgang there was deep snow on the summit, and the rack railway had not commenced its summer service. I was however to ride on another splendid mountain railway at a later date.

The principal main lines of the Austrian Federal Railways of today are now electrified on the same traction system as that of West Germany and Switzerland, 15,000 volts alternating current at $16^2/_3$ cycles per second. The modern electric locomotives make short work of the heavy grade out of Salzburg where the line is working its way round the northern flanks of the Salzkammergut mountains. This is one of the most picturesque stretches of the Vienna main line, though the distant views of fine ranges do not compare with the rugged scenery on the all-Austrian line to the Tyrol, via Bischofshofen and Kitzbühel, still less with the tremendous mountains of the Tyrol itself west of Innsbruck. The line to Vienna is more pastoral and at Linz enters the broad valley of the Danube. The travelling today is a great deal faster than in the era of steam locomotives, and the quickest service over the 316 kilometres between Salzburg and Vienna is by the railcar-type train 'Transalpin', operating through from Basle. In Austria it stops only at Feldkirch, Innsbruck, Salzburg and Linz, and takes only 3 hr. 10 min. over the 316 kilometres, with a 2 minutes intermediate stop.

These railcar-type trains, despite the comfort of the seating and the service of meals and refreshments to each individual seat, always seem to me to have the confinement of a long distance aircraft, and I am old-fashioned enough to prefer the traditional corridor train that includes a walk to the dining car at meal times. On some of these international trains in Europe, it is not as though the journey times are particularly short. I travelled first on the 'Transalpin' from Zürich to Innsbruck, a run of exactly four hours, and the total time from Basle to Vienna is $10^3/_4$ hours. The 'Orient Express', which has left Paris at 22.15 on the previous evening reaches Salzburg just over twelve hours later, and provides a very pleasant run to Vienna, stopping intermediately at Attnang-Puchheim, Wels, and Linz. The journey time is 4 hr. 8 min., inclusive of 8 minutes spent at the three stops. The running average speed is 79 km./h. with a final start-to-stop run at 91.5 km./h. over the 189 kilometres from Linz to Vienna. It is a very enjoyable run, with fine views across the Danube valley, and a magnificent sight of the great monastery of Melk, before the beautiful final stretch through the Vienna Woods is entered upon.

Both railway enthusiasts and pure sightseers should endeavour to obtain a seat on the left-hand side of the train, because this not only provides the best viewpoint for the scenery but it also gives a brief, though intriguing glimpse of three preserved steam locomotives as the train is pulling away from Linz. Two are 0–6–0 tender engines, and the third is a 2–4–0 tank. They stand in the railway garden beside the line, and while they have been partially restored to their original condition some of the fittings have been removed by vandals, and the colours in which they are painted have no historical justification. Nevertheless, the locomotives themselves are important relics, and provide links with some of the earliest days of railway operation in Austria. The engine 'Fusch' distinguished by its enormous spark arresting chimney, dates from 1868, and was one of a class of 69 working on the Kaiserin-Elisabeth Railway, as the line from Vienna to Worgl was known until it became part of the State Railways in 1882. The second 0–6–0 came from the Südbahn, and is one of a class of 171 locomotives built between 1860 and 1872. Although an important relic this former Südbahn locomotive is not quite such a relic as 'Fusch', because at least one other of the class was still in revenue-earning service on the Graz-Köflacher Railway in 1969. I photographed it myself there in 1966, when it was 106 years old!

The third engine standing in the garden at Linz is the oldest of them all, and is one of a class built between 1848 and 1853 for the Kaiser Ferdinand's Northern Railway, which despite its name was a private company. It was one of three railways running northward from Vienna, competing for the traffic to and from Berlin, and all eventually feeding into the Saxon State Railways at Bodenbach. The Kaiser Ferdinand was the centre one of the three, having the Imperial Royal Austrian State to the west, and the Austro-Hungarian State Railway to the east. Now, most of the mileage of all these three lines is in Czechoslovakia. At Emms, about ten kilometres down stream from Linz a branch line crosses to the left of the Danube. If one has the time it provides a very charming alternative route to Vienna, by a slow train, steam hauled, while there is the further alternative of the river steamers.

Having progressed this far on what used to be one of the most important steam routes in Austria it is time to refer to the later development of the Gölsdorf compound locomotives. Not the least remarkable feature of this interesting epoch is that both father and son were simultaneously chief mechanical engineers of the Südbahn and the State Railway respectively. Furthermore, Karl Gölsdorf also became Chief of the Locomotive, Carriage and Wagon section of the Austrian Railway Ministry, and in this capacity he acted as consultant and designer to all the Austrian railways. As such he gained the distinction of introducing the first locomotive of the 'Atlantic' type to run in Europe, which was built for the Kaiser Ferdinand's Nordbahn, in 1894. These engines were somewhat apart from the normal Gölsdorf line of development in having outside frames. But it was about the turn of the century that he paid a visit to England, and was so impressed with the neatness of outline of British locomotives that his own products began to partake of a new look. The finish and standards of maintenance had always been beyond reproach, but the overall effect had been functional in the extreme.

In 1902 the first of a new series of 'Atlantics' was built at the First Bohemian Moravian Machine Works, Prague, for the Austrian State Railways, and they were the first main line passenger engines in which the characteristic double-dome arrangement was abandoned. They were large 2-cylinder compounds with 1902 mm. coupled wheels designed for the fast trains between Vienna and Prague, and between Vienna and Salzburg. These locomotives have a special place in Austrian railway history in that on this basic design Gölsdorf three years later introduced his system of compounding with four cylinders, instead of two. On a fast running locomotive having two cylinders, each of different size, outside the frames there was an inherent degree of unbalance that would produce swaying and general unsteadiness at high speed. On his new 'Atlantics' of 1905 there were two high pressure cylinders, inside, and two low pressure outside. Externally there was little to distinguish the 4-cylinder from the previous 2-cylinder machines — except when seen from the front, when the difference in diameter of the cylinders of the latter would be clearly apparent. The 4-cylinder engines were a great success, and thereafter Gölsdorf built none other for heavy main line work, both passenger and goods.

He attained his greatest heights of elegance in design in 1908 with his 2–6–4 express engines which came near to rivalling some of the Dutch 4–6–0s for the honour of being the most handsome-ever of Continental locomotives. His use of the 2–6–4 instead of the more popular 4–6–2 wheel arrangement can be appreciated from the placing of the large driving wheels ahead of the wide firebox, which in its turn was conveniently supported by the trailing four-wheeled truck. At the front end the low pressure cylinders were outside, surmounted by the enormous piston valves. Gölsdorf was evidently determined to have no restriction to the flow of steam through the valves. These were of special design, distributing steam to both high and low pressure cylinders. The boiler barrel was markedly tapered, after the practice of G.J. Churchward on the Great Western Railway of England, and a further characteristic of all Gölsdorf's work was retained in the double smokebox door, hinged vertically at each side, and fastening together on the vertical centre line.

The use of no more than a two-wheeled leading truck on a fast express locomotive would have caused some eyebrows to be raised, but for a special feature of design used by Gölsdorf. The 2–4–2 and 2–6–2 wheel arrangements had been used on certain American locomotives designed for high speed work, but had to be abandoned because of unsteady riding, due to lack of guiding effect from the leading two-wheeled truck. Gölsdorf surmounted this difficulty by use of what is known as the Helmholz leading truck. In this ingenious design the two leading wheels, and the leading pair of coupled wheels are mounted on a bogie frame, and provide in effect a leading bogie, of unusually long wheelbase, and pivoted centrally. To compensate for the slight lateral movement of the leading pair of coupled wheels, in relation to the second and third pairs, the coupling rods are jointed vertically at the crank bosses. The original engines of the class were fitted with steam driers, but the later group built between 1911 and 1916 had Schmidt superheaters. They were designed to haul 406 tonnes trains, but no one, not even the industrious J.P. Pearson, seems to have taken any detailed notes of their work for publication.

136

Gölsdorf died during the First World War, in March 1916 at Semmering, within sight of the remarkable Südbahn main line to the south, for which he had provided some very successful locomotives. But before turning to the truly mountain sections of the Austrian railways reference must be made to some notable post-war designs for the greatly reduced system of the Austrian Federal Railways, serving the new republic. A main line locomotive of greater capacity than the Gölsdorf 2–6–4 was needed, and new engines based on a wartime design of 4–8–0 for the Südbahn were built for general service. Whether Gölsdorf himself had anything to do with these engines is not known, and the question naturally arises because they were in so many ways a negation of all his earlier work. Until the outbreak of war in 1914 he had been in constant correspondence with the editorial staff of the *Locomotive Magazine* in London, who frequently referred to him as their 'esteemed friend and correspondent'. This contact ceased with the war, and it was indeed not until four years after his death that the news reached England. Then, although many interesting items were found among his private papers there was apparently nothing concerning the Südbahn 4–8–0 of 1915. Only two were then built, but in working over the heavy gradients of the Semmering pass they were very successful, and a further 40 of modified design were built between 1923 and 1928.

The 4–8–0 is an ideal type for heavy grade work, but these large, rather ungainly locomotives were 2-cylinder simples, and full advantage was taken of the height of the Austrian loading gauge, pitching the boiler high, and having the large firebox above the rear two pairs of coupled wheels. They were intended as mixed traffic engines, with a maximum speed in ordinary working of 100 km./h., as well as being reliable mountain climbers. In contrast to the smoothness and well-balanced action of the Gölsdorf 4-cylinder compounds these 4–8–0s had all the harshness of the basic 2-cylinder simple, which is a general purpose work horse, rather than a 'Rolls-Royce'. But the times had changed, and an essentially simple machine with all its working parts outside and readily get-at-able was needed in the austere conditions of post-war Austria, and these 4–8–0s fulfilled the need admirably. They slogged their way over the 1 in 36 gradients of the Semmering pass with reliability, if not speed. It was a design that influenced the locomotive practice of Poland, Czechoslovakia, Hungary and the Soviet Union. In later years most of those working in Austria had their performance characteristics notably enhanced by fitting of the Giesl ejector. Some very fine work over the Semmering pass was done by the modified engines.

The final development of Austrian steam locomotive practice came in the late 1920s, when the proposal to electrify the main line between Vienna and Salzburg had to be postponed because of the high capital cost. Train loads were very much on the increase and if double heading was to be avoided larger locomotives than either the pre-war Gölsdorf 2–6–4s, or the later 4–8–0s were needed. In any case the 4–8–0s were not suitable for the faster stretches of the Vienna-Salzburg line. Just as the French and the American railways advanced from the 4–6–2 to the 4–8–2, so in Austria the development eventually decided upon was from the 2–6–4 to the 2–8–4, with a similar form of the Helmholz truck at the front end, to provide good guiding effect. Experience with the 2-cylinder simple 4–8–0s had however been such that this engine layout was preferred to the Gölsdorf 4-cylinder compound. An important difference was that the new 2–8–4s had oscillating cam poppet valves, actuated by Walschaerts valve gear. The first of the new engines was put into service in 1928, and simultaneously strong representations were made by one of the manufacturing firms in favour of 3-cylinder propulsion. It was much in favour in England at the time, and to a lesser extent in the U.S.A. A second 2–8–4 was accordingly built for comparative trails.

After three years of intensive comparison the 2-cylinder version was accepted as the future standard. Six more engines of this type were put to work in 1931, and a further six in 1936. These, together with the original engine of 1928 and the experimental 3-cylinder example met all needs of traffic on the Vienna-Salzburg main line, until the political upheavals of 1938 brought all normal progress to an end. Although not numerous these 2–8–4s proved a very successful class, and one which had its greatest sphere of activity outside Austria. The Rumanian State Railways adopted the design as a standard, and no fewer than 79 engines were supplied by Austrian firms. The basic dimensions were, cylinders 650 mm. diameter by 720 mm. stroke;

coupled wheels 1940 mm. diameter, and boiler pressure 15 kg. per sq. cm. They were among the most powerful passenger locomotives in Europe.

The specification of performance for these locomotives had been a guaranteed speed of 60 km./h. up a gradient of 1 in 100 with a load of 550 tonnes, this being the steepest inclination westbound through the Vienna Woods, and eastbound out of Salzburg. They were also required to haul 620 tonnes at 110 km./h. on level track. Both requirements were comfortably surpassed, and in recording this two features of the design must be specially mentioned — both due to Dr. A. Giesl-Gieslingen, then a young engineer. The first was a greatly improved exhaust arrangement, foreshadowing what Giesl was to do in the way of front-end design after the Second World War, with his now famous oblong ejectors. The second feature was the successful balancing of the engine, by applying the drive to the third pair of coupled wheels. Although the 13 Austrian 2–8–4s were made redundant by the electrification of the main lines after the Second World War one of these great engines has been preserved, and is in store pending the setting up of the Vienna railway museum.

CHAPTER TWELVE

Austria — railway mountain climbing

In the gracious capital city of Vienna the exhibits in the technical museum take one back into the very earliest days of railway operation in Austria, revealing the early British and American influences; but to any one interested in the indigenous locomotive practice of the country by far the most striking exhibit is a Gölsdorf 2-cylinder compound 0–10–0, designed originally for the Klostergrab-Moldau line in Bohemia, where heavy coal trains had to be hauled over gradients of 1 in 37. The opportunity the museum gives to walk round and study all the detail features of this fine locomotive is a fitting prelude to journeys over two routes where Gölsdorf's skill in engine designing was brilliantly applied to the surmounting of steep gradients. The construction of the Semmering line, through the tumbled wilderness of mountains through which the main line of the Südbahn was carried through to Styria and beyond, was an epic in itself, fit to rank with that of the Western Ghats in India, with the Canadian Pacific through the Selkirk range, and of the Settle and Carlisle in England.

The cab of a modern electric locomotive is an unrivalled vantage point for appreciating the geography of a difficult route — far better than the footplate of a steam locomotive, from which the lookout ahead is inevitably half cut off by the large boiler and firebox extending so far ahead of one's own position. To me, however, on a memorable ride, even with the advantage of such an uninterrupted look-out in such a jumble of rugged hills, so thickly covered with trees, there were many times when our likely way up to the Semmering tunnel was impossible to descry. The railway swings this way and that, over lofty viaducts, round jagged bluffs, through short tunnels, while all the time giving breathtaking glimpses of deep valleys, distant mountain ranges, and occasionally of trains speeding down the gradient, bursting into sight unexpectedly round curves. The maximum steepness of gradient is 1 in 40 over the 21.5 kilometres from Payerbach to the summit, where the average is 1 in 52 throughout; but quite apart from this, and the effort needed to haul heavy trains, as a civil engineer I thought even more of the task the first surveyors faced in such a countryside in trying to establish anything of a route at all. More than a hundred years ago, with no modern aids like aerial surveys to help, the pioneer had to do everything from ground level. It is not as though a straightforward mountain pass had to be climbed. There is a confused welter of crags, ravines and steep slopes that form no ordered geographical pattern, and so densely wooded that it must have been incredibly difficult to do any long-range sighting. And all the time the prophets of woe were chorusing ever more loudly that even if the line were built at all it would never be possible to design locomotives to climb the gradient!

How the engineering skill and indomitable spirit of Karl Ghega got the line built is one story; those who were at first responsible for providing engine power seemed a little overawed by the task, and a number of unconventional designs were proposed. In the famous competition of 1850 all the four locomotives entered were able to fulfil the stipulated conditions of haulage, but in the opinion of the judges none of them gave any expectation of the reliable service that was needed over such a route; and as the line was not then ready for opening to traffic, much additional scheming went on. It was not until 1870, when Karl Gölsdorf's father had been in charge for several years that a truly reliable type of locomotive was introduced. This contained no freakish innovations, no fancy schemes of frame articulation, as in the competing locomotives of 1850; it was a simple, straightforward design of 2–4–0, soundly constructed, with a good boiler, ample bearing surfaces, and everything readily accessible for maintenance. This was followed by an enlarged version, with the 4–4–0 wheel arrangement, which proved the backbone of the operation over the mountain section for upwards of thirty years. I photographed one of these great veterans, then nearly 70 years old, when I was at Graz, in 1966. One of them has been preserved, and is in store ready for display in the Austrian railway museum.

It was Gölsdorf the younger who, in 1897, made the greatest advance in mountain motive power for the Austrian railways, with the '170' class 2-cylinder compound 2–8–0. This was originally designed for passenger working over the Arlberg Tunnel route of the State Railway where the eastern ramp, from Landeck to St. Anton-in-Arlberg, is both longer and more steeply graded than the Semmering line. It was however built at a much later date in 1884, when no railwayman had any qualms about operating on 1 in 38 gradients. The '170' class was one of the most successful of all Karl Gölsdorf's designs. No fewer than 908 of them were built, construction continuing for three years after his death, in 1916. They were used on goods and mixed traffic service all over the old Imperial Austria, and on passenger trains on the most severe mountain sections. In 1966 when I was in Styria several of them were still working on the privately owned Graz-Köflacker Bahn, including one with the original spark-arresting device on the chimney. It is interesting that it is one of these celebrated engines from the Graz-Köflacker Bahn that has been earmarked for preservation, while the class that was developed from them, the 2-cylindered compound 0–10–0, is already so handsomely displayed in the technical museum at Vienna. As an example of how Austrian motive power had advanced in less than 50 years, the specification laid down for the original Semmering competitors was the haulage of a load of 140 tonnes up the 1 in 40 gradient at 13 km./h.; the Gölsdorf compound 2–8–0s would take 250 tonnes up at 20 km./h., or even faster.

The line south of the Semmering summit is not so steeply graded, and is less of a mountain railway. Electric traction continues to Bruck, and south westwards to Klagenfurt; but the international main line leading south through Graz into Jugoslavia, was worked by steam or diesel power when I was in that region in 1966. I rode south from Bruck to Graz on the footplate of one of the powerful '78' class 4–6–4 tank engines, of which the first were built in 1931. They are 2-cylinder simples, with the Lentz oscillating cam poppet valves, actuated by outside Walschaerts gear. They belong essentially to the post-Gölsdorf era, and have the angular functional appearance of the 4–8–0 passenger engines. They represent the last new design of steam locomotive built for the Austrian railways. They were excellent machines in traffic, and construction of them continued during the German occupation of Austria. Their appearance, never very elegant, has suffered from the addition of the German type of smoke deflectors, the same short type that made hideous the last years of the Gresley 'Pacifics' in England. Looks apart No. 78–614 on which I rode was a perfect 'Rolls-Royce' of a locomotive, riding smoothly and silently at speeds up to about 100 km./h. and gliding with ease round the numerous curves on this line, and making light work of an express train of 220 tonnes. The engine was then fitted with the Giesl ejector, and the exhaust was colourless to the point of being invisible throughout the run. Dr. Giesl himself came with me on the footplate, and was an absolute mine of information on Austrian locomotives.

We alighted at Graz, for I was to be taken to the station and running sheds of the Graz-Köflacker Bahn. There indeed I was in the living presence of Austrian locomotive history. At the time of my visit the railway was operating about 30 steam locomotives, which were not only working all the freight trains, but assisting in the rush hour passenger traffic. The year was 1964, and it seemed almost unbelievable to find in the same locomotive yard, in steam and smartly kept, several Gölsdorf 2-cylinder compound 2–8–0s, a Class '17c' 4–4–0 of the Südbahn, and above all one of the truly ancient '29' class 0–6–0 tender engines. The GKB then had four of these veterans, all built in 1860, and then 104 years old. Like the ex-Südbahn 4–4–0s these 0–6–0s had outside link motion, of the Allan type. Of the Gölsdorf 2–8–0s on shed at Graz one had the distinctive spark-arresting chimney, which however enhancing to a vintage specimen did not exactly improve its appearance.

We must now retrace steps along the line to Vienna as far as Leobensdorf, in the comparatively level country north of Wiener Neustadt, which is the junction for the branch to Puchberg. This charming little sub-Alpine village is at the foot of the Schneeberg (snow-mountain), up which there climbs a very splendid little rack railway. The upper station, Hochschneeberg, is 1795 metres above sea level, and although not commanding such a dramatic prospect as that from the Scharfberg in the Salzkammergut, it is entrancing enough, and has the attraction of an especially interesting railway ride on the ascent, maintained throughout the winter. The maximum gradient is about 1 in 5, and the sturdy little tank locomotives each propel two cars. Originally they had conical type spark-arresting chimneys, but when I made the trip in 1966, they had all been fitted with Giesl ejectors and micro-spark arrestors. The descent is controlled by a counter-pressure brake. Naturally progress is not rapid in either direction of travel. My wife and I were accompanied by Dr. Giesl and his elder daughter; she as an expert mountaineer decided to walk down, rather than ride, and she reached Puchberg at the same time as the train!

In Gölsdorf's day the main line northwestwards into what is now Czechoslovakia was an express route equally as important as the present main line from Vienna to Salzburg, and the first batch of the 4-cylinder compound 2–6–4s were put on to the Prague run. In the late 1920s however when only the Salzburg line remained as a fast route it was over this latter, with its fairly moderate gradients, that the performance requirements of new express locomotives were studied. In light of the known capacity of the compound 2–6–4s, and the 4–8–0s that were being used with much success on the Semmering line, the first thoughts were towards an enlarged 2–6–4 — a blend of the two existing designs, but a 3-cylinder simple, with all cylinders driving on to the central of the three coupled axles. But although it was to have been a fast express engine the tractive effort would not have been so great as that of the existing 4–8–0, and so eventually the big 2–8–4 materialised.

When bound for the Tyrol and so to Switzerland it is always pleasant to break the journey, because on a route of such continuous scenic charm one can eventually become completely saturated, with just looking; and some of the finest mountain country is passed through towards the end of the journey. So, on several occasions we have left Vienna at mid-afternoon on the 'Orient Express', and when proceeding to Switzerland stayed the night in Salzburg. From there the mid-morning train westwards is an ideal one for sightseeing, not too fast, making a number of intermediate stops, and in summer crossing into Switzerland before sundown. The somewhat circuitous route from Salzburg to the junction with the Südbahn line at Worgl is a continuous pageant of rugged country, plunging in a few kilometres from starting point into a deep gorge of dramatic rock formation.

Then comes Bischofshofen, and 15 kilometres further on is Schwarzach St. Veit, where the important international route to the south, via the Tauern Tunnel diverges. This is taken by the principal express trains from West Germany to Jugoslavia and Greece. It was to cope with the heavy gradients on this line that Karl Gölsdorf's last major locomotive design was built, a huge 2–12–0, in 1911.

The route to the Tyrol makes a winding course to the west, past Zell am See and the popular skiing resort of Kitzbühel. I have seen this wild country in all kinds of weather, and I must confess thay my recollections of it are mostly of storm and sleet, when the higher slopes of the mountains were shrouded in mist, parting only to show expanses of uninviting snow; the rivers so many torrents, and the wide lake at Zell bleak and windswept. On the railway it is not a fast stretch at the best of times. Our train takes all but three and a half hours to cover the 194 kilometres from Salzburg to Worgl, with six intermediate stops, and the 'Arlberg Express' — the present successor to the one time 'Arlberg-Orient Express' — making only four stops, just manages to get through in three hours. These averages of no more than 57 and 65 kilometres per hour give some idea of the running difficulties of the route. The three fastest trains from Salzburg to Innsbruck now take the original route through Germany, and are known as 'Privilege Trains'. They make no stops in German territory, and passengers holding special through tickets are not subjected to any customs formalities. The effect of this arrangement is that while the 'Arlberg Express' takes 3 hr. 34 mins. from Salzburg to Innsbruck by the all-Austrian route, the 'Transalpin' takes 2 hr. 11 min. non-stop, while the high speed railcar trains 'Bodensee' and 'Tirolerland' take 2 hr. 12 min. and $2^{1}/_{4}$ hr., including one and two stops respectively.

I must admit that I do not regard such very fast services as an entirely unmixed blessing. The average speeds between Salzburg and Innsbruck are around 100 km./h. and this means much rapid negotiation of curves. However good the super-elevation may be, and the safety of travel beyond any question, one is nevertheless conscious of the swinging round, and often frequent changes of direction. My own experience is that these types of trains provide a kind of travel that is neither one thing nor the other. It is neither the leisurely perambulation of a mountain country in the style of the 'Arlberg Express', nor the sustained swiftness of the 'Etendard' or the 'Mistral' in which the travelling conditions are so stable, that one can forget all about travelling and settle down to work, read or sleep. I could never concentrate on anything for long in the 'Transalpin'. In writing of these fast railcar trains however I have jumped the 60 kilometres of the old Südbahn line from Worgl to Innsbruck, and I must retrace steps a little, because between the two, at Jenbach, junction is made with two fascinating little narrow gauge lines. To the north goes the short, but steep Achensee rack railway, while southwards runs the Zillertalbahn. When I was travelling this way last both were still steam operated. They were great favourites with railway enthusiast photographers because of their comparative nearness to Innsbruck; in any case most of the main line trains stop at Jenbach.

By Innsbruck the railway is penetrating into the very heart of the Tyrol, and there can be few important railway centres set in such sublime mountain scenery. The technical features of its new colour light signalling caused the Institution of Railway Signal Engineers to pause there for two days on a Summer Convention bound eventually for Vienna, though really in the first place that pause was to take breath after twenty two hours of continuous travelling, and fourteen of them in the same carriages from Calais! The position of Innsbruck at the junction of the Arlberg and the Brenner routes is of much importance, and the re-arrangement of the track layout at the western end, to avoid the conflicting crossings, removed a source of delay and enabled trains from the Arlberg and Brenner routes to arrive and depart simultaneously. Today the entire operation is electric, but there is a reminder of steam days in a large roundhouse. Unlike many of its kind, which have been allowed to become derelict, this one is still in a good state of repair, though housing no more than a few electric locomotives. Nowadays the idea of locomotives of any kind — electric and diesel-electric anyway — being in a shed for any length of time is anathema to a running superintendent, whose aim is to secure maximum utilisation out of every unit on the strength. A modern motive power depot is more like a roadside filling station than a garage!

It might nevertheless seem like sacrilege to talk about colour light signals, electric points, and the philosophies of modern locomotive usage in an arena such as that of Innsbruck, ringed with great snow-clad mountains, with forests extending far up their slopes, and when the sun shines a sky so blue as to be almost unbelievable. There are some famous resorts, having strong railway interests, where one can get out on the line and become thoroughly absorbed in technicalities; but not so at Innsbruck. The mountains tower over everything — a mighty backdrop in every direction. The modern electric locomotives of the Austrian Federal Railways, smartly turned out in dark blue naturally do not provide the individual interest and human appeal of steam, especially when they were such a striking collection as those of the old 'Imperial Royal' State Railway. But for such gradients as we are soon to ascend, on our way through to Switzerland electric locomotives are ideal. The largest passenger type, carried on two six-wheeled bogies, may not have such opportunities for high speed as their contemporaries in West Germany, or France; but they are doing a great job in the mountains. And so, with a heavy train we glide out of Innsbruck, round the new Konzert curve away from the line to the Brenner Pass, and head westwards through the Inn Valley.

The scenery is tremendous. The mountains rise to great heights on both sides of the line, but form no mere continuous walls. There are frequent intermissions, where smaller ravines debouch, and breathtaking sights where a major valley like the Ötzthal joins in. At first the gradients are not severe and speed is brisk, and while enjoying the landscape and the well-ordered farms and homesteads along the route, the railway enthusiast will also note with appreciation the massively built country stations, and the neatness of all the ancilliary equipment. In this part of Austria one does not see any tumbledown sheds, sidings overgrown with weeds, harbouring derelict rolling stock; everything is smartly kept, and obviously in use. When one leaves the railway, and climbs the hillsides the overhead electric traction wires and their supports are so unobtrusive as to be almost invisible. The line is single-tracked from Innsbruck, with colour light signalling throughout. So, at Landeck, 72 kilometres west of Innsbruck, the foot of the great eastern 'ramp' is reached, whence for another 27.5 kilometres the ascent is continuously at 1 in 38.

Landeck is a busy country station, but it used to be a place of major railway significance. In steam days rear-end banking assistance had to be provided for all heavy trains, and a considerable stud of the Gölsdorf 2-cylinder compound o—10—os of the type displayed in the technical museum at Vienna, was stationed at Landeck specially for the job. Though not an out-and-out railway colony, the snug little town set so deep among the mountains depended to a large extent on the railway when it was so vital a steam locomotive centre. The design of the o—10—o engines was influenced as much by the curvature as by the gradients of the line, because although a ten coupled locomotive was desirable from the tractive point of view, so relatively long a wheelbase could be a hindrance rather than a help. Gölsdorf solved the problem by giving the first, third, and fifth axles freedom to move laterally 28 mm. each side of the centre position. They were thus able to ride the curves with freedom and ease. These engines, of which many more were stationed at Blüdenz, at the foot of the western 'ramp' to the Arlberg Tunnel, were not exclusively bank engines. At one time there were 208 of them, and they were used in heavy goods traffic on most parts of the old Imperial Royal State Railway, and also on the Südbahn.

In referring to the engines still in service at Graz, I wrote in appreciative terms of the 2-cylinder compound 2—8—os. These were originally designed for the Arlberg route, as general purpose locomotives for passenger and freight trains alike. It became a very popular route, and the weight of trains increased accordingly. Even with rear-end assistance, either from Landeck or Bludenz, there were times when the 2—8—os could not manage the heavy trains unassisted over the other parts of the line, and in 1906 Gölsdorf designed his enormous 4-cylinder compound 2—10—o specially for the Arlberg line — not only for the mountain section, but to have sufficient capacity for speed to be able to work through between Salzburg and Bludenz, via Kitzbühel. The coupled wheels were 920 mm. diameter and this, combined with large cylinders, high boiler pressure, ample heating surface and high degree superheating, produced an outstandingly successful engine for these difficult conditions. In view of the many and various Austrian steam locomotives preserved for eventual display in the national railway museum it would be graceless to ask for still more; but one would have liked to see one of these great

148

engines included, rather than one of their 2-cylinder simple successors built from 1912 onwards.

In Landeck one naturally falls to discussing high powered mountain climbing locomotives, but our modern train has not proceeded far up the great incline towards the Arlberg Tunnel before coming to one of the great masterpieces of European railway civil engineering, the Trisanna Bridge, over the gloriously wooded gorge where the rivers Rosanna and Trisanna meet, before tumbling their combined waters into those of the Inn. The gorge required a bowstring girder bridge of 119 metres, carrying the railway at a height of 86 metres above the river. Mere words cannot convey much of the beauty of the scene: it is best left to the photographs. The lower inverted girder was added in 1923 to provide additional strength to carry the electric locomotives then projected. Later, in 1964, complete reconstruction was made, with the Langer type bowstring arch, with a much greater depth of main girder. The location is made doubly attractive by the railway passing adjacent to the romantically perched Wiesberg Castle on the southern slopes of the gorge.

So the train continues without apparent effort up the continuation of the steep gradient, though it does not need a great deal of imagination on the part of a locomotive lover to conjure up something of the cacaphony of sound that used to prevail when a couple of Gölsdorf 2-cylinder compounds, one in front and one in rear, were slogging it out with a heavy passenger train of 70 years ago. By sound alone the speed could well have been judged much slower than it actually was, because with only one low-pressure cylinder these engines had only two exhaust beats per revolution instead of the normal four. On a long train there are frequent glimpses of the head end, and on a 1 in 38 gradient there is no doubt — we are definitely going uphill! Often in May there is snow lying near to the railway, and in nearing the summit at St. Anton-am-Arlberg the altitude is almost that of the summit of Ben Nevis. Although the Arlberg is the shortest of the great tunnels in the Alps it is the highest of them all, with a summit level of 1315 metres, against the 1240 metres of the Lötschberg line. So, threading the tunnel, we pass from the Austrian Tyrol into the district of Vorarlberg, and at Langen enter upon a precipitous descent.

The Arlberg tunnel passes under one of those watersheds that seem to act as a barrier betwen different weather systems. One can enter in bright sunshine, and emerge in rain, fog or snow. So it was on a journey by the mid-morning train from Salzburg to Zürich. It was nearly 17.30 when we had run through St. Anton. Clouds were low on the mountain sides, and the slopes had the forlorn appearance that comes with great expanses of melting snow. Although it was May everything suggested an early nightfall. Then when we emerged at Langen the skies were clear in the west, and the long view ahead down the valley gave promise of a pleasant finish to the journey. But after more than six hours of travelling through so great and varied a countryside as that between Salzburg and St. Anton-am-Arlberg, there comes irresistibly a feeling of anti-climax when the last major summit is passed. I always recall the words of a Canadian friend, an avid notetaker on locomotives, who said he always felt like throwing his pencil and notebook overboard when a place like Shap Summit, Druimuachdar Pass, or the Connaught Tunnel in British Columbia had been attained. I must say I had something of the same sentiments, though not to the extent of throwing my notes away (!), as we went zig-zagging our way down the hill to Blüdenz, often on gradients as steep as 1 in 32. But we should fairly soon reach the frontier station at Buchs, and the Swiss Federal Railways would take over haulage of the train. Before reaching Buchs, however, one can go one of two ways. At Feldkirch a line goes off to the north to Bregenz, Lindau, and the north shore of Lake Constance; but our own route, through Buchs, leads to Sargans, and a junction with the main line of the Engadine. Thence in the gathering dusk, as the train sweeps along by the still waters of the Wallensee, one has said farewell to Austria.

CHAPTER THIRTEEN

Switzerland — all electric railways

Riding westwards in the 'Arlberg Express', leaving the mountains behind, and seeing the many lights twinkling in the dusk across the pale iridescence of the Lake of Zürich, it is a moment to reflect upon the wonderful railway system on to which we have so lately entered. One can become so engrossed and enthralled by the scale and majesty of the greater engineering works, by the splendour of the trans-Alpine routes, as to lose something of the true significance of the Swiss railways. Soon after the establishment of the Swiss Confederation in 1848 the Government approached Robert Stephenson, and asked for his recommendations for a national railway system. At that time there was little thought of any international connections, except that the famous 'Spanish Bun' Railway had already been built between Zürich and Basle. Stephenson proposed a national main line connecting Geneva, Lausanne, and Olten with Basle, from which connection to the eastern part of the country would be made over the 'Spanish Bun' line, through Baden. And it is over the Geneva, Lausanne, Zürich 'axis', proposed by Stephenson, that by far the greatest railway activity in Switzerland is to be found today. It runs through fairly level country, and is the scene of much fast running.

Switzerland can claim some remarkable railway statistics. In terms of train kilometres per kilometre of route its tracks are by a considerable margin the busiest in Europe, while the number of train journeys made for every citizen of the country is more than *twice as many* than that of any other European country. It is sometimes said that statistics can be made to prove anything, but a brief sojourn at any one of the main stations is enough to show the popularity of the very fast inter-city trains. The spectacular TEE services, and the great international expresses that run by night have a prestige of their own, but it is the comparatively local trains that carry the Swiss people. To a railway enthusiast, particularly one with historical or nostalgic leanings the outward aspect of the busiest parts of the network might appear to be rather dull, in its uniformity and precision; but as an example of closely co-ordinated modern railway operation it is outstanding. The Swiss, like the Dutch, have developed the push-and-pull, fixed formation electric trains to a high degree of utilisation, and one of the operating diagrams shows how a typical set covers 2610 kilometres in three days, in a total running time of 37 hours or an average of 70.5 km./h. Considering that the services worked make numerous intermediate stops this is very smart going.

It is, of course, in the co-ordination of all engineering activities that the Swiss railways have been able to achieve such success. And it is important to emphasise that in addition to the nationally owned Swiss Federal Railways there are several important, and equally efficient private ones that contribute notably to the impressive statistics already quoted. The electrification of the Federal system was completed in 1960. Until the year 1919 no more than a few pioneer installations had been made, mostly in connection with the opening of the Simplon Tunnel in 1906, and using different systems of traction current supply. The Italian railways had been using the three-phase system which provides for running at constant speed, and it was understandable that the link through the tunnel, and its Swiss continuation down the valley of the Rhone as far as Sion, should have been similarly equipped, by way of a trial. By 1919 indeed the Swiss Federal Railways were operating nearly 75 kilometres of route on this system. Except for two short experimental sections the rest of the standard gauge network was operated by steam, and in 1915 had reached its peak, with 1224 locomotives. In the meantime however the privately owned Bern-Lötschberg-Simplon Railway had been opened through the great Lötschberg Tunnel in 1913. It was all-electric from the outset, and equipped on the single-phase 15,000 volt alternating current system, at $16^2/_3$ cycles per second. It proved so successful that when the Swiss Federal Railways began the systematic conversion of their entire network to electric traction this was the form they also adopted. In Stage One of the national plan, covering 55 per cent. of the entire route, it was interesting to find that the first section to be equipped was that from Berne to Thun, to link up with the Lötschberg line.

At the outset it was determined that three different types of locomotives would be needed. The Gotthard line, with its long sections of very severe gradients had the highest priority in the programme of electrification, and the mountain section between Erstfeld and Bellinzona was completed as early as April 1921. Following the launching of Stage One of the programme, the three different types of locomotives required were:

1. Haulage of heavy freight trains.
2. Haulage of express passenger and stopping trains in level country.
3. Haulage of express passenger and stopping trains on the Gotthard line.

For category '1' a locomotive of distinctive, but not entirely original design was introduced. At that time in the history of electric locomotive development there were many features of design derived from steam practice. The traction motors were connected to the road wheels by means of coupling rods, and in these locomotives there were four motors to provide the requisite kilowatts — about 1640. The motors were arranged in pairs, each pair driving the wheels in two bogies. These each had six-coupled driving wheels and a leading two-wheeled truck. The body of the locomotive containing the driving cab was carried on a cradle resting on the two powered bogies, rather like an electric locomotive version of a Beyer-Garratt articulated steam engine. These Swiss electric locomotives, class 'Ce6/8[11]', had a rated maximum speed of 65 km./h. In level country they could haul 1200 tonnes at 40 km./h. and on the 1 in 38 gradients of the Gotthard line haul 450 tonnes at 36 km./h. They are still to be seen in service on the Swiss Federal Railways.

In the passenger locomotives, both for the Gotthard line and for the level routes in the high speed 'corridor' between Geneva and Zürich the different manufacturers were permitted to introduce design features of their own, and while some adhered to the coupling-rod form of drive the Ateliers de Sécheron used flexible individual drives on to each axle, thereby starting the trend towards the present standard practice. The 'Ae3/6¹' class of which 114 were built was a very successful early example of individual drive, with a wheel arrangement of three driving axles, a leading four-wheeled truck, and a two-wheeled trailing truck. They had a one hour rating of 1570 kilowatts and a maximum speed of 110 km./h. This class was developed into the 'Ae4/7', which was the same, but with four driving axles, and a rating of 2328 kilowatts at 65 km./h. The maximum speed was 100 km./h. The Swiss Federal Railways have always looked with particular favour on this class, of which there are 127, even though they have now been superseded by later and much more powerful designs. The 'Ae4/7' class are no beauties. Essentially functional in appearance they have nothing of the sleek streamlined exteriors of the modern Swiss electric locomotives; but as solid reliable workhorses they have earned every bit of the affection in which they are held by the running staff.

While this Chapter is essentially about electrical matters, I cannot altogether ignore steam, and mention of the locomotives that carried the traffic so well until Stage One of the big changeover to electric traction began in 1919. Although the Gotthard Railway became part of the Swiss Federal system in 1909 its locomotive practice remained quite distinct, right up to the time of electrification. It was the Jura-Simplon Railway, before it became part of the Federal system that covered the network originally recommended by Robert Stephenson, and had, as its name suggests, a line leading from the shores of the Lake of Geneva up the Rhone valley to where the Simplon tunnel was being built. In 1902 this company introduced a design of 4-cylinder compound 4–6–0 that, with later additions such as the Schmidt superheater, remained the standard express passenger locomotive on all Swiss lines except the Gotthard. They had the von Borries system of valves, with its simplicity in starting. For its very heavy gradients the Gotthardbahn adopted at first the de Glehn system of compounding in a 4-cylinder 4–6–0 design that looked very French. With heavy international express trains these locomotives had often to be used in pairs. When larger locomotives were needed the railway management turned to the Bavarian firm of Maffei, and purchased a number of large 4-cylinder compound 4–6–0s in which the drive was in the usual Maffei style with all four cylinders driving on to the leading coupled axle.

Reverting again to electric traction, while the mountain locomotives of both the Swiss Federal Railways and the Lötschberg had done excellent work, the increasing weight of the international express trains, needing more powerful locomotives, led to studies by the Lötschberg railway as to how power could be increased while at the same time avoiding the need for increasing the weight of the locomotives themselves. The Swiss Federal 'Ae4/7' class had a weight in working order of 120 tonnes, while the Lötschberg 'Be6/8' and 'Ae6/8' had an all-up weight of 142 tonnes. The latter had two bogies, each with three powered axles and a leading two-wheeled truck. Two motors drove on to each of the powered axles, and the adhesion weight was 120 tonnes. The earlier series dating from 1926 had an hourly rating of 3357 kilowatts and a maximum speed of 75 km./h., while the later series dating from 1939 had an hourly rating of 3950 kilowatts and a maximum speed of 90 km./h. These latter locomotives took the road just at the time when international traffic had greatly diminished because of the outbreak of the Second World War, and being rather too powerful for ordinary passenger service were used mostly on freight trains.

It was towards the end of the war that the Lötschberg engineers gave urgent consideration to an all-adhesion type of locomotive, and one incorporating all the latest techniques in electric locomotive design that would permit of a major reduction in all-up weight. The result was the epoch-marking 'Ae4/4', which placed on two four-wheeled bogies and no other wheels, a locomotive of 2984 kilowatts, weighing no more than 80 tonnes. Thus in a tractive unit of 2984, instead of 3357 kilowatts, a weight of no less than 62 tonnes had been saved; and this meant that an additional weight of nearly this same amount could be hauled up the steep gradients. There was even more to it than this. A great deal of research had been put into the bogie design, so that although there was no leading truck ahead of the driving wheels the new locomotives were permitted to run up a maximum speed of no less than 125 km./h. They constituted a 'world first', as the first really high speed locomotive without any carrying, as distinct from driving wheels. This was the second time that this relatively small private railway had set a new world standard; because on its opening in 1913 it had been the first in Europe to adopt high tension single phase traction, 15,000 volts alternating current at $16^2/_3$ cycles, subsequently adopted by the Swiss Federal, and the state railways of Germany and Austria.

The new 'Ae4/4' locomotives created immense interest, and they have indeed become a world prototype, developed for greater power into the Co – Co type on two six-wheeled bogies. It was two of these derivatives in France, one Bo – Bo, and one Co – Co that made, on successive occasions the present world speed record on rails of 332 km./h. between Bordeaux and Dax. The British Bo – Bo series on the London, Midland Region, another direct derivative of the Lötschberg 'Ae4/4', operate the most intensive high speed passenger service in the world, with huge daily mileages run regularly at 160 km./h. On the Lötschberg itself there are, ironically, no opportunities for such high speed running, though occasionally maximum rates of more than 110 km./h. are attained on the straight and almost level length of the great tunnel itself. The fastest regular running in Switzerland is over the central main line between Zürich and Geneva over which the crack trains cover the 289 kilometres in 3 hr. 16 min. with intermediate stops at Berne, Fribourg and Lausanne. There is however some cautious running needed in the approach and departure from stations like Berne, because of the complicated track layout, and some high speed is needed intermediately to keep such timings as 34 minutes for the 59.75 kilometres from Lausanne to Geneva, or 90 minutes for the 130 kilometres from Zürich to Berne, with a severe intermediate slowing through the junctions at Olten. The maximum speeds attained by the Bo – Bo electric locomotives adhesion' locomotives, of the Bo – Bo type have a rate of 1716

While the change from steam to electric traction came rapidly in Switzerland, and by 1929 more than half of the total route mileage of the Swiss Federal Railways had been converted, there was at first no corresponding change from semaphore to colour light signals. In due course however electric traction brought higher running speeds, and the need for greater braking distances; the distant or warning signals had to be placed at a greater distance before their associated stop signals — up to 600 metres — and this introduced a difficulty in mechanical working. In Switzerland as in Germany and Holland the double-wire system of mechanical actuation was standard; and since the distant signals were in the same double-wire transmission that operated the stop signal, with both signals changing position together, it became difficult to operate them at such a distance from the cabin. A change to colour light signals was therefore initiated. Viewing the policy so far as the entire network was concerned it was clearly impossible to change all the mechanical signals into light signals at one stroke, it was realised that many years would have to pass during which the two types would have to function side by side. On this account the new colour light aspects were made the same as those displayed at night by the semaphore signals. It was not until 1929 that any colour light signals were installed in Switzerland.

Electrification did however lead to a very important safety development in Switzerland. A number of accidents due to drivers of fast trains misinterpreting or disregarding signals led, in the early 1920s, to the development of an ingenious system of automatic train control, known as the Metrum. It was based firstly on the indication shown by the distant signals, which as previously explained were co-acting with their associated stop signal. It depended upon an inductive pick-up between locomotive and track equipment though the latter, connected to the adjacent signal, did not require any power supply of its own at the lineside — an important feature. The two electro-magnets in the track were activated only when a locomotive passed over, and then the inductive link between the locomotive and track magnets found the locomotive equipment, in effect, asking the question: 'Is the signal clear, or at warning?' If it was at 'warning' a horn was sounded in the driver's cab. Immediate acknowledgement was required, otherwise, after travelling about 60 metres the emergency brakes would be applied and the train stopped. This system proved so successful that in 1934 a decision was taken to equip all electric locomotives, and multiple-unit trains. Agreement was also secured that on all units so equipped a second man in the cab was not required. Most locations to which this system of train control were first applied were semaphore; but the system itself has become a national standard.

In Switzerland elimination of mechanical interlocking between levers came considerably later than in England; but in years after the Second World War, with the changeover to electric traction nearly completed rapid strides were made in power signalling development. A notable feature of many new installations was the use of a control console built up by units, rather than having the representation of the track layout to be controlled painted on a solid sheet of steel. Early experience with the push button and thumb switch type of control panel had emphasised the difficulty and costliness of making additions or alterations once the plant was in service. Accordingly a series of standard units, or dominoes, was devised each corresponding to a standard track feature, such as a pair of points, a simple crossing, a slip road, buffer stop, section of plain line and so on. Each unit had behind the 'domino' facade the necessary miniature lamp units for

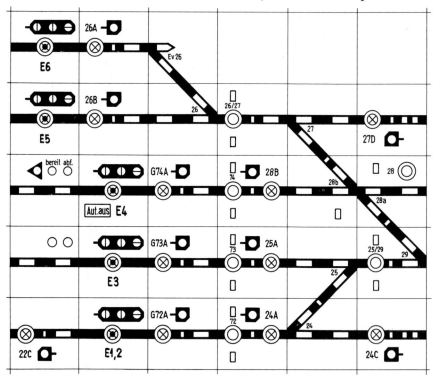

18. Domino type of control panel on Swiss railways

providing the appropriate indication lights. The advantage was that if an additional feature had to be introduced, such as a new crossover road, an extension to a siding, or on the other hand redundant connections had to be removed, all that was necessary was to substitute the domino unit corresponding to the changed layout. One of the most impressive recent examples is at Zürich-Altstetten, on which the electronic features include automatic route setting, and enable two signalmen per shift to handle 400 trains a day.

Track circuiting is an almost universal feature of all modern signalling installations, but there are certain localities where the operation would be difficult, and the 15 kilometre long Gotthard tunnel is certainly one. Until 1938 the tunnel formed one long block section, but in that year it was divided into two, and in 1947 a remote interlocking with a scissors crossover was put in at mid-tunnel, controlled from Göschenen. The long tracks on either side of the central crossover station are equipped with axle counters by which devices all axles of a train are counted when entering and leaving a section. If no vehicle has become detached in the transit of that section the counter shows 'zero', and the corresponding signal will be cleared for the next train. The same is, in the ordinary way, performed by the track circuit; but in the Gotthard Tunnel there would be complications because of the length, and the adverse physical conditions inside.

Mention of the Gotthard Tunnel, and by inference the heavily graded lines leading up to it, brings me once again to locomotives because the ever-increasing loads of the passenger and freight trains over this route demand ever-increasing haulage capacity. On the long 1 in 38 inclines leading up to the tunnel, including several lengths of spiral tunnel on both sides, the maximum permitted speed is 75 km./h. and operating requirements demand the maintenance of that speed with the heaviest trains. There is, of course, no distinction between passenger and freight trains, because all the stock used on the latter is fitted with continuous automatic air brakes and can be run at passenger train speed, uphill and down. For the Gotthard line the basic all-adhesion type derived originally from the Lötschberg 'Ae4/4' has been developed into the tremendous new 'Re6/6' class, which has a rate of 7699 kilowatts. No more striking example could be chosen to demonstrate the advance in design technique of electric locomotives than to compare these latest machines with the 'Ae4/7' of 1928; both weigh about 120 tonnes, yet the latter has a rate in kilowatts of only 2334 — a 3.3 times increase in power for the same total weight.

Not all the most interesting Swiss developments in electric traction have taken place on the standard gauge lines. In the less frequented parts of the country there are some splendidly equipped metre gauge lines. One of these is the Brünig Railway connecting Interlaken with Lucerne. It runs through beautiful country, and having to surmount the Brünig Pass intermediately involved some true mountain climbing. This is not a case of ordinary steep gradients such as the ascents to the Arlberg, Gotthard and Lötschberg tunnels, but long sections of 1 in 10, 1 in 9 and even 1 in $8^1/_2$. These cannot be climbed by adhesion even with the powerful modern metre gauge locomotives, and these very steep pitches are climbed by rack and pinion methods. This is the only metre gauge section of the Swiss Federal Railways, and in 1942 it was electrified on the standard 15,000 volt single phase alternating current system, followed by a substantial acceleration of the train service. Until then with steam haulage the run of 74 kilometres between Interlaken and Lucerne took around $3^1/_2$ hours. The rack sections necessarily took a long time to climb and descend, with the changes from ordinary to rack working.

Now, with electric traction and with one locomotive throughout the journey is completed in about two hours. The special 'rack and adhesion' locomotives, of the Bo − Bo type have a rate of 1716 kilowatts. The design of electric motors is of a simple type that, by the engagement of a special set of gears, can be used for rack as well as adhesion working. When working wholly by adhesion the maximum speed is 50 km./h., while on the rack it is 33 km./h. While high power is needed for mounting the heavy gradients into the Brünig Pass, it is perhaps even more important to retain the most rigorous brake control on the descents, and these locomotives have no less than five independent brake systems, namely:

1. The automatic air brake on locomotive and train for normal adhesion running.

2. Straight air brake on the locomotive only.
3. Electric resistance brakes for controlling downhill running on the rack sections.
4. A special disc brake acting on the cogged wheels engaging with the rack.
5. Hand brakes operated from the cab.

These very powerful and efficient locomotives weigh no more than 54 tonnes. The Brünig Railway has also a number of combined locomotives and luggage vans, with the Bo – Bo wheel arrangement. This type of locomotive was used when the line was first electrified. The maximum rated speeds are 18.6 km./h. rack, and 46.6 km./h. adhesion.

While mentioning the versatile 'rack and adhesion' locomotives of the Brünig Railway one is tempted to venture far into the mountains to the astonishing route taken by the 'Glacier Express' between St. Moritz and Zermatt, metre gauge, and over the tracks of no fewer than three private railways in succession: the Rhaetian, the Furka-Oberalp, and finally the Brig-Visp-Zermatt. All the locomotives employed have to work at times on both rack and adhesion and purely as a sightseeing route, including the novelty of a dining car being operated over gradients of 1 in 9, the run could scarcely be surpassed; but from the viewpoint of electrical engineering, with which this Chapter is mainly concerned, it is the Brig-Visp-Zermatt section that is of the greatest interest. The renowned Alpine resort at the terminus of the line is no more than 44 kilometres from the important main line junction of Brigue (or Brig, to give it the German spelling) making connection with the Swiss Federal main line through the Rhone Valley to the Simplon Tunnel, and also with the Lötschberg line. There are times when the metre gauge line between Brigue and Zermatt is very busy, and on this account special attention has been given to its train control system and signalling.

The line is single-tracked throughout, but in the distance of 44 kilometres there are no fewer than ten crossing places while, to enable trains to follow each other at close headway, there are additionally eleven block posts. For example, on the section between Kalpetran and St. Nicklaus, which is almost entirely rack, there are three intermediate block posts, so that between crossings at those two stations there could be three trains following each other up the rack. To complete the picture of physical conditions on this remarkable line, there is a difference of altitude of 955 metres between Brigue and Zermatt. The traffic on the entire line is regulated from a single control panel, and it is indicative of the way that modern railway operation is conducted without the need for the men concerned to see any trains, that this panel is not in the station at Brigue, but in the headquarter offices of the company, several blocks of buildings away. The controller — one cannot call him a signalman — has a panel diagram before him covering the entire line, on which the movements of trains are shown by lights at the appropriate places on the track diagram, while signal and point operation is by push button. At the rear of the control panel displayed prominently on the wall is the timetable diagram of the entire 24 hours' working.

Automatic operation is the normal procedure at the passing loops. A train entering the last block section nearest to a station causes the entrance route and the home signal to set up for the train movement. Provided that the right of way is available for the line section following the station — the line being clear to the next passing loop — the exit signal is cleared also. But if the section ahead is occupied by a train coming in the opposite direction, the exit signal remains at danger until that train has arrived in the loop. The controller at Brigue merely exercises a watching brief over the working. In exceptional circumstances, however, he can over-ride the automatic working and regulate train movements from his panel. One can quite believe however that the vast majority of passengers using these brilliant red electric trains have little thought for such technicalities, for this splendid little railway is bringing them to one of the most famous tourist centres in all Switzerland; and as the ascending train rounds the last curve before coming to Zermatt station, suddenly there appears over a shoulder of one of the mountain sides flanking the railway, that most spectacular of all Swiss mountains — in some respects the most spectacular mountain in the whole world — the Matterhorn.

CHAPTER FOURTEEN

The great north to south mountain routes

Among the many grandly picturesque railway routes of the world, those in Switzerland hold an outstanding and in one respect a unique place. One can think of many great scenic lines, some containing engineering works of world renown, but most of them represent secondary or branch lines, like the West Highland, and the Callander and Oban Railways in Scotland; but two of the most important trunk routes in Switzerland carrying an ever-increasing volume of international passenger and freight traffic pass through such stupendous mountain scenery, that it can only be called sublime. These two routes, the Gotthard and the Lötschberg, have already come prominently into this account of Swiss railway working from the problems in traction that they provide; and now, heading towards Italy the tremendous nature of their engineering and traffic working must be discussed. In singling out the Gotthard and the Lötschberg I am not forgetting the main line of the one-time Jura-Simplon Railway which, coming into Switzerland at Vallorbe and reaching the shores of the Lake Geneva at Lausanne, itself makes a picturesque course up the Rhone valley to Brigue.

I have, indeed, pleasant recollections of this particular line on several long railway journeys in Europe, notably one on the 'Direct-Orient Express' in a through carriage from Calais to Milan. There was a tremendous feeling of adventure upon joining such a train, and even the leisurely perambulation of the Petite Ceinture Line in Paris anticipated the marshalling up of the train to its full compliment, with through carriages to Athens and Istanbul. But it was nearly midnight before departure from the Gare de Lyon, and unless luckily one had slept well, it was a jaded and travel-weary passenger that gazed out of

the sleeper window when the train drew into Lausanne at seven
o'clock next morning. But then again, for how long could anyone
remain listless and feeling jaded on a brilliant morning in late Spring
as the train raced along beside the upper reaches of the Lake of
Geneva, one saw the Castle of Chillon, and the Dents du Midi across
the lake; and although the Rhone valley is broad it runs between
increasingly high mountains and has all the charm, on the first day
out from England, of rural Switzerland. From the railway point of
view, however, both in construction and operation, it is an easy
route, and the fast trains make start-to-stop average speeds of around
100 km./h. between Montreux and Sion; and Sion and Brigue.

Nearing Brigue the Lötschberg line can be seen coming
precipitately down the northern wall of the valley, and the situation

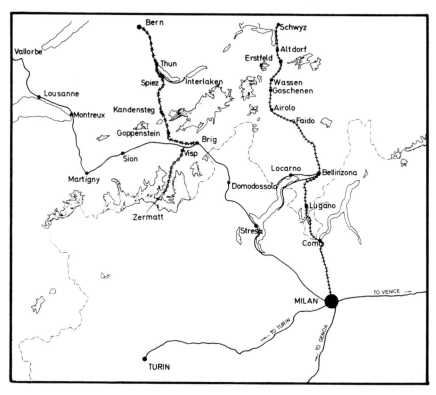

19. The lines through Switzerland to Milan

of the three great routes that all eventually converge upon Milan can be seen from the accompanying sketch map. Only the principal through lines are shown, but the general traffic pattern needs some explanation. The line through Lausanne and up the Rhone valley is the main route from France, while most of the traffic converging at Brigue from the Lötschberg line originates in the Swiss capital city of Berne. The Gotthard line, which has the heaviest traffic of all, is fed from two directions. The main international route from Germany and Eastern France comes south from Basle, through Olten to Lucerne, and joins the second route from Bavaria, through Zürich at Arth-Goldau. Thence it plunges into the mountains. International traffic from the north passing over the Lötschberg line mostly consists of through carriages for Interlaken, which do not run over the really mountainous section of the line. The dates of completion of the great Alpine tunnels were Gotthard 1882, Simplon 1906, and Lötschberg 1913. Until the opening of the Simplon Tunnel traffic from France to Northern Italy had to move via Basle and the Gotthard line, or avoid Switzerland altogether by going through the Mont Cenis Tunnel direct into Italy, and arriving in Turin, instead of Milan.

Although I have now travelled over many of the great scenic routes of the world, the Lötschberg and the Gotthard still remain among my greatest favourites of railway rides, especially when one has the privilege of a place in the driver's cab; and one can hardly imagine a more delightful starting point than beside the Lake of Thun, with its distant glimpses of that mighty trio of the Bernese Oberland, the Eiger, the Mönch, and the Jungfrau. The mountain section of the railway from Spiez to Brigue is only 74 kilometres long, but from whatever way one looks at it — of railway engineering, stupendous mountain scenery, or efficient traffic working — I always find it second to none. It is just as well to dispense with the statistics first; then the ride itself can be enjoyed to the utmost. In profile the line is just one huge gable, as shown in the accompanying diagram. The gradients have a maximum inclination of 1 in 67 as far as Frutigen, after which the rise is at 1 in 37 continuously for 18 kilometres to Kandersteg, at the northern end of the great tunnel, in which the gradients are no more than slight. At mid-tunnel the summit level is reached, 1239.7 metres above sea level. Then from Goppenstein the descent to Brigue is continuous and severe, averaging 1 in $41\frac{1}{2}$ for the entire 25.7 kilometres. The line is double tracked through the main tunnel, but the two approach ramps are single-tracked. As will be seen from the diagram there is a large number of shorter tunnels.

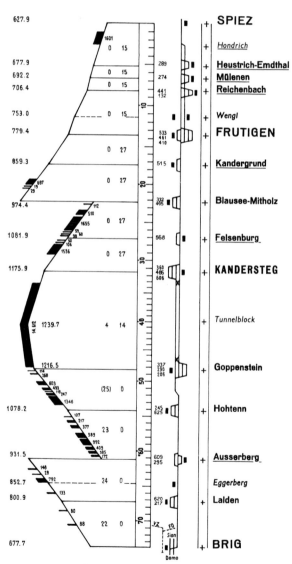

20. Profile of the Lötschberg line

The traffic pattern is based on the ability of all trains, passenger and goods alike, to run at the maximum line speed of 75 km./h. uphill and downhill alike. There is no concession to such tremendous inclines as that between Frutigen and Kandersteg; everything has to climb it at 75 km./h. The Lötschberg has never been anything but an all-electric line, and its gleaming red-brown locomotives, with their aluminium painted roofs, are a decoration in this majestic countryside as well as having tractive power enough to be master of the most severe haulage demands. The latest type, on two four-wheel bogies, and weighing no more than 80 tonnes have a rate of no less than 4655 kilowatts, which is enough to haul 600 tonne trains up the northern 1 in 37 ramp at 75 km./h. A southbound express train makes light work of the opening section from Spiez to Frutigen, on such 'easy' gradients — for the Lötschberg! — of 1 in 67. It is a glorious Alpine countryside of immaculate villages and green tree-clad slopes; but then we come to Frutigen, and statistics tell that it is only 8 kilometres, as the crow flies, to Kandersteg, and that we have to climb 390 metres in that short distance to reach the northern entrance to the great tunnel — an average rise of 1 in 20$\frac{1}{2}$. Such a gradient would, of course, have been completely impracticable on a heavily used main line requiring a basic speed of 75 km./h. by all trains.

The great principle of the spiral tunnel had already been exploited to great effect on the Gotthard line, and more recently in the Kicking Horse Pass on the Canadian Pacific Railway; but I do not think it has ever been used more spectacularly than on the Lötschberg in the neighbourhood of Blausee-Mitholz and Felsenburg. To stand almost spellbound one really has to walk the road along the floor of the valley, rather than ride the trains. On the line it all seems too easy, as that mighty pocket-pistol of a locomotive goes purring up the gradient. But stand below and watch. At one place, just to the north of the picturesque village of Felsenberg three levels of the railway can be seen on the mountainside to the east. Such is the difference in altitude that one might think they were three entirely separate railways; but wait, a train is coming out of the tunnel at the lowest level. It crosses the valley and disappears, but then, from another tunnel beneath the ruin of Felsenberg Castle it emerges higher up the hillside, and coming towards us. It crosses a lofty stone viaduct and disappears again into the trees. Then a few minutes later there it is again, at the highest level, and going the opposite way. Between the second and third levels it has negotiated a long spiral tunnel in the mountainside, all the time ascending on a gradient of 1 in 37, at the basic Lötschberg speed of 75 km./h. This is no toy train; no light railcar, but a heavy international express, weighing between 400 and 500 tonnes, with the sunshine flashing on the silvery roof of the smart red-brown locomotive.

Meanwhile from the cab the sight ahead is almost overpowering in the massed grandeur of the heights of the Bernese Oberland. From the topmost level above Felsenburg the last kilometres up to Kandersteg are quickly mounted, and from this gigantic arena there is indeed no way ahead, but to tunnel; and the Lötschberg line tunnels in no half-hearted style. The railway itself is now nearly 1200 metres above sea level, but the mountain into which it plunges, the Balmhorn, towers another 2200 metres above the railway. These are impressive statistics, but I have in front of me a typical Swiss Alpine photograph showing the twin snow-clad peaks of the Balmhorn and Altels rising in all their awe-inspiring majesty, and at the very bottom left hand corner of the picture is a tiny black speck — the entrance to the Lötschberg tunnel! Against such a manifestation of nature the results of railway engineering effort could well tend to sink into insignificance — were it not for the vivid stories of human endeavour that went to the making of that tunnel.

My own memories are of modern operation. With commendable foresight the tunnel was made large enough to carry a double track line. The distance between the stations of Kandersteg and Goppenstein at the south end is by far the longest of any between adjacent stations on the line, and had it been single-tracked the tunnel could well have become a bottle neck. On my first trip in the cab I was riding one of the older 1–Co + Co–1 type locomotives and in mid-tunnel we met a northbound train. In the approach to this passage the two drivers courteously dipped their headlights. On a second occasion I was travelling north on one of the very powerful 'Ae4/4¹¹' class, and we had made light work of a 400 tonne train up the 'ramp' from Brigue. When we reached Goppenstein we found a brand new locomotive of the same class undergoing its final commissioning trials. They were going to couple on ahead of us for the return run to Berne. The older Lötschberg electric locomotives were limited to a maximum of 100 km./h., but these latest ones are designed for 125 — not that one can run at such speeds on the mountain ramps. On the straight double track through the tunnel however one can 'let rip', and the engineers on the leading loco-motive wanted to make a trial. They asked the driver of the second locomotive to shut off power altogether after the immediate start, so that the leading one would have 400 tonnes of train, and an 80 tonne locomotive. I was invited to go on to the leader, and away we went, on one of the most exciting engine tests I have ever witnessed. From Goppenstein the acceleration was terrific and in the depths of the tunnel, before even we had reached the midway point, we were doing the 125 — $77^1/_2$ m.p.h., with 2200 metres of mountain above us!

The scenery at the two ends of the Lötschberg tunnel is in extraordinary contrast. Kandersteg, for all the immense array of mountains that encircle it is a typically charming Alpine resort of bright chalets, gardens, and lush green meadows at the foot of the crags. Goppenstein on the other hand is set in a grim, desolate gorge, down which the railway begins at once to descend. There are no spiral tunnels here. The line was blasted out of the treeless, rocky hillside, and is protected in many places by avalanche shelters. There are many short tunnels, and then a much longer one. A sightseer should always be sure to obtain a seat on the right hand side of the carriage when going south over the Lötschberg line; but if such is not available a short sojourn in the corridor is a 'must' after Goppenstein, for on coming out of that longer tunnel, about three minutes' run down the Lonza Gorge, there is *the* surprise of the whole trip. Spread out below, many hundreds of metres down, is the smiling expanse of the Rhone valley — a sight as beautiful as it is well-nigh breathtaking in the change from the forbidding and desolate Lonza Gorge. Far below can be seen the straight track of the Jura-Simplon line of the Swiss Federal Railways, along which express trains run at 130 km./h., while we are winding our way down the hillside at the statutory 75 km./h. From Hohtenn, where we came out of that long tunnel and saw the great view, it usually takes about 18 minutes to negotiate the last $19^1/_2$ kilometres down into Brigue. But what a ride!

* * * * * * * * *

If one should arrive in the gracious city of Lucerne by any form of transport other than the railway, and then walk down to the lake front, a large and handsome building adjacent to the steamer piers will immediately catch the eye. It is in the most elegant style of the nineteenth century; impressive without being ostentatious, and to those who perhaps are not so minded it might come as a surprise to learn it is the main railway station. Swiss stations generally are notable for their pleasing architectural styles but at Lucerne, with more functional and less sympathetic treatment, a great station in such a location could so easily have been an eyesore. In fact, one could hardly wish for a finer gateway to what I would place as the most scenic railway in the world. The delights of the Lötschberg are mostly confined to the sections between Thun and Kandersteg, and the final pitch from Hohtenn to Brigue, whereas those of the Gotthardbahn are sustained not only from Lucerne for practically the whole way to the Italian frontier at Chiasso, 140 kilometres, but onwards through Como. And there is no one ideal place for a sightseer in a Gotthard train. The enthusiast, whether of railways or mountain scenery must be prepared to switch from one side of the carriage to the other at short notice, and this will not always be easy. The trains are no leisurely locals, but TEE 'flyers' and great international express trains travelling the length of Europe, with through carriages from Calais, Ostend, the Hook of Holland, and the big West German cities to Milan, Venice and Rome.

The scenery is entrancing from the very start, after the train has left its terminus by the lakeside and made a circuit of the back areas of the city to approach the northern shores of the lake. Before finally leaving Lucerne however I would counsel any enthusiast, railway or otherwise, to visit the brilliantly contrived transport museum by the lakeside. Both in situation and in the display of the exhibits it is a joy. It is as well to go to the museum first, before starting on a journey by the Gotthardbahn, because there can be seen the very beginnings of Swiss mountain railway engineering. The story of the rack railways, their vicissitudes and the development of their motive power, would fill a book of their own, and I can only commend to the connoisseur of steam traction the curious little machines that clawed their pioneer ways up shapely Pilatus, seen so finely across the Lake of Lucerne, and up the Rigi the base of which the Gotthard train will soon be skirting. For some years now both these mountain rack railways have been electrically worked. At Arth-Goldau, base station for the Arth-Rigi rack railway the main line from Lucerne is joined by that from Zürich, and the occupation of the line thence forward becomes intense. It is double tracked throughout, and equipped with colour light signalling. This railway is not everywhere subject to the speed limit applying to the Lötschberg, and until the northern ramp to the Gotthard Tunnel is reached, at Erstfeld, the express trains can make some fast running. I have noted speeds up to 118 km./h., with the big 'Ae6/6' electric locomotives hauling trains of nearly 600 tonnes.

I rode south over this lovely railway in the cab of one of these great locomotives, accompanied by the section-chief from Erstfeld. This little town of some 4500 people set deep in the mountain is an out-and-out railway colony. There was a village farming community there before the construction of the Gotthardbahn, but what made the Erstfeld of today was the northern ramp. It is at this point that the profile of the railway changes from one of gentle ascent to real mountaineering on a 1 in 37 gradient, and in steam days heavy trains stopped to attach a second engine, or perhaps a third pushing in rear. Such conditions prevailed for the first forty years of the life of the Gotthardbahn, and at Erstfeld were stationed many locomotives whose only work was assisting on the 'ramp'. Now of course no such assistance is needed with the passenger trains, and few of them even stop. But it is a different matter with the freights and the railway community there is still strong with about 400 men in regular employment on the line.

The northern ramp is a fascinating piece of railway particularly where it comes to the double spirals of Wassen, and one passes that picturesque landmark — the village church, three times viewing it from below, then level, and finally from above on the way up. The crest of the great incline is reached at Göschenen which has lately become a traffic centre of greatly enhanced importance. One of its most vital activities is unseen and probably quite unknown to the vast majority of travellers by train, for about two-thirds of a kilometre from the station at the further end of the village is a great underground power station, using hydro-electric energy to furnish

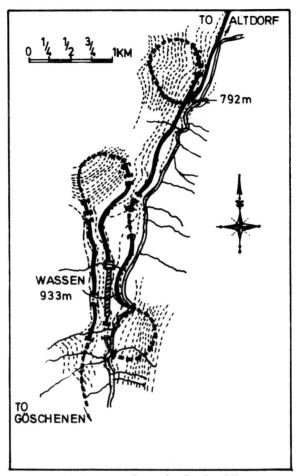

21. Spiral tunnels on the Gotthard line

power for a large section of the Swiss Federal Railways. In a vast hall, like some subterranean cathedral the great turbines whirr constantly. Like the majority of Swiss industrial plants it has been built with every regard to beautiful appearance; and to interested parties it is one of the unexpected showpieces of the neighbourhood. The station is unusually large, with a palatial dining room and other offices, and a visitor standing on the platforms would not be long in appreciating why it has been so developed. It is certainly a junction with a metre gauge link to Andermatt, and the east-west Furka-Oberalp metre

172

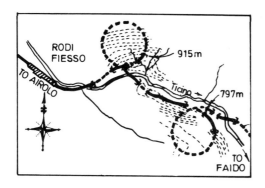

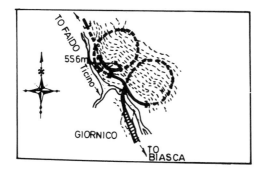

gauge line. This link line can be seen rising steeply to the right of the entrance portals to the Gotthard Tunnel.

The railway through the tunnel has come into prominence recently in another connection. During the winter the highway over the historic St. Gothard pass is blocked with snow, and for the benefit of motorists a car ferry service is operated through the tunnel to Airolo, at the southern portal. With the heavy ordinary passenger and freight traffic on the Gotthard the car ferry trains have to take their turns, and the large station dining rooms, which were built in the days before restaurant cars, often provide welcome fare to those waiting their turn to ride in their cars through the tunnel. In earlier days the refreshment stop at Göschenen was as much an institution on the Gotthard line as it was on the Anglo-Scottish expresses at Preston, or

173

York. The tunnel itself is about 15 kilometres long, and to secure maximum line capacity special signalling arrangements have been installed. The line is double-tracked, and at mid-tunnel there are crossovers and a remote controlled interlocking. Both tracks can be used in either direction, and trains crossed from one to the other, if need be, in mid-tunnel. Maximum speed is limited to 105 km./h., while on the approach ramps the speed is 75 km./h., as on the Lötschberg line.

The descent into the Ticino valley is equally steep and includes two sets of spiral tunnels, and the remarkable location of these is shown on the sketch maps reproduced here. At Giornico in particular the entrance to the upper spiral and the exit from the second are little removed from vertically above each other, yet the difference in altitude is about 100 metres. The Giornico spirals are perhaps the most spectacular for the passenger, because on approaching the upper tunnel both the middle and lowest levels of the line can be seen immediately below; and on the open sections the train is travelling in the same direction on each line, unlike the Lötschberg trains in the celebrated Felsenburg location. In studying the maps one can be fairly consumed with admiration for the skill of the surveys, and the precision of the boring that drove these spiralling tunnels in the solid rock of these rugged mountain-sides. The distance by railway round the various spirals, from Airolo to Biasca, is 46 kilometres though the foot of the southern ramp comes at kilometre post 123, just below Giornico station.

Riding in the locomotive cab one sees occasionally that touch of precision in operating that characterises the Swiss railways. On the first day I went through the Gotthard there was an advance section of the train running and at Faido, a station midway between the two sets of spiral tunnels, we had been stopped having closed in upon the first part. At intermediate stations the stationmaster is always on the platform to watch a non-stopping train pass through, and at Giornico despite the stop at Faido we were a minute early. Although signals were clear the stationmaster gave us a hand signal to slow down a little, as the preceding train was not far ahead. I have seen the same done on the Lötschberg line, just because a train was running slightly ahead of time. Between Biasca and Bellinzona the line is relatively straight and level, and one can usually note some fast running up to about 110 km./h., still in a deep and picturesque mountain valley.

Bellinzona is an important divisional point. On through express and freight trains drivers are changed, and the new man is usually Italian speaking. It is a major junction, serving routes that run westwards to both sides of Lake Maggiore. The northernmost of these lines passes through Locarno. The frontier between Switzerland and Italy is extremely meandering in this tumbled mountain country, following in most places the crests of the ranges; but the Gotthard line stays in Swiss territory for a further considerable distance. There is some hard climbing once again, at 1 in 39 up to the Monte Ceneri tunnel to clear the ridge that separates the lakes of Maggiore and Lugano, and so, after a precipitous descent the train comes into one of the most popular resorts south of the Alps. The TEE 'Gottardo', by which I travelled on another occasion runs non-stop between Zürich and Lugano, covering the 218 kilometres in 168 minutes, an average of 77.5 km./h. Although running up to 120 km./h., on suitable stretches of line, this lightweight streamlined train is also subject to the 75 km./h., limit on the mountain ramps.

On leaving Lugano for the south the railway traverses a particularly beautiful stretch of country, taking first a winding course past Paradiso station that gives superb views up the Lake of Lugano, and then comes to Melide. Nature did not give much help to the engineers who built the Gotthard railway, but here they had a stroke of luck; they discovered the remains of a glacial morain extending right across this otherwise very deep lake. Moreover the ridge was very little below water level, and it was an easy matter to dump the necessary filling to make an excellent causeway across to the eastern shore, which they needed to attain in order to continue the line towards Como. Near Melide itself there is a bridge to permit of navigation between the upper and lower parts of the lake, much frequented by pleasure steamers in the tourist season. Railway enthusiasts with a taste for modelling ought certainly to break their journey at Lugano if for no other reason than to visit 'Swiss Miniature' at Melide, where there is a very extensive and superbly equipped outdoor model railway, fully operational, and including all the present day forms of motive power on the Swiss Federal Railways.

Capulago — the head of the lake — is another intermediate station where one might pause, for this is the base station of another mountain rack railway, up Monte Generoso. Until quite recently it was steam worked; but now that it has been 'modernised' one of the steam locomotives has been preserved and stands, beautifully restored, on a pedestal by the lakeside. So eventually we come to Chiasso, the frontier station and the end of the Gotthard line. It is a frontier point in every way between the Swiss and Italian railways, between two different systems of electric traction, and all the problems of freight exchange, customs examination, and all other problems at such a post. Except for the TEE trains which are equipped for working on any of the European traction systems all trains have to change locomotives from the dark myrtle green Swiss to the mustard coloured Italians. Recently too, an extensive new marshalling yard, for storage of freight wagons prior to customs formalities and interchange between the two national systems, has been brought into operation.

Chiasso, only 5 kilometres short of Como, and with Milan another 50 kilometres ahead is a good place to take leave of the Swiss railways, at the southern end of its most remarkable line. And I can well end, as I began, with one arresting item of statistics. The Gotthard line represents only 13.8 per cent. of the total route mileage of the Swiss Federal Railway system, but it now carries more than 40 per cent. — *forty per cent!* — of the total freight traffic — an astonishing record for what can equally be regarded as a scenic railway.

CHAPTER FIFTEEN

Italy — convergence on Milan

It is obviously axiomatic that one's attitude to any activity should depend upon the way it is used. Families or friends visiting the theatre in gala mood would regard a play or opera in a very different light from that of a hardened critic who had to dash off a report in time to appear in the next morning's newspaper. So it is with a railway system. A meandering outdated narrow gauge steam line may be fascinating to the seeker after railway lore, but sheer purgatory to anyone who has to use it in the absence of any other form of transport. It has so happened that nearly all my railway journeys in Italy have been made with the simple object of getting to the other end, for holiday or business convention purposes. Italy is the one country within the area covered by this book where I have not just 'gone for the ride'. Of course anyone as interested in Railways as I have been all my life could not fail to take note of much that can be seen from the carriage window; but that interest has been detached, rather than professional in most cases. Nevertheless 'who runs may read', and after early experiences I did read up all the old articles in the *Locomotive Magazine*, in the *Railway Magazine*, and in nineteenth century engineering literature so that by the time I made my third visit I had some solid background on which to make a more critical appraisal of what I saw and experienced.

The two journeys into Italy that prompted the slightly cynical opening to this Chapter were perhaps rather unfortunate, and I hope exceptional. My very first introduction to the Italian State Railways came at the end of a long overnight journey by sleeper from Calais. On a morning of beautiful sunshine the run through the Valais had revived my flagging energies somewhat, and emergence from the

Simplon Tunnel into Italy brought all the natural eagerness to see a new country. Our train was still in the efficient hands of the Swiss Federal Railways and then, roughly 40 kilometres from Brigue, we came to what John Russell has called 'the filthy hump of Domodossala'. This is the exchange point on the Simplon route between the Swiss and Italian railways, with customs examinations, and so on. It is not an attractive place, but there was the consolation that Milan and the long journey's end was then only 125 kilometres ahead, with the prospect of some pleasant scenery where the line skirts the shores of Lake Maggiore. By the time we did eventually get away from Domodossala however, the fair weather was vanishing. There were numerous delays on the run, and although the Swiss had handed over the train punctually, the Italians contrived to be forty minutes late on arrival in Milan — not a good introduction!

On our second venture into Italy we came along the Cote d'Azur. To avoid prolonging the journey from Paris to the point of exhaustion, we stayed overnight in Nice, and caught the express from Hendaye and Cerbère, which goes through to Rome, next morning. Again there was that eagerness upon entering Italy, sampling the gastronomical delights of an Italian dining car, and the anticipation of a run beside the Mediterranean coast as far as Genoa. But, oh, the tedium of that journey! The run of 152 kilometres from Ventimiglia to Genoa by this important international express was scheduled to take just three hours — not exactly a heroic average of 50 km./h. — but actually it took much longer. There were lengthy stops, intermediate checks, and when we did eventually arrive in Genoa it was to sit far longer than our scheduled half hour, in the sweltering heat of a crowded train, before all was ready for us to move off along the continuation of the coastal route to Rapallo, Yes, indeed: there was only one object in this journey — to get to the other end! An old joke about travel in Italy could well have applied to this train. One could alight at the first suburban station of Sampierdarena, make a quick sightseeing tour of Genoa, and rejoin the train at Nervi an hour later. The distance between the two stations is only ten kilometres. Another early experience came one day when we were travelling to Milan from the south. After many checks on the approach lines the train drew up outside the station, amid passengers from several other trains, who were humping their luggage along the tracks. The station itself was in a state of wild confusion — what about I never discovered — but never have we been more relieved to see the name COOKS on the cap of the friendly courier who was meeting us, and who escorted us through the milling throng to a hired car.

All this is perhaps a rather unkind introduction to a railway system I have since learned to appreciate. Once arrived in Milan however, whether in the thunderstorm that greeted us from Domodossala, or in the melée of our later arrival from Genoa, our only thoughts were to get away from railways, and everything to do with them as quickly as possible. As we drove away neither of us thought to give a backward glance towards what Jasper More in *The Land of Italy* has described, with tongue in cheek I fear as:

... the greatest masterpiece of the early Fascist style. Built in ferro-concrete with a great façade towering above the station square, this station seems to have been designed to impress the traveller rather than to facilitate his journeys. The resources of modern sculpture have been freely drawn on to adorn the exterior; angry ferro-concrete beasts glare at the passing trams, and two considerable cart-horses are only restrained by their muscular attendants from plunging from the roof on to the heads of the crowds below.

But away from the immediate frustrations of travel, which can be experienced even on the best and most efficiently run of railways, the Italian system can be seen in its broader perspective — very interesting historically, significant in its technical developments, and as a carrier by which we have journeyed to some delightful holidays in the sunshine.

Looking back into history, at the beginnings of the railway age, the Italy that we know today just did not exist. What is now the industrial north formed part of the Kingdom of Sardinia; Venice and Lombardy were under Austrian rule; Naples and the south was a kingdom of its own, while between north and south the Papal States formed an uneasy buffer. The Risorgimento movement, which inspired the unification of Italy did not achieve its major objective of the nineteenth century until 1870, when the exertions of Garibaldi led to the occupation of Rome. The British railway world became briefly aware of the earlier steps towards railway construction in Italy at the time of the Royal Commission on Gauges in 1845. The great Isambard Kingdom Brunel came under heavy cross-examination by the Commissioners over his choice of the 2130 mm. gauge for the Great Western Railway, the choice that had led to the entire controversy. The Commissioners felt that his case for the broad gauge was much weakened by his having recommended use of the standard 1435 mm. gauge for other railways he was building, and one of these was the line from Genoa to Turin, under the Sardinian Government. In reply to much questioning Brunel said:

'The reason which led me to adopt it was this, that I did not think that either the quantities or speeds likely to be demanded for many years to come, in that country, required the same principle to be carried out that I thought was required here: and I thought it very important that they should secure the goodwill of certain other interests which would lead into and out of this railway; and, as a question of policy as much as of engineering, I advised them to adopt that gauge. I thought it was wise to conciliate the interest of the Milan and Venice Railway and others which are likely to be connected with us.'

'But', the Commissioners queried, 'they are not yet in operation, are they?'

Brunel replied: 'Yes, the Milan and Venice is being constructed; and the part between Padua and Venice is open'.

Asked if he was likely to come into connexion with that line, Brunel said:

'To join at Milan I hope; but there is a short space of Austrian territory between Milan and the Sardinian frontier, and I thought it likely that the connexion between the two railways would be facilitated by our offering to adopt the same gauge'.

Brunel was examined in October 1845, and it would have seemed by then that he had considerably changed his tactics since he had set the Great Western at defiance against all established railways in England, when it was quite clear that connexion with them would very soon occur at many places. But Brunel's work on the Genoa-

180

Turin line is most interesting, because physically it includes one of the most difficult pieces of railway in the whole of Italy, the Giovi Incline. Referring to the railway in the reverse order to that in which it was built, the gradients from Turin are easy until coming to the range of the Ligurian Alps, that form a continuous barrier only a short distance inland from the Mediterranean coast. Up this mountain range from Genoa Brunel took his railway on a gradient of 1 in 27, an inclination that puts his worst banks in South Devon completely in the shade. Whether he hoped to work this part of the line on the Atmospheric principle we do not know; but before the Italian line was finished the Atmospheric had failed disastrously in South Devon, and the north of Italy had been convulsed by an abortive revolution. It was not until 1855 that the line up the Giovi Incline was opened with some curious little 0–4–0 saddle tank engines built in England by Robert Stephenson & Co., and used in pairs, back to back, with two drivers and one fireman to stoke both engines.

It is a very difficult location, and short of making a very long zig-zagging detour a heavy gradient could hardly be avoided. About the turn of the century a second and easier line was constructed, getting a better gradient of 1 in 60 by going underground some distance short of the old summit, and having a bore seven kilometres long in the Ronco Tunnel. Progressively larger steam locomotives were designed for working heavy trains up these inclines, culminating in a class of huge 2-cylinder compound 4-8-0s put into service in 1903. But the only really satisfactory answer was electrification, and this came in 1911; though before coming to this stage of Italian railway development some mention is needed of early happenings elsewhere in the country. Seeing that a unified Italy did not exist until 1870, it is not surprising that railway constructional enterprise was at first somewhat haphazard. Brunel evidently looked forward to some co-ordination in the north, and it was really surprising how much was actually achieved considering the disturbed state of the country.

Austria, as Brunel hinted, was a thorn in the side of Italian aspirations, but when the great Piedmontese patriot Count Cavour managed to persuade Napoleon III, Emperor of France to help, a war in 1859 resulted in a defeat of the Austrians, and the province of Lombardy was annexed to Piedmont. The small Milan and Venice

Railway referred to by Brunel blossomed into the Lombardo-Venezia, and this together with the 'Adriatico' purchased many locomotives from England. The level nature of the country traversed by most of the early Italian railways was in striking contrast to that fearsome incline northwards from Genoa, and the locomotives imported, variously from Sharp, Stewart & Co., Robert Stephenson & Co., and Beyer, Peacock were all of the 2–2–2 type, of the design once christened by Hamilton Ellis as 'Old English', having outside frames to all the wheels, including those of the tenders. These pretty little single-wheelers were ideal for the light work and moderate speeds of the early Italian railways, on which, one must add, punctuality was non-existent. Neither did matters improve much with the introduction of larger locomotives and more commodious carriages, and among ordinary travellers as distinct from those who did much railway note-taking, the late running of Italian trains was proverbial.

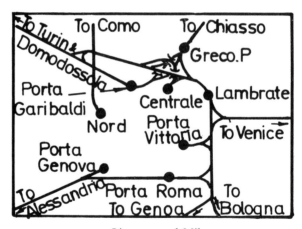

22. Lines around Milan

The complications around Milan have always been such as to breed unpunctuality. No fewer than six major routes converge upon the city — moving round the centre clockwise, from Genoa, Turin, the Simplon Route, Como and the Gotthard Route, Venice and Trieste, and finally the main south line to Bologna, Florence, Rome and Naples. The large Central station, with the rather overwhelming façade, is a terminus, and the important international express trains like the 'Direct Orient', the 'Riviera Express', and the 'Italia Express' spend anything up to a full hour within its precincts, while direction of travel is being reversed. Only the 'Simplon Express' (Paris to Belgrade) takes the avoiding line, and makes its Milan call at the Lambrate station. This is a similar instance to that of certain expresses calling only at the Enge station in Zürich, or at Antwerp East, to avoid going into the central terminal and having to reverse direction. The accompanying sketch map shows how the connections are arranged at Milan from the various lines of approach. During the Fascist regime what amounted to a decree was issued by Mussolini's government that trains would run on time. It sounded as simple as that, and there certainly was a great improvement. But then mark what Jasper More wrote, in 1949:

The traditional trains of Italy — the wooden thirds, the grey-rep seconds and the red plush firsts decorated by reproductions of old masters chosen strictly according to the standards of Vasari — were already yielding, even before their general destruction in the recent war, to new species of steel torpedoes in silver and blue; and though for the trains of non-Fascist Italy it will doubtless be a point of honour to be unpunctual, there is no reason why the expresses should not continue both comfortable and swift.

This form of travel, which necessarily limits tours to the most important centres, is unquestionably convenient for non-Italian speakers. A knowledge of the language is not necessarily an advantage, for in this country nothing succeeds like stupidity; the waves of Latin eloquence beat helplessly upon the rocks of Anglo-Saxon incomprehension. A little knowledge of Italian can be a dangerous thing, and budding linguists may be warned in particular not to seek practice in arguments with the Venetian gondoliers ......

I once saw this myself in a different, but very amusing way. We were travelling eastwards along the Cote d'Azur, and had in the carriage an American entering Italy for the first time. He confided to us that he had been studying Italian, and had some questions to ask when we reached Ventimiglia. He was rehearsing his little speech most assiduously during the last few kilometres, and when the train stopped, out on the platform he stepped where he delivered it faultlessly. A typically Latin railway official answered him in a positive deluge of words, at great length, with innumerable gesticulations, leaving poor Uncle Sam bewildered almost to the point of collapse. For my own part, when the game of stupidity has been played from the opposite side, towards the English language, I have always found that a little schoolboy French works wonders!

It is, I suppose, symptomatic of the impressions given by the Italian railways that one should fall to gossiping about the incidentals of travel rather than of technicalities, and one last memory must be injected before I get on to the sterner business of steam and electric locomotive engineering. Earlier in this Chapter I rather summarily brushed aside the Italian end of the Simplon route, which I saw in gathering mist and rain. Some years later my wife and I were travelling on the morning express from Milan to Paris, and looked forward to seeing it in pleasanter conditions. The weather was certainly beautiful, and from Arona Lake Maggiore was seen in all its glory with every detail of the fascinating Borromean Islands standing out clearly. But we had as travelling companions three Italian ladies, unknown to us, and unknown to each other before the start of the journey. English people are regarded as reticent, even unsociable travellers, but not so the Latin race! Before we had even reached Arona the three ladies were in animated conversation, and so it continued in a positive torrent for the whole journey. We thanked the powers that be that it was not a TEE with meals served at one's seat, and we eagerly sought escape to lunch in a distant restaurant car. When we returned they had fallen asleep, out of sheer exhaustion we suspected. But the sight of the Lake of Geneva revived them, and the cataract was resumed, and continued without another pause to the very outskirts of Paris. Our blinding headaches were not improved by the brinkmanship of the Parisian taxi driver!

Turning now to engineering matters, one of the most distinctive of all Italian steam locomotive designs was Signor Plancher's cab-in-front 4-cylinder compound 4–6–0 of 1900. It was a time when the size of locomotives was increasing to such an extent that in single-tracked tunnels, of which there were plenty in Italy, the bore was filled to such an extent that exhaust steam and smoke made things uncomfortable to the point of near-asphyxiation for those on

23. Plancher's cab-in-front locomotive

the footplate, while in open country when steaming lightly the exhaust from the chimney would beat down and obscure the lookout ahead. In the U.S.A. the quaint-looking 'Mother Hubbard' type of locomotive, with the driver in a separate cab perched astride the middle of the boiler, had a spell of popularity, until boilers got so large that a cab amidships would have fouled the loading gauge. Plancher turned the locomotive back to front, keeping the driver and fireman together, and having a trailer tender carrying only the water supply. An inconvenient feature of these ugly locomotives was the provision of coal bunkers on either side of the firebox, from which it must have been damnably awkward to extract the coal, when the supply nearest to the shovelling plate had been used up. These engines achieved a measure of success, and the initial batch was followed by several more. It must however be borne in mind that the demands then made on Italian passenger locomotives were light compared to those of France and Great Britain in the early years of the twentieth century. The sustained speeds on level track were around 90 km./h. with trains that were not often very heavy. The firing rate on Plancher's 4-cylinder compounds would not be very high and firemen would have time to go digging into those narrow side bunkers.

185

It was another matter on the Giovi incline, and to a lesser extent on the original main line to the south, before the construction of the long Apennine Tunnel, part of the Bologna–Florence direct line; and Italy was early in the field with railway electrification. The firm of Ganz in Budapest was one of the strongest protagonists of the three-phase alternating current system of traction. It was in fact a strong competitor for the job of electrifying the Inner Circle railway in London. The case argued in favour of three-phase alternating current was a more economical method of power transmission, though it had certain features that could in particular conditions prove inconvenient in railway traction. It needed two overhead wires, while the traction motors ran at a constant speed. The last mentioned feature was in some ways an advantage in a locality like the Giovi incline. The electric locomotives introduced in 1911 could be run at two speeds 50 and 25 km./h. The former was used for passenger trains ascending the Ronco line, on 1 in 60, and for all trains descending, while 25 km./h. was the speed for ascending freight trains, or for passenger trains taking the original line.

In due course the three-phase alternating current system, at 3000 volts, was later installed on the line along the Mediterranean coast from Genoa to the exchange station with the French railways at Ventimiglia, and on this the locomotives were geared to run at a maximum speed of 100 km./h. With numerous stops, and no higher speed than this intermediately the overall progress was not very rapid. In 1925 however experiments began with the use of 3000 volts direct current; these were not concluded until 1934, but then it was decided to standardise on direct current for all future work. The coastal route from Ventimiglia, and the Ronco and Giovi inclines were still being worked three-phase alternating current into the early 1960s. Until quite recently Italian electric locomotives, whether a.c. or d.c., were purely functional in appearance, and painted a mustard yellow colour. In standardising on 3000 volts d.c. the new electric locomotive designs envisaged much faster running than anything previously attempted in Italy. The first, introduced in 1927, had a rated maximum speed of 110 km./h., while later designs provided for 140 km./h. As will be discussed in the next Chapter however the fastest services operated since the Second World War have been provided by railcar-unit types of trains rather than with heavy rakes hauled by electric locomotives.

Concurrently with these developments in electric traction came some interesting work in steam locomotive practice that had influences far outside Italy. Engineers, anxious to secure higher thermal efficiencies, have always felt hamstrung to a degree by the inter-related valve events of conventional valve gears such as the Stephenson link motion and the Walschaerts radial gear; but the use of poppet instead of piston valves, actuated by rotating cams after the fashion of an automobile engine, enabled independent timings to be given to inlet and exhaust valves, and a degree of weight reduction made possible in the gear operating the valves. The Italian engineer Arturo Caprotti spent all his earlier years in the motor industry, and it was not until 1915 when he was 34 years of age that he designed a locomotive valve gear. The Caprotti valve gear was widely adopted by the Italian State Railways and gave very good service. It created a good enough impression to be adopted on a limited scale on British railways, notably the London Midland and Scottish, though British experience was that although providing a very free running locomotive, the thermal efficiency was not superior to that obtained with a well-designed layout of the conventional Walschaerts radial valve gear.

Apart from the use of poppet valves Italian steam locomotives during the Fascist era, and after, were mostly of conventional types, except in the case of a class of 2–6–0s which had inside cylinders but outside valve motion. A development as unconventional as that of Plancher's cab-in-front compound 4–6–0 had its origin in 1937 with the construction of an experimental articulated locomotive. During the war the interesting form of boiler fitted to this machine was developed for application to ordinary fixed frame locomotives by Dott. Ing. Piero Crosti, and in due course the Crosti boiler was applied to many Italian locomotives and also to a batch of the British Standard 2–10–0s of Class '9F'. The peculiar feature of the Italian engines so equipped is that they had no conventional chimney. This was quite incidental but it gave them a most curious appearance. The principle of the Crosti boiler was that the hot gases of combustion after passing through the flue tubes of the main boiler to the front end were drawn backwards through the tubes of the preheater in which the feed water was heated before it was introduced to the main boiler. Because the hot gases arrived at the rear-end, after having passed through the tubes of the preheater, the chimney was placed on the side of the boiler towards the rear and in the Italian examples, of which there were many, there was no ordinary chimney on the smokebox. The sight of one of these engines, which were to be seen working around Venice, always reminded me of the ghost who carried his head under his arm. The British 2–10–0s so equipped had a chimney on the smokebox but it was used only for lighting up. Many Italian engines of the 2–6–2 and 2–8–0 type were so fitted, and they were reported to show considerable savings in fuel over the conventional boilered locomotives of the same type. By the time the British 2–10–0s were built the steam locomotive was already on its way out in Great Britain, and the time these locomotives were in service was really insufficient for any definite conclusions to be drawn as to the effectiveness of the Crosti boiler.

My only personal experiences of steam hauled trains in Italy were between Milan and Turin, hauled by the inside-cylinder 2–6–0s with outside valve gear. With light trains they ran swiftly and very quietly though, as was so frequently the case, there were numerous checks from adverse signals and any appraisal of the sustained performance capacity of those interesting engines could not be made. The route is very easily graded throughout. On local freight and shunting work many steam locomotives were to be seen at Venice in the early 1960s, while on the branches extending from the Milan-Venice main line most of the local passenger trains were still steam hauled at the same time. Today, a fine collection of preserved steam locomotives is to be seen at the Leonardo da Vinci Museum of Science and Technology in Milan, and in addition to examples of the locomotive designs mentioned in this Chapter, there is one of the big 4-cylinder simple 'Pacifics' of 1914 vintage, and a 4-cylinder compound 2–8–2 of 1922. The Plancher cab-in-front type is represented not by one of his 4–6–0 express locomotives but by an 0–10–0 freighter designed for heavy grade working. Although, in general, Italian steam locomotive practice did not 'hit the headlines' to the same extent as that of France and Austria, in the long history of railway traction the names of Plancher, Caprotti and Crosti will always retain honoured places.

CHAPTER SIXTEEN

Milan to the south

It would not, I suppose, be far off the mark to suggest that Rome is the greatest tourist attraction in the whole world. And one can get there so easily today by air from all parts, that there is a strong temptation to skip all the intermediate stages. By rail Rome is almost the same distance from Milan as Edinburgh is from London, and this inevitably invites comparisons in speed and conditions of service. I must say at the very beginning of this Chapter that when the opportunity came to travel to Rome, and farther south, the traffic operation that I criticised in the preceding Chapter had vastly improved. By the year 1965 punctuality was once again the order of the day. Even by train one could be tempted to skip all the lines between, using such luxury trains as the 'Super-rapido', the 'Freccia del Vesuvio', or above all the 'Settebello'. These trains however are all first class, involving prior reservation of seats, with of course the disadvantage to the railway sightseer of being confined to one seat, mealtimes included. In the course of our own travels our journeys were broken at Bologna, Florence and at Rome, and the intervening stages were made in different kinds of trains. It was only on one of our return journeys that we travelled in the same carriage through from Naples to Milan.

The first stage, from Milan to Bologna, level and largely straight, through uninteresting country is one of the fastest stretches in Italy. Even quite ordinary trains cover its 220 kilometres in less than two hours, and the real flyers, like the 'Freccia del Vesuvio' and the 'Settebello' take no more than 100 and 108 minutes — the former a breathless average of 132 km./h. The locomotives used on the ordinary express trains are the 'E 646' class, with the Bo-Bo-Bo wheel arrangement, and having a one-hour rating of 4197 kilowatts.

The Italian State Railways have remained quite distinct in their preference for the use of three four-wheeled bogies on their express passenger and fast mixed traffic locomotives, instead of the generally favoured Co-Co, with two six-wheeled bogies. Some of the express trains load heavily, to more than 500 tonnes, but even with this the 'E 646' class have such a capacity for acceleration that I have seen the 220 kilometres from Bologna to Milan covered in 135 minutes in spite of six severe slowings for engineering work. The maximum speed did not exceed 120 km./h.

It is at Bologna that the really interesting part of the journey south begins. Until just over forty years ago travelling between Bologna and Florence used to be something of an adventure. In negotiating the great mountain range of the Apennines a most difficult single-tracked line was used, having steep gradients, incessant curvature, and rising to a summit level 620 metres above sea level. The distance between the two cities by this route is 132 kilometres, and the non-stop trains took about 2$^1/_2$ hours — only 53 km./h. As long ago as 1902 the need was felt for something better, but it was not until 1913 that a start was made on a new direct line. Then war intervened, and it was not until the Fascist regime was established that work was rapidly pushed forward. It was a tremendous task that was then resumed, none other than the driving of a well-nigh straight line clean through the mountain range. The principal tunnel is no less than 18.55 kilometres long, only one kilometre short of the Simplon, the longest main line railway tunnel in the world. In the 81 kilometres of the new line, between Bologna and Prato, where the old line is rejoined, there are in all 30 tunnels, and in addition to the Great Apennine there is another 7.2 kilometres long under Monte Adone.

Even the ordinary passenger could not fail to be aware of a rugged mountainous country, as the train dashes into and out of tunnels, sweeps across lofty viaducts; but no less than 58 kilometres of the line are dead straight, and even with the ordinary express trains speeds are often around 120 km./h., with the ascending gradients to the great tunnel climbed at a steady 100. The fastest trains cover the 100 kilometres from Bologna to Florence by the new route in 55 minutes. The working through the Apennine Tunnel is similar to that in the Gotthard in that there is a crossing place in the middle; but in the

Apennine the crossing, named Precendenze, was until recently a manned interlocking operated from a cabin in a recess hewn out of the tunnel side. Some years ago I had an opportunity of seeing this most unusual signalbox. I was familiar with many cabins on the London Underground railways, deep below the surface, and many of them seeing no trains all day except on their illuminated diagram; but this one, 9 kilometres from daylight at the Vernio end, and many hundreds of metres below the crest of the mountain range above, was distinctly awesome. In the operation there used to be more to it than just crossing trains from one through line to the other. At Precendenze there are two long refuge sidings on each side of the line, in single line tunnels that each run for a distance of 610 metres. At the time the Apennine Tunnel was built these were intended to provide refuges for slow moving freight trains to enable them to be overtaken by faster traffic. Now however they are seldom used, and in any case the Precendenze interlocking is now controlled by CTC from Bologna.

The main station in Florence is a terminus, named Santa Maria Novella after the great church on the opposite side of the square. Thus, as in so many large centres on the continent of Europe, through trains have to reverse direction. The line to the south is one of the most sinuous in all Italy so much so that the present distance by rail from Florence to Rome is no less than 35 per cent. greater than that of the crow's flight. It was built piecemeal between 1859 and 1875, and because most of the construction was in progress before the unification of Italy the earlier national interests tended to dictate the line to be followed by individual sections, rather than having any regard for the route as a whole. It runs through very hilly country, and in linking up the towns the location of the line was in most cases chosen so as to minimise constructional costs. The distance by rail is 314 kilometres, and today the 'Rapido' trains make the run in three hours, while the ordinary expresses, locomotive hauled, take about $3^{1}/_{4}$ to $3^{1}/_{2}$ hours. This is extraordinarily good going, seeing how many intermediate slowings have to be made for curves. The scenery is very fine, and of great variety, at first winding among some of the highest ranges of the Apennines, and one never ceases to delight in the picturesquely situated hill towns always, seemingly, clustered upon some large eminence. Castiglione is very prettily situated on a knoll overlooking Lake Trasimento. We travelled this way first in a 'Rapido' of the TEE type, but my numerous notes include a reminder that there were some steam locomotives at work at Chiusi.

Although there had been numerous dashes up to 120 or 130 km./h., the curves and slowings over bridge works prevented our making a very high average. We took $64^1/_2$ minutes to cover the first 89 kilometres out of Florence to Arezzo, and Chiusi, 152 kilometres was passed in $94^1/_4$ minutes. The average up to this point was thus 96 km./h. From Orvieto, beneath lofty chalk cliffs that reminded me of the Folkestone Warren, we entered the winding valley of the River Tevere (Tiber), and as if the curves in the line were not enough hindrance, we experienced slowings to dead slow speed, for permanent way work at Attigliano, Orte and near Stimigliano. Between these the speed did not rise much above 100 km./h., though acceleration from each check was certainly very rapid. The train rode comfortably, though there was always the feeling of 'airliner' confinement that I get in rolling stock of this kind. Down the final stretch, fairly straight beside the Via Salaria, we made good speed, running at 110 km./h. for some distance, and then finished with an easterly circuit of the 'Eternal City', to arrive in Rome in the relatively new terminal station, 314 kilometres from Florence in 3 hours $16^1/_4$ minutes — an average of 97 km./h.

Today even the very fastest of the 'Rapidos' do not average more than 105 km./h., and allowing for the six checks we experienced to 10 km./h. or less, our net running average would not have been very much less. But nowadays city to city averages, even of 105 km./h. are just not good enough; the speed has got to be 140 or 150 km./h. *at least*, and to upgrade such a line as that between Florence and Rome to permit of such running would be a colossal task — one moreover that would cause fantastic dislocation of existing traffic while the work was in progress. Even so, when it was finished, would speeds of 140 to 150 km./h. be acceptable in this modern age? In Japan the construction of the Shinkansen network is showing how the travelling public responds to really high speed inter-city train services, and in France and West Germany, after introduction of trains with a maximum running speed of 200 km./h., the conclusion has been reached that entirely new railways should be built to permit of *average* speeds of *two hundred* kilometres per hour. So it is in Italy. As a first and mighty big step towards a super high speed service between Milan and Rome, an entirely new line between Florence and Rome is now in an advanced stage of construction, by which the distance between the two cities will be reduced to 254 kilometres, and the time of the fastest trains to 145 minutes — 175 km./h.

From what I have already written about the nature of the intervening country, it can well be imagined that some tremendous engineering work has been involved. The physical conditions, in relation to those of the old line bear quite a striking resemblance to those of the New Tokaido line in Japan. In this latter case the old line, on the 1067 mm. gauge, was built at minimum cost, and meandered round the coast on its way from Tokyo to the south. The new high speed line was driven level and practically straight regardless of obstacles — over the valleys and through the mountains, as the Florence-Rome 'Direttisima' is being done, in Italy. On this new line there will be no fewer than 525 bridges, or major viaducts; and no less than 74.5 kilometres, or nearly 30 per cent. of the entire route will be in tunnel. An English writer, devoted nostalgically to earlier days on the Italian railways, once said that he found the scenery on the Bologna-Florence 'Direttisima' about as inspiring as that of the Inner Circle, in London. The proportion of tunnel to total distance on the Bologna Line is almost as high as on the new line now under construction — 37 kilometres, out of the total of 130. But I suppose that when one's sole object in travelling is to 'get to the other end', the scenery is of little consideration.

One feels that to those who love railways for their own sake the main interest in the Florence-Rome 'Direttisima' will be in viewing its magnificent civil engineering, from the neighbouring countryside. There will certainly be little opportunity for appreciation at the speeds that are proposed, with an average speed from end to end of 175 km./h. and maximum speeds of 250 km./h. — 155 m.p.h.! One of the most spectacular works on the line is the viaduct over the valley of the river Paglia, to the north of Orvieto, which is 5375 metres long — nearly 4.5 kilometres! The bridge structures generally are functional rather than artistic in appearance, and conform to the uninspired

193

'rectangular block' style, rather than to the exquisite grace in railway bridge construction that so distinguishes the railways of Switzerland. It is only when crossing large rivers, as in the viaduct over the Tiber and at Settebagni, that the piers are rounded, to suit the flow of deep water. One of the longest tunnels, 10,954 metres, is being built to cut across the broad salient to the east that comes just after leaving Florence. This is the Saint Donato, while another lengthy tunnel near the southern end of the line, the Saint Oreste, 5173 metres, passes under Mont Soratte.

It is not only the urge to provide much faster through passenger services that has prompted the construction — at vast expense — of this new line. The existing line is so heavily used by both passenger and freight traffic as to be approaching saturation. It was evident on my own journeys that passenger trains were being run at the maximum practicable speeds, and that no speeding up could be made to provide some relief to line capacity. The 'Direttisima' has been described as a 'quadrupling', and it is certainly intended to continue heavy utilisation of the old line. The 'Direttisima' will be retained for fast through traffic, though connections with the existing line are being laid in at Chiusi, Orvieto, and Orte. These connections are in the 'motorway' style, with separate linking lines, some little distance north and south of the stations on the old line. It will thus be possible to run fast intermediate express trains using the 'Direttisima', and looping off to call at such of the three stations as required.

While the heavy civil engineering work is progressing important developments in locomotive practice show clearly the intentions of the Italian State Railways for traction on the 'Direttisima'. In the 'BB-E444' electric locomotive a departure was made from the three-bogie type, used successfully in the 'BBB-646' series, and thus bringing Italian developments into conformity with those in Germany, Switzerland and France. But more particularly for the 'Direttisima' and for sustained running at 200 km./h. a very powerful new design is in hand, designated 'CC-E666'. As its distinguishing prefix letters indicate, this is carried on two six-wheeled bogies, and will have a one-hour rating of about 6341 kilowatts. This is comparable with the French '6500' class used on the 200 km./h. runs of the South Western Region, to Toulouse and

194

Bordeaux. With the introduction of new types of locomotives, even before these most recent developments, a departure into much gayer colour schemes has been made on the Italian State Railways. From the long standing mustard yellow there was a change to silvery grey and bright green; but the 'BB-E444' series have been finished in the same silvery grey between two broad bands of sky blue, and the new 'CC-666' locomotives will be finished likewise.

Referring to locomotive and train decor, I cannot leave the line from Florence to Rome without further mention of the de-luxe 'Settebello' train — the 'lucky-seven'. No more than 160 passengers are conveyed on this seven-car electric train, but the front and rear coaches are in the way of observation saloons and are not included in the ordinary seating. They have been most ingeniously contrived after the style of the prow of a 'Jumbo Jet' — only the 'Settebello' came first. On the Italian train the driver is accommodated on an upper 'flight deck', and the observation saloon for passengers is carried to the very front, giving an unrivalled view of the line ahead. There is no extra charge for a visit to either the forward or rear observation saloon, and for my own part I should always make for the forward one. From experience of travel in the beaver-tail observation car of the 'Coronation' on the LNER in the years 1937–1939, I think the rear saloon of the 'Settebello', at speeds up to its maximum of 180 km./h. would be rather overpowering, especially on such a curving line as the present one between Florence and Rome. Like the 'Coronation' used to be, the 'Settebello' does most of its running in darkness, leaving Milan at 17.50 and not arriving in Rome until 23.40. The northbound journey is however entirely in daylight, leaving Rome at 10.50, and reaching Milan at 16.36.

Lines from all directions lead into the one terminal station in Rome, just inside the Aurelian Wall of the ancient city. This involves a series of complicated junctions outside, shown on the sketch map on page 196. Until 1927, when the new line to Naples was opened, the line to the south took as meandering and difficult a route as the present one between Florence and Rome. There is not such a great difference in distance to Naples Central, 216.5 against 242 kilometres, but the difference in time is tremendous. Today while the so-called 'Fast' trains by the old route take $4\frac{1}{4}$ to $4\frac{1}{2}$ hours, the 'Rapidos' by

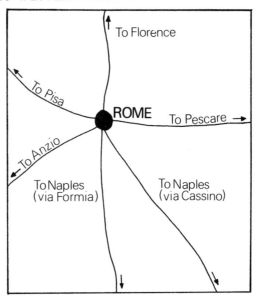

24. Lines around Rome

the new route positively 'eat up' the 210 kilometres to Naples Mergellina in $1^1/_2$ hours — an average of 140 km./h. It goes without saying that the old route is much more picturesque, passing through Frosinone, Capua and Caserta, and at Cassino running beside one of the greatest Italian battlefields of the Second World War. The Abbey of Montecassino, the original home of the Benedictine Order, on its height overlooking both the railway and the Via Casilina, was a natural strongpoint from which to hold up the Allied advance from the beaches of Salerno, and it suffered almost total destruction in consequence. Happily it has now been completely rebuilt. This old route certainly has its points, unless one is in a desperate hurry to 'see Naples' — and perhaps to die! Even the 'Fast' trains stop at the ancient pre-Roman city of Capua, while at Caserta the palace and its vast landscape gardens have been described as one of the greatest architectural achievements of all time. But readers of this book may well be more concerned with the railways themselves rather than the places they serve; so we had better retrace steps to Rome Terminus.

The Rome–Naples 'Direttisima' was one of the national 'prides and joys' in Mussolini's earlier years. Certainly it has now been

196

developed into one of the really fast express routes of continental Europe. In 1965 we travelled by the non-stop morning 'Rapido', which was a six-car electric railcar set, and we ran the 210 kilometres in $115^1/_2$ minutes. The present schedule of this train is 108 minutes. The line at first runs across the Pontine Marshes, never very far from the Appian Way. Several kilometres to the east is the range of the Lepini mountains, behind which the old line makes its sinuous way; on the other side the marshes extend featureless and limitless towards the sea. It is however a grand place for a straight and fast running railway, though because of temporary engineering speed restrictions we did not really get going until we were 50 kilometres out of Rome, and it took 29 minutes to pass Cisterna. Beyond this we got up to 140 km./h. but this was quickly followed by a brief stop for adverse signals at a station called Latina. Actually the town of that name, originally Littoria, is now a provincial capital, and lies about half way between the Appian Way and the sea, and a good 10 kilometres from the railway station. The 60 kilometres from Rome to this out-of-course stop had taken us 36 minutes.

Once clear of this hindrance we settled down to a fine spell of sustained fast running, covering 87 kilometres in $39^1/_4$ minutes, at an average speed of 133 km./h. We swept along at an almost unvarying 135 km./h., diving spectacularly beneath the Ausoni mountains that mark the end of the Pontine Marshes, and continuing at full speed round the curves past Fondi and Itri and down to the sea at Formia. More running, now at 140 km./h. and after Sessa Aurunca a headlong plunge straight into the mountainside beneath Monte Massico. There was some slight easing of the speed after this, but we nevertheless passed Villa Literno, 121 kilometres from our restart at Latina, in $59^1/_4$ minutes. It is at Villa Literno that the alternative route into Naples diverges. The railway geography of this great city of the south is rather complicated. The line on which our 'Rapido' was travelling takes the coastal route, diving underground before reaching the first stopping station, Mergellina, and then continuing entirely underground to Piazza Garibaldi. The alternative route through San Marcellino and Aversa terminates in the Central station, and the distance from Rome to this station and the distance from Rome to Piazza Garibaldi is the same.

Central, like most major Italian city stations, is a terminus and it is used by those trains on which remarshalling and the attaching and detaching of through carriages is involved. South of Naples there are two main lines, one running down the west coast to Villa san Giovanni and the ferry to Sicily and Palermo, and the other runs east to Foggia, where it joins the line along the east coast to Bari, Brindisi, and Lecce. The 'Treno Azzurro' by which we travelled north conveys through carriages from Taranto to Rome, while other trains have through carriages from Reggio, Siracusa, and even from Palermo. It is the trains that terminate at Naples, like the 'Super Rapidos' that use the coastal line, and do not run beyond Mergellina. We used that station on our journey south rather than the Piazza Garibaldi, because it was nearest to the hotel where we were staying. It also serves an elegant residential district. Trains of fixed formation like the morning 'Rapido' from Rome use the Piazza Garibaldi, and at the present time that train continues to Villa San Giovanni, whence one section continues on the mainland to the terminus at Reggio, while two cross the Strait of Messina by ferry, and divide in Sicily; one section goes to Siracusa and one to Palermo.

After having travelled, in two stages, the entire way from Florence to Naples in the railcar 'Rapido' type of train it was interesting to return by an ordinary express, locomotive hauled. The 'Treno Azzurro' (the Blue Train), originates at Taranto. At the time when we travelled it left Naples at 11.14, but departure is now at 12.00, having started from Taranto at 06.33. The present overall time from Naples to Milan, 850 kilometres is exactly $8^1/_2$ hours — a precise average of 100 km./h. At the time of our own journey the time was a full hour longer. We kept exact time, despite no fewer than eighteen slowings and out-of-course stops for engineering and other work. We were hauled throughout by locomotives of the 'BBB-E646' series, the units being changed only at the stations where direction of running was reversed; i.e. at Rome and Florence.

The journey began in somewhat dramatic fashion. We were not 15 minutes on our way when vandals stoning the train broke some windows, and a stop was made to investigate. Because of this it took $34^1/_2$ minutes to cover the first $35^1/_2$ kilometres to Villa Literno, just before which we had joined the 1927 'Direttisima'. After this we went ahead in good style making an average of 116.5 km./h. for 30 kilometres leading to Fondi. After this we went very slowly through the Monte S. Biagio tunnel prior to a special stop in the open country. Single line working was in operation beyond, and we had to cross over on to the south-bound line, run much more slowly than normal, and then slow to cross back again on to the regular northbound line at Priverno. Then at last we got a spell of really fast running. The powerful electric locomotive could make light of our ten coach train, weighing with passengers about 420 tonnes, and for 47 kilometres we made a steady average of 132 km./h. But yet another drastic slowing was necessary before we began to approach Rome, right down to 7 km./h. over a bridge under repair. In all these circumstances we did well to run the complete 216 kilometres from Naples Central to Rome Termini in $133^1/_2$ minutes — average 97 km./h.

From Rome, with a fresh '646' class engine in charge and load increased to 455 tonnes, the difficult run to Florence was even more interesting than in the fast railcar train by which we had travelled south. The heavy corridor coaches rode the curves elegantly, and of course there was ample tractive power at the front end. We climbed the gradients up the valley of the Tevere (Tiber) at 90 to 100 km./h., and after passing a summit beyond Orvieto ran up to 120 and occasionally 130 km./h. on favourable stretches. There were places where we pulled up dead slow for engineering work on the line, but the 314 kilometres from Rome to Florence took 200 minutes — an average of $94^1/_2$ km./h. and very creditable too. Yet a third '646' backed on to what had been the rear of the train, and this one took us through to Milan, with the one stop at Bologna. It was now after 17.00 and I must admit that my note-taking became a little less intense. I could not, even then, subscribe to the view that the scenery on the Florence-Bologna direct line was only matched by that of the Inner Circle! It was early summer, and the broad vistas as we climbed high among the mountains were magnificent, even when travelling at 100 km./h. We were slowed to 20 km./h. at Vernio, the entrance to the Great Apennine Tunnel; but once inside our big locomotive accelerated like lightning, and we threaded its 18.55 kilometres in $10^3/_4$ minutes, despite the slow start. After Bologna our interest in the journey became centred on the pleasures of the dining car, and beyond noting that between various slowings we were running regularly at 115 to 120 km./h., our arrival in Milan was, most satisfyingly, dead on time.

On this occasion we were bound for Paris by the Simplon Route, and so to prepare the entree for the next Chapter, I have to side-step smartly to Genoa, and trust ourselves once again to the three-phase line along the Mediterranean coast. The westbound direction is unquestionably the more advantageous in which to make this run. One is hardly clear of the industrial purlieus of Genoa before there are enticing glimpses of high mountains ahead, rising straight out of the sea; and although the journey is still long, even now that the standard system of Italian electrification is installed, the scenery gets more exciting mile by mile. And as one takes farewell of the Italian State Railways it is perhaps a good place to pay a farewell tribute to the old three-phase constant speed electric locomotives that handled the traffic on this line for so long. Uninspiring and functional in appearance, and inflexible in operation because of their constant speed characteristic, they nevertheless represented an important phase in the history of railway traction. I should add in conclusion that the passenger locomotives had four speeds at which they could be operated up to a maximum of 100 km./h., and with one of these mustard-coloured 'tin boxes' wheeling us into Ventimiglia it is time for the SNCF to take over once again.

CHAPTER SEVENTEEN

Cote d'Azur — PLM

The entry into France from Ventimiglia — or Vintimille, as we should call it, once across the frontier — is one of sheer delight, both to the railway enthusiast and to the lover of magnificent scenery. We spent a short holiday at Menton while the line along the Cote d'Azur was still steam operated, and it was then that I came to appreciate as never before the merits of the ultra-simple steam locomotive, with no more than two outside cylinders, a large boiler, and a complete absence of frills. Yet 'Les Americaines', as the local *cheminots* used to call them were about the most un-French engines that ever ran the rails, and withal, among the most highly prized! It is nevertheless inappropriate to burst in at the very tail end of the steam locomotive history in these parts, even though it is my own most vivid memory. One should go back nearly a hundred years, to the days when the strangely picturesque Henry 2–4–2s were laboriously wheeling their caravans of four-wheeled dog-boxes along the line from Marseilles.

For much of its length it is a gloriously picturesque route, whether amid the stark limestone heights between Marseilles and Toulon; in running along the Riviera coast line, through a chain of resorts highly favoured by English visitors in Victorian and Edwardian times; and then most spectacularly in winding round the rocky cliff faces of Monaco and Monte Carlo to that most extraordinarily placed station on a ledge just below the mighty gilded casino, perhaps the most famous gaming house in the world. It always seemed to me that the station was so placed by design to aid a quick get-away, for good or ill! Casinos apart however, the view seawards from the station, over the harbour to the rock and palace of Monaco is entrancing, though now, unhappily in some respects, denied to the traveller by train.

That sharply curved track carried on a ledge cut out of the solid rock was not only slow, and because of the curves expensive to maintain, but uneconomic in that the stations of Monaco and Monte Carlo, so close together, virtually duplicated the facilities. Furthermore, we now live in an age when conservation has become a key word. In such an age the idea of trains making their laborious ways amid a scene of such beauty has been abhorrent. Our fathers, and grandfathers were quite content to have smoky steam locomotives puffing their way along; but our own times cannot tolerate the pollution of the diesels, or the catenary wires of 25,000 volt electrics. So a new line has been built, almost entirely in tunnel, beneath Monte Carlo, to keep the trains out of sight.

Talking of pollution, when we were staying at Menton the American 2–8–2 engines working on the Cote d'Azur were all oil-fired, and for the most part their exhausts were absolutely clear and colourless. French enginemen, whether drivers or firemen, are among the most expert and professional in the world and make it almost a point of honour to deal with the smallest detail on their locomotives with the utmost care. Now oil-firing inevitably results in some sooting up of the tubes, and as with many of the most recent coal-fired locomotives the equipment included a 'sand gun' for blowing a fine spray of sand through the tubes and clearing them of soot. From some of the many vantage points in Menton where we used to laze away the summer days, I could see the trains pounding their way up the stiff gradient past the Italian frontier, and without fail, once they were clear of French territory on would go the sand gun, and their entry into Italy would be signalised by a tremendous cloud of black smoke! Those engines would be finishing their eastbound run at Vintimille, and waiting there an hour or so before picking up a return load; and the cleaning of the tubes at that particular moment was logical enough. But it always struck me as amusing how precisely they waited until they were in Italy before they did the job.

It is nevertheless a far cry from the oil-fired American 2–8–2s to the 2–4–2 express engines that handled almost the entire express service of the Paris, Lyons and Mediterranean Railway from 1876 to the end of the nineteenth century, including the often mountainous

202

COOKS CONTINENTAL TIMETABLE

CENTENARY ISSUE 1873-1973

Indicateur Européen Cook

25. Cover of Cook's continental timetable

sections along the Cote d'Azur. These once very familiar and famous engines were of two varieties, and were derived from a batch of fifty

203

2–4–os dating from and built to replace the old Cramptons, which had borne the brunt of the express service of the PLM for many years. The 2–4–os of 1868 however had an unpleasant, and at times dangerous pitching action at speed, and when larger locomotives were needed, Monsieur Marie, then Chief Mechanical Engineer, used the 2–4–2 wheel arrangement with the pair of trailing wheels under the firebox providing a steadying action against pitching. Sixty of these engines were built between 1876 and 1878, and then in 1879 Monsieur Henry, who had then succeeded to the office of Chief Mechanical Engineer, produced his improved version of which no fewer than 290 were built, 40 indeed in England, by Sharp, Stewart & Co., then in Manchester. The Henry 2–4–2s were so numerous, and so familiar to English travellers visiting the resorts on the Riviera, that they became virtually synonymous with travel on the continent of Europe. Indeed, when Thomas Cook & Son celebrated the centenary of their greatly appreciated Continental Timetable, in 1973, a beautiful drawing of one of these engines formed part of the attractive cover design.

Today these celebrated engines would be regarded as quaint rather than handsome. Certainly they would look very angular and functional against their neat contemporaries in Great Britain and their counterparts in Holland. On the basis of nominal tractive effort they were very powerful engines for their day, having cylinders 500 mm. diameter by 620 mm. stroke at a time when few British locomotives had advanced beyond 450 mm. diameter. The boiler pressure used was relatively high for the year 1879, namely 10 kg. per sq. cm. But in those last years of the nineteenth century the work they were called upon to do was not exactly heroic. The 'Train de Luxe' ran in the winter only and, largely for the benefit of English visitors, had start-to-stop average speeds only between 59 and 66 km./h., making stops at Laroche, Dijon, Macon, Lyons, Valence and Avignon — an overall average of only 60 km./h. over the 863 kilometres between Paris and Marseilles. Most of the intermediate runs were quite long, such as Paris to Laroche, 155 kilometres, Lyons to Valence, and Valence to Avignon, over dead level routes. And this was by far the fastest train on the line.

Professor Foxwell and Lord Farrer had some scathing comments to make about PLM running in 1885–1900:

Though great improvements have been brought about here of late years induced by the competition of the Est and Gotthard on one side and Orleans Companies on the other, the general results on this system — the longest and most powerful in France, perhaps in Europe — are still the worst of all. Low speed, few expresses, and a great want of third class do not make up a pleasant picture. It is a fact, though it seems hardly creditable, that there is not a single train along the Riviera between Marseilles and Ventimiglia, winter or summer, which attains to the rank of an express according to our definition (twenty nine miles an hour stops included), while one train between Cannes, Monte Carlo, and Mentone labelled 'express', first class only, does the journey at the magnificent speed of eighteen miles an hour.

One train — the 10.10 p.m. from Marseilles to Paris — labelled 'Direct' — takes twenty five hours to do the 537 miles — not 22 miles an hour.

I should interpose here that the joint authors set a standard for an 'express' train as one which averaged 40 m.p.h. (64 km./h.) from end to end including stops. This was all very well so far as Great Britain was concerned; but they had to drop the level to 29 m.p.h. (47 km./h.) to collect any trains at all on the continent of Europe when they made their survey in 1889. It was undoubtedly the leisurely timings of the long distance passenger trains that helped to make the longevity of the Henry 2–4–2s. Their long rigid wheelbase and overhanging cylinders were not ideal for a fast running engine, especially for a line like the PLM which had much curvature. In 1893 the new chief mechanical engineer, Monsieur Baudry, rebuilt one of them so drastically as to be quite unrecognisable, save for its number plate. The result was an orthodox-looking 4–4–0. Even the main frames were new, and this rebuild was the prelude to an entirely new era in PLM locomotive practice.

This rebuild was a 2-cylinder simple, but in 1898 the PLM brought out the celebrated 'C 61' class of 4-cylinder compound 4–4–0 in the de Glehn style, but most strikingly fashioned externally. They were probably the first locomotives anywhere in the world to have any form of external streamlining, and although by the end of the century there had been a great improvement in express train timings on the PLM, the view of some English commentators of the day was that the aerodynamic fairings on the 'C 61' class were not really justified. Neither they were, so far as ordinary running conditions went. But the PLM has somewhat exceptional physical circumstances to contend with in the Rhone delta. Between Avignon and the approach to Marseilles the line runs across a very flat and exposed countryside, subject to the furious wind of the Mistral, and the new locomotives were designed and described as 'wind-cutters'. Apart from this however, they were most skilfully designed engines and, mainly due to their large low pressure steam passages which permitted a very free exhaust, they proved the most powerful and swiftest of all French 4–4–os. One of them reached a maximum speed of 153 km./h., while another of them making up time with the 'Rome Express', sustained 130 km./h. on level track, with a train weighing 170 tonnes. Both these spectacular feats of running were not publicised at the time because the legal speed limit in all France was then 120 km./h.; but they were well known among railwaymen.

The Rhone delta, and Marseilles itself may not be among the most attractive tourist areas in France, but from the railway viewpoint they have features of exceptional interest. In the present age Marseilles is the junction point between the earlier standard 1500 volt d.c. electrification, and the new 25,000 volt a.c. system, which is installed along the coast to Vintimille. The main city station, St. Charles, is a terminus, and thus a convenient place for changing from the 1500 volt d.c. locomotives that have brought the Riviera expresses down from Paris to the 25,000 volt a.c. types that continue the run along the Cote d'Azur. There are stationed at Marseilles a number of locomotives that can work on either traction supply. In Marseilles also there are wide ranging traffic and electrical supply control centres; and while it is always fascinating to see the latest ingenious engineering devices for regulating power supply, and remote signalling controls, I must confess always to be drawn towards the graphic records of the actual train running that are being plotted minute by minute by skilled regulators, as reports of train movements are received. At Marseilles I watched the gradual building up of the day's record on the main line across the Rhone delta to Avignon, which carries additionally, as far as Tarascon, the important traffic to the Spanish frontier at Cerbère, and trains destined for Toulouse, Bordeaux, and Hendaye. Nowadays the principal express trains between Marseilles and Paris do not actually pass through Tarascon, but take the avoiding line, outside the town.

The ancient and grandly historic city of Avignon, with its sight of the great Palace of the Popes and the machicolated towers and parapets of the city ramparts, so tantalisingly near yet unattainable to the traveller who is just passing through, will to me always be memorable for my first introduction to the great 4–8–2 compound locomotives of the '2–4–1P' class. The PLM had been the first French railway to adopt the 4–8–2 type, a special purpose 'monster' for the section through the Cote d'Or mountains between Laroche and Dijon, and in 1930 a new express passenger prototype was received from the Schneider works at Le Creusot. Although in no more than an experimental stage, this engine, No. 241.C.1 did well in an important series of tests on the Nord in 1932–1933. But at that stage no additions were made to the type. At the end of the war however when new passenger locomotives of maximum power were needed urgently an order was placed with Schneider for 35 4–8–2s. Time did not permit of a major re-design, and the new engines had the characteristically light frames traditional of the PLM, 280 mm. thick, but reinforced somewhat in the new engines. Improvements were also made to the cylinder, valve, and boiler design, and with the superb workmanship traditional of the Le Creusot works of Schneider, and careful handling by the enginemen they did much first class work.

On the PLM they were always handled on a fairly light rein. I shall always remember my first experience of them, when a heavy train of around 700 tonnes was taken over from the electric locomotive that had brought the train down from Paris. We glided very slowly and silently out of Avignon, gradually gathering speed, yet taking nearly 8 minutes to do the first 6 kilometres; but the speed went on increasing till we were tearing across the level track of the Rhone delta at 120 km./h. — with the engine all the time as silent as any electric. Baron Vuillet tells an amusing story of how one of these engines came to make a record run with the southbound 'Mistral', when the changeover to steam took place at Lyons. With a train of about 470 tonnes, the 106.2 kilometres to Valence were covered in $61^3/_4$ minutes start-to-stop, but then as the train was restarting a passenger arriving late and more than slightly drunk, tried to board the train, but could not open the door; and while the speed rose to 120 km./h. he hung on *outside* until he was spotted by a signalman, and the train stopped at Livron. A newspaper report next day aptly described the sequel:

'Cette aventure l'ayant, parait-il, dégrisé, le voyageur a continue sa route'.

Sobered up indeed! How, in such a befuddled state, he managed to cling to the outside of a *streamlined* coach baffles the imagination. Afterwards, the driver and fireman doing their best to make up the lost time coaxed their big engine over the 120.7 kilometres from Avignon to Marseilles in $67^3/_4$ minutes.

In the years between the two World Wars, despite the introduction of the 4–8–2 locomotives, the PLM depended almost entirely on the 'Pacific' for its express passenger services. This type had been developed to a high state of perfection over many years of experience, and after trials of various systems of propulsion. The earliest engines of the type, dating from 1912, were actually 4-cylinder simples, and the compound variant appeared first in 1913. In those early years there were in all 20 simples and 85 compounds; but the developments from 1922 onwards were all compounds. They were beautifully designed engines and gave splendid service on their own line. They could not, however, stand thrashing. Like the big 4–8–2s one had to treat them gently, and allow them to find their own pace — which was hot enough once attained. The flexible frame theory that persisted on the PLM was unfortunately exposed in its weakness when some comparative trials were made between Paris and Calais between Nord and PLM 'Pacifics' in 1933. To provide a severe comparison the regular load of the 'Golden Arrow' was augmented, and in trying to keep the exacting schedule the PLM engine overtaxed its strength as it were, and fractured one of its frames. As Baron Vuillet commented:

The merciless Nord schedules had therefore demonstrated the inadequacy of the flexible frame theory.

At the gracious city of Dijon the PLM line, hitherto an almost continuous racing ground on easy gradients, reaches the foot of the Cote d'Or range, and in beautiful scenery climbs on a 1 in 125 gradient to Blaisy Bas Tunnel. Apart from its situation as an engine-changing point on the line from Paris to Marseilles, Dijon featured, just before the First World War, in a piece of competitive railway building which from 1920 altered the pattern of international traffic from Paris to the South-East. Until the year 1915 the route from Dijon to Lausanne followed by trains for the Simplon Route had been very roundabout. It was meandering enough in the tumbled country foothills of the Jura Mountains, but then from Frasne eastwards it followed the line heading for Neuchatel and Central Switzerland as far as Portarlier and then making a right-angled turn to the south to enter Switzerland at Vallorbe. The distance from Frasne to Vallorbe in a direct line is 22.5 kilometres, while by the railway route then operating it was 38.5 kilometres. The opening of the Lötschberg line in 1913 tempted the Eastern Railway of France into direct competition for the Simplon traffic, by running through carriages off their own line from Belfort to Berne, via Delle. To combat this the PLM embarked upon the building of a cut-off line from Frasne direct to Vallorbe, with a long tunnel under Mont d'Or. This line was however not completed until 1915, and did not influence the tourist traffic until after the war; it then became the route of the Simplon-Orient express.

The 159.3 kilometres of line northward from Dijon to Laroche, because of its severe gradients through the Cote d'Or mountains, became a natural testing ground for PLM locomotives. I have already mentioned the '241 A' class. It was the usual practice for expresses to the south to change engines at both Laroche and Dijon, and with the new 4–8–2s available, 'Pacifics' were used between Paris and Laroche and south of Dijon, leaving the mountain section to the bigger engines. These latter were also used between Dijon and Vallorbe where there were also some heavy gradients. The PLM flexible frame theory was a point of some significance there, because it was a route of extreme curvature for much of its length, and of beautiful scenery. It was on the southbound ascent to Blaisy Bas that many famous French locomotives were subjected to full capacity testing. After an hour of gradual uphill running from Laroche came the 31.3 kilometres from Les Laumes to the summit, on an average gradient, allowing for curvature of 1 in 172. The concluding 6 kilometres are inclined at 1 in 125 (or 1 in 118 equivalent taking curvature into account). The following table, gives details of the performance of some famous engines:

Engine Number	Type	Date	Load tonnes	Average speed km./h.	Minimum speed at Blaisy km./h.
220 C 62	4–4–0 PLM	1899	220	74.8	68.2
241–A1	4–8–2 PLM	1927	809	75.2	61.0
231 H 141	4–6–2 PLM	1933	430	109.2	98.4
241 C 1	4–8–2 PLM	1932	588	99.2	90.5
232 S 3	4–6–4 NORD	1941	710	111.2	99.2
240.P5	4–8–0 PO	1941	810	107.2	95.2
242 A 1	4–8–4 OUEST	1948	743	114.2	112.2

The first five of the above results concern locomotive types already discussed, and the advance in standards of performance is certainly impressive from the wind-cutting 4–4–0 to the 4–8–2s. Of these latter, the 'A' class was found capable of taking nearly four times the load of the very competent 4–4–0 at much the same speed, while the prototype 'C' class in 1932 took 588 tonnes over the summit at $90\frac{1}{2}$ km./h. The work of the 'Pacific' 231 H 141 was also magnificent, representing the highest development of the PLM 'Pacific' type up to the year 1939. The Nord 4–6–4 was one of the De Caso streamliners referred to in Chapter Six, and a design of outstanding capability. The references to 240 P5 and 242 A1 should be pigeon-holed in the mind, and will be referred to in the concluding Chapters of this book.

The section between Dijon and Laroche has a significance of a different kind. From Paris to the north end of Blaisy Tunnel the line is quadruple tracked, but through the tunnel itself, and the steep descent of 26.5 kilometres into Dijon, there are only two running lines. Because of the very heavy engineering works and mountainous country it would have been very expensive to widen the line. Yet there were times when the line was saturated and subject to reactionary delays. It was however a well known characteristic of PLM traffic that the heaviest pressure southbound was in the late evening through the procession of sleeping car expresses, while a corresponding flow northbound occurs in the early morning. Arrangements were made for complete resignalling of the section between Dijon and Blaisy Bas to permit of what is known in France as *banalisation* — in other words, use of either track in both directions, instead of the usual 'down' and 'up' lines. By this, for example, both tracks could be used for southbound trains simultaneously, or both for northbound, and track facilities were installed at the intermediate stations not only for crossing from one to the other, but for berthing a slower train between the two main lines. The sketch diagram shows how this was done. The whole section between Dijon and Blaisy Bas is controlled from an electric signalling panel, with the usual illuminated track diagram, and a remarkable instance of how these facilities are now used came to my own notice. A fast express for Paris arrived at Dijon about ten minutes late. It would normally have been followed by a train making a number of stops, but this was sent away ahead of the express on line A. The express followed on line B, but at the second intermediate station a remarkable manoeuvre was set up. A southbound freight train was approaching in the opposite direction on line B, under caution signals of course, and while the stopping train was at the platform in line A, the express running under clear signals, was switched through the centre road and on to line A, thus leaving line B clear for the freight to continue.

This line, like practically every other main route in France, suffered terrible damage in the concluding stages of the Second World War, when strategic bombing by the Allied air forces aimed at disrupting every possible line of communication to the enemy forces resisting the invasions from the Channel coast. When the time came for recon-

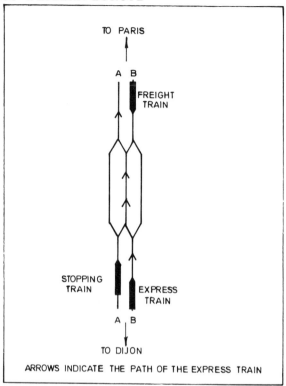

26. Crossing loop — Blaisy-Dijon section

struction very great care was taken to re-align major junctions like Laroche, Montereau and Melun so that in future they could be run through without any reduction of speed. With the electrification programme every consideration was given to making the former PLM a really high speed route, with colour light signalling throughout. The traction system was to be 1500 volts d.c., as most successfully used on the Paris-Orleans-Midi line in the years between the two World Wars. The original intention also was to use a direct development of the Orleans type 2–D–2 electric locomotive. In the meantime however the great engineer who had done so much to advance the steam locomotive on the Orleans railway, André Chapelon, had made an almost sensational step forward towards post-war steam practice in France by rebuilding a 4–8–2 of the Western Railway as a 4–8–4. Into this great engine were packed all the features that had been so carefully developed on the Orleans, but on a much enlarged scale; and on trial in 1948, on the favourite Laroche-Dijon test route, this great engine put up a performance that not only delighted all steam lovers but which shook the electrical men to their foundation.

In the table on page 210 it will be seen that 242 A1 took a train of 743 tonnes from Les Laumes up to Blaisy Bas at an average speed of 114.2 km./h. — moreover going over the summit at 112.2 $(69^1/_2$ m.p.h. on a 1 in 125 gradient!). No wonder the electrical pundits were astonished, because this not only equalled, but slightly surpassed the performance they were planning with the new electric locomotives. Some urgent reconsideration of the design took place, with the result that the rated power output of the new locomotives for the PLM line became about 746 kilowatts greater than was originally intended. This was probably the only instance anywhere in the world of steam locomotive prowess strongly influencing electric locomotive design. Good though these units were, the French National Railways were not long in adopting the all-adhesion type, so successfully pioneered on the Lötschberg line, and subsequently developed on the Swiss Federal Railways. What the earlier French examples of this epoch-marking design could do in the way of high speed is told in the final Chapter of this book; but in what seems a very short time the French advanced to the beautiful and immensely powerful 'CC 6500' class, on which I have had the privilege of making a number of runs in the driver's cab.

In view of what I have written earlier in this Chapter about speeds in climbing to Blaisy Bas Tunnel the work now demanded on a train like the 'Mistral' is interesting. The time allowance over the 315 kilometres between Paris and Dijon is 138 minutes, an average of 141.5 km./h. and when I rode in the cab we averaged 145.5 km./h. between Les Laumes and Blaisy Bas, and we were actually travelling faster at the summit than on the approach gradients — 153 km./h.: for old-time English readers, 95 m.p.h. up 1 in 125, with a trailing load of 715 tonnes! Not even such mighty power units as the 'CC 6500' can cope with every condition that sometimes affects railway working; and on this very trip we were heavily delayed between Valence and Avignon by a series of tremendous thunderstorms. The damage, which we could see included widespread flooding, and interruption to the railway traction supply; and this very powerful locomotive was brought to a stand in open country for lack of power in the overhead line. It took eventually 122 minutes to cover the 124.5 kilometres from Valence to Avignon where we arrived 72 minutes late.

A fellow traveller unkindly remarked: 'We should have done better with steam!' Not necessarily so. The line between Lyons and Avignon seems to be particularly susceptible to interference from thunderstorms, and Baron Vuillet tells of an occasion when Train 51, hauled by a '241 P' 4–8–2 was heavily delayed between Lyons and Le Peage-de-Roussillon. On both the steam and electric occasions gallant attempts were made to recover time after Avignon. The steam 4–8–2 took its 800 tonne train over the 120.5 kilometres to Marseilles in $75^1/_2$ minutes, while on the electrically hauled 'Mistral' we took no more than $54^3/_4$ minutes with a load of 715 tonnes. A fortnight later I timed, from the driver's cab, another of these remarkable 'CC 6500' class locomotives to cover the distance back from Marseilles to Avignon in $57^1/_2$ minutes with a load of no less than 820 tonnes. These runs, back again in the Rhone delta, do indeed highlight the almost phenomenal advance in locomotive tractive power that has taken place in the last twenty years in France. One has the comparison between a superb steam locomotive, with a driver and fireman out to do their level best, and one of the latest electrics; and the times with roughly equal loads over the 120.5 kilometres between Avignon and Marseilles were $75^1/_2$ and $57^3/_4$ minutes: respectively start-to-stop averages of 96.1 and 125 km./h. I need not say more!

CHAPTER EIGHTEEN

Saga of the 'Orleans'

There was surely never a great railway whose title was more geographically modest than the Paris-Orleans. It became much more comprehensive after 1934 when it was amalgamated with the Midi, and the activities of the enlarged company extended from Paris to the Spanish frontier; but among English travellers the original 'Orleans' was perhaps the least known among the French main line railways. Even those who went to holiday resorts on the Basque coast would sleep through the night, and awake to find themselves travelling on the Midi. In its earlier days however the Orleans provided one of the very few instances in France of strongly competitive routes. The original concessions made to the railway builders had neatly parcelled out the country so that competition should be minimised, but the accompanying map shows how the opening of the State line to Bordeaux set up immediate competition with the Orleans, while on the eastern side the PLM via Clermont Ferrand at one time provided the recognised route from Paris to Barcelona. The Midi on the other hand enjoyed a position of complete monopoly, controlling all the routes to the Spanish frontier, and was in a position to take traffic from the State, the Orleans and the PLM. The result was that in the nineteenth century the train services of the Orleans became the fastest and most enterprising in the whole of France.

There is no doubt that the attitude of the Midi played a big part in creating this situation. In taking traffic for Cerbére, connecting for Barcelona and eastern Spain, it was much more advantageous to have this handed over by the Orleans Company at Bordeaux, rather than taking it from the PLM at Sète on the Mediterranean coast. The Midi got a far greater mileage. So they struck up so profitable an alliance with the Orleans that the service from Paris to Barcelona, via

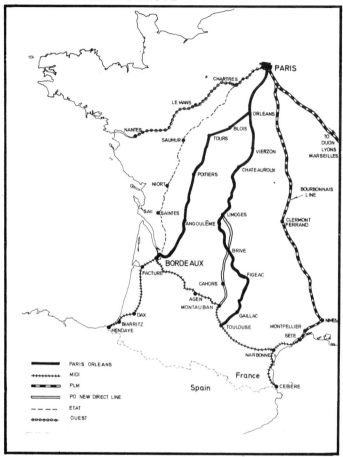

27. The 'Orleans' and its competitors

Bordeaux, Toulouse and Carcassonne was nearly one hour quicker than that by the PLM, although the distance was about 100 kilometres greater. One has only to look at the map to appreciate this disparity. At that time the train service over the Central France line, running directly south from Orleans and through Limoges to Toulouse, had not been developed to the express standards. South of Limoges it is very hilly, and it was much quicker to go from Paris to Toulouse via Bordeaux, than direct. The main line of the Orleans, continuing south through Tours, Poitiers, and Angoulême is for the most part a fast route through easy country and was ideal for the

216

building up of an enterprising service. The main city stations at both Orleans and Tours are termini, and connections with the through express trains are given at Les Aubrais and Saint Pierre des Corps, as shown on the sketch maps.

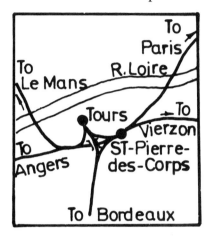

28. Lines around Tours (above) and Orleans

The Orleans had many runs scheduled at speeds of 67 to 71 km./h. start–to–stop in the 1880s, and it needed good going with an express like the 10.40 from Paris to cover the 231 kilometres to Saint Pierre des Corps in 3 hours 35 minutes with six intermediate stops totalling 17 minutes standing. In 1897 there was an excellent train to the south which had the following timings:

Distance kilometres	Section	Time mins.	Average speed km./h.
118.9	Paris–Les Aubrais	92	77.8
113.9	Les Aubrais–St.Pierre	83	82.2
103.6	St.Pierre–Poitiers	80	78
112.8	Poitiers–Angoulême	88	76.9
81.7	Angoulême–Coutras	65	75.5
51.2	Coutras–Bordeaux	42	45.3

The standard passenger locomotives of the Orleans at that time were of the 2–4–2 type, but of rather different design to those of the same wheel arrangement on the PLM. The design was due to Monsieur V. Forquenot, and was long lived and successful. Some of them were still in service in 1949. Their most distinguishing external feature was the brass-jacketed boiler, always kept scrupulously clean.

Until well into the twentieth century the Orleans Company ran a very large number of four-wheeled coaches on their principal express trains; but for the most part these were very different from the little 'dog-boxes' found elsewhere. They were relatively large vehicles with a long wheelbase. J.P. Pearson has given a detailed description of one of the first class compartments which is worth quoting:

The compartments reached by sliding doors from off the corridor were upholstered in white cloth, which had trimmings along the top of the cushions and — to prevent these latter being soiled — removable lace slips were provided as head rests. A long narrow mirror was fixed under the luggage racks, but its narrowness made it of little use and I think its purpose was merely ornamental. Three-seat places were given each side, there were three windows looking on to the corridor and two large ones looking on to the track, and all of these had curtains. These windows, as well as those in the corridor, were divided by a horizontal moulding which gave a fair sized upper portion of the window, with a much larger main window below. White blinds were fitted to the corridor window. Altogether, most comfortable and artistic looking compartments, but with one fault and that was the lighting, which was oil, and similar in its application to that curious sidelong flickering light which just rendered darkness visible on our own Midland and Great Northern lines.

The load of most of the fastest Orleans expresses at the turn of the century was around 150 to 170 tonnes, and the little Forquenot 2–4–2s had to be skilfully driven and fired to make good time on the relatively fast schedules maintained. On level track the speed had to be about 90 km./h. They were less powerful engines than the Henry 2–4–2s of the PLM having cylinders 440 mm. diameter and 650 mm. stroke, but they had a better record of service. Moreover when they had been taken off regular work on the best expresses there was still plenty of useful work for them. Down in the south the 'Orleans' had a business service between Bordeaux and the town of Bergerac, about

218

75 kilometres to the east. The trains were light, rarely more than about 120 tonnes, and the old 2–4–2 engines proved entirely adequate — in fact more economical than heavy modern engines that would necessarily need to be worked much inside their maximum power. The little 2–4–2s used to skip merrily along at speeds up to 100 or 102 km./h. on the level track. They continued on this duty until 1939, and then after the electrification of the main line into Bordeaux they were taken off, and relegated to the branch line east of Bergerac to Sarlat, where they worked until 1949.

Baron Vuillet logged an interesting run from Les Aubrais to Paris, when one of them was put on to pilot one of the 4-cylinder de Glehn compound 4–6–0s of the '1700' class, which had an enormous train of 20 four-wheeled coaches weighing over 400 tonnes. With three intermediate stops the train was booked to run the 119 kilometres in 105 minutes. The two engines gained 5 minutes on schedule, and ran at 90 to 95 km./h. on level track. Technicalities apart, what a picture the two of them would have made, with the brass-jacketed 2–4–2 leading, and the typical small wheeled de Glehn compound behind. The Orleans had some compound 'Atlantics', which were a larger version of the celebrated Nord '2641' class, but the greatest locomotive development on this railway began in 1907, when the very first European tender locomotive of the 'Pacific' type took the road. It preceded, by only three months, a Baden State engine of the same type, and was followed early in 1908 by the third European 'Pacific', 'The Great Bear', on the Great Western Railway of England. Before discussing the Orleans 'Pacifics' in any detail something must be said of the heavy road south of Limoges, for which they were expressly introduced.

Among the principal main lines this is one of the most picturesque in France. It cuts through the western flanks of the Massif Central, and is already deep in the mountain country well before Limoges is reached. The steep gradients begin at Argenton, but at first it is an upland rather than a mountainous country. So far as the railway is concerned the climbing is continuous to Forgeville, much of it on gradients of 1 in 100. When riding in the cab of one of the modern electric locomotives one can appreciate the constant curvature, and also the tunnel entrances picturesquely-built in splendid masonry.

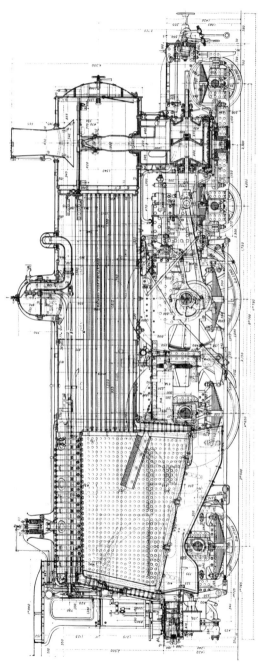
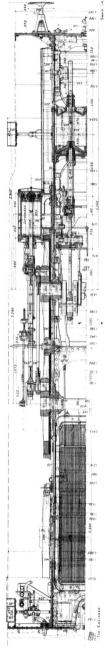

FOUR-CYLINDER COMPOUND LOCOMOTIVE. PARIS-ORLEANS RAILWAY

SOCIÉTÉ ALSACIENNE DE CONSTRUCTIONS MÉCANIQUES, BELFORT, ENGINEERS

29. Drawing of the Orleans 'Atlantic': one of the finest of early de Glehn designs

The Tunnel de la Jeraphie, just beyond La Souterraine, is a particularly fine example. Soon after passing St. Sulpice the long and steep descent into the valley of the Taurion begins, and at a distance of almost exactly 400 kilometres from Paris the train draws into Limoges. Seen from the engine cab Limoges-Benedictins is one of the most spectacular stations I know. Many have splendid buildings alongside, great clock towers and such like, while others have huge and graceful arched all-over roofs; but Limoges has an all-over roof crowned with a gigantic cupola in the centre. As one approaches from the north and prepares to dive in immediately beneath it the effect is terrific. Limoges is a through station, and in these days with the one electric locomotive working through from Paris to Toulouse, it is a place where drivers are changed.

South of Limoges the traffic pattern has changed completely from that of the nineteenth century. On the map reproduced on page 216 the Paris-Orleans route to Toulouse is shown taking the old meandering through route, swinging westwards via St. Yrieix to reach Brive, and then going south through Figeac, Villlfranche, and Gaillac to come straight into Toulouse from the northeast. In their work of 1889, Foxwell and Farrer mark this as a line over which 'express' running was performed, thus signifying that there were trains making an overall average speed of at least 47 km./h. But the present direct line from Limoges over the summit at La Porcherie to Brive, and thence via Cahors to a junction with the Midi line at Montauban is not even marked, let alone dignified by express running. It was actually built in 1893 and its emergence as a first class main line came in the early 1900s. South of Limoges, and throughout to Montauban it is scenically magnificent, but very difficult from the locomotive point of view. There are no gradients steeper than 1 in 100 but the continuously severe curvature makes them equivalent to about 1 in 87. In steam days the heaviest express trains passed through this region in the early mornings, when there was often mist and low cloud to affect the adhesion. To ride through in the cab of an electric locomotive is as thrilling a railway experience as one could wish for, seeing the deep wooded glens, the line carried high on ledges cut from the solid rock, in and out of tunnels, across graceful viaducts, rounding curves at 110 km./h.; all as exciting as when the same locomotive was doing 200 km./h. in the open country north of Les Aubrais! The profile of the line is like the edge of a saw: from Brive up to Gignac; down to La Chapelle-de-Mareuil; up to Thedirac, down to Cahors, up to Cieurac, and finally down to join the Midi line at Montauban.

It was the difficulty of working over this route that led the Orleans Company to introduce the first 'Pacific' engine to run in Europe. Delivery of the first of the type, No. 4501, was taken in July 1907 from de Glehn's works at Belfort. Because of the physical conditions on the line south of Limoges the coupled wheels were made no more than 1850 mm. diameter, instead of the more usual 2000 or 2030 mm. for express engines. The prototype and its successor No. 4502, received from the builders in September 1907 proved admirable engines on the heavy gradients of the Central France line. During early trials No. 4502 hauling a load of 22 four-wheelers (415 tonnes) averaged 58 km./h. up the severe 40 kilometres northbound from Alassac (Brive-Limoges section), where the average adverse gradient is 1 in 119. The two original 'Pacifics' proved so satisfactory that orders were placed for another 68, and all of these were in traffic by the end of 1909. These engines were not superheated. A further batch of 30 purchased in 1910 were superheated, and were used on the faster stretches of line north of Limoges. Although very powerful, and ideal for the heavily-graded sections of the Central France line, neither the 4501–4570 series nor the superheated 4571–4600 class were very successful as real express engines. They were poor runners on level or favourable stretches of line, and rarely exceeded 105 km./h. As the Orleans was developing some very fast services on the Bordeaux line this was not good enough, and in 1912 a new series was introduced with 1950 mm. coupled wheels and, while having the same boiler as that of the earlier engines, there was a much improved cylinder and valve design. These engines, the '3521' class, could haul trains of 400 tonnes at 116 km./h. on level track.

Mention of the Bordeaux line brings me down to the southern end of the Orleans system, as it was before amalgamation. As at Toulouse, the Paris-Orleans entered Bordeaux by running powers over tracks of the Midi. Actually both the Paris-Orleans and the State system had their own terminal stations in Bordeaux backing on to the

Quai Deschamps on the river Garonne; but all the through trains went into the Midi station, St. Jean, which as headquarters of the latter company was an appropriately magnificent affair. The map on page 216 shows the route of trains from the State system running over Paris-Orleans metals to enter Bordeaux. This was then the normal way of getting into St. Jean station; but after nationalisation in 1938 the position was reversed, and although the old Etat station was closed some re-arrangement of tracks was made to enable Paris-Orleans-Midi trains from the north to use the former Etat approach to the city, as it provided an easier entrance to St. Jean. The former Midi line is continuous through this big station coming in from the south west, and then swinging round eastwards to form the important international route to Toulouse and Narbonne, with continuations thence to Spain on the one hand and Italy on the other.

The Midi was a very interesting line, and prior to its amalgamation with the Orleans in 1934 one with a strong individuality. Its two main lines from Bordeaux were very different in physical characteristics. The western line, running over a dead level course passes through the forest country of the Landes de Bordeaux, planted in the eighteenth century by Nicolas Brémontier to check the wind-blown sand from the coast from spreading inland and turning the countryside into a veritable desert. At Facture, just inland from the lagoon of Arcachon the line turns due south, and almost dead straight to form the greatest high-speed railway test track in the world. The forest lands continue almost to Dax, and provide some shelter from winds, and assist in making the line so suitable for extra high speed running. The Midi was one of the first French railways to begin main line electrification. The proximity of the Pyrenees, and the readiness with which the mountain torrents could be harnessed for power generation was a strong influence; it is interesting that despite what was currently being done in Italy and elsewhere, the Midi engineers decided upon the single phase a.c. system of traction. In 1920, however, the French Government ruled that the 1500 volt d.c. system should be standardised. It was used for later schemes on the Midi, and later by the Orleans Company, and for a time looked like becoming the standard system for the whole of France — and Great Britain too. The earliest Midi electrifications were on the heavily graded

223

secondary lines in the Pyrenees, in 1910–1914. War conditions prevented any developments for a time, but by 1925 the line from Dax to Toulouse via Pau and Tarbes was electrified, and by 1930 the main line between Bordeaux and the Spanish Frontier at Hendaye had been similarly equipped.

This relatively early changeover to electric traction naturally halted the development of steam locomotive practice on the Midi, which had followed a notable course since 1908. Then, having noted the success of the first two 'Pacifics' on the Orleans they took delivery, in 1908, of four compound express 'Pacifics' of very similar design but with coupled wheels of 2050 mm. diameter. Tests showed that 500 tonnes trains could be hauled at start-to-stop average speeds of 80 km./h. and a further 12 were purchased in 1909–1910. Further tests showed that with trailing loads of 520 tonnes speeds up to 115 km./h. could be attained on level track — a remarkable performance for that period, particularly as these locomotives were not then superheated. The work of these Midi compound 'Pacifics' was in many respects better than that of their contemporaries on the Orleans itself. In 1910 also, the first of the superheated compounds was introduced — an important and successful development. Then in 1914 there came a surprising move in that a new series of powerful 'Pacific' engines was introduced, not as compounds but as two-cylinder simples, with cylinders 630 mm. diameter by 650 mm. stroke. The outbreak of war in 1914 halted this development, but the general impression at the time was that the 2-cylinder simple engines were slightly less powerful than the superheated compounds, and not so economical. The simples were mostly used on the cross-country line from Bordeaux to Toulouse and Cette, and between Narbonne and Port Bou. The overall assessment in years after the First World War put the three varieties of Midi 'Pacific' as follows:

Type	Coal consumption Kg. per 100 tonne/km.
non-superheated compound	6.29
superheater compound	5.01
2-cylinder simple	5.29

Against the lower coal consumption of the compound the 2-cylinder simple, with less machinery and all of it outside, would doubtless have been a cheaper locomotive to maintain.

The early conversion of the main line between Bordeaux and Hendaye to electric traction fairly soon after the end of the First World War took away the chances of seeing what the Midi 'Pacifics' could do in the way of sustained high speed running. Their activities became concentrated on the line between Bordeaux and Narbonne, and there nothing in the way of high speed could be made. On a typical run with the eastbound night mail, one of the 2-cylinder simple 'Pacifics', working up the gradually ascending gradients with a train of 460 tonnes covered the 136 kilometres to Agen in a net time of 98 minutes, taking into account various checks en route. It continued over the 70.5 kilometres to Montauban in $53^3/_4$ minutes, start-to-stop, and concluded by running the last 50.3 kilometres to Toulouse Poteau station in $39^1/_4$ minutes. Maximum speed on the whole journey was 103 km./h. but the heavy rate of firing, 4 tonnes in a journey time of $3^3/_4$ hours, is enough to emphasise the severe nature of the working. After the electrification of this line from Toulouse to Sète and the consequent restriction of steam operation to the line west of that city the activities of the Midi 'Pacifics' became progressively less. After the amalgamation of the railway with the Orleans in 1934 the programme of steam locomotive modernisation which had begun five years earlier at Tours, was continued afterwards purely on ex-Orleans engines.

No more than two years after the Ministerial decree of 1920 as to electrification systems the Midi had the first 1500 volt. d.c. locomotives in France running between Pau and Tarbes, and as early as 1927 work on the main line to the south was sufficiently advanced for a high speed test run to be made from Bayonne to Bordeaux, 198.5 kilometres in 104 minutes — an average speed, almost sensational for that period, of 114.3 km./h. start-to-stop. It was certainly prophetic of future events that this notable new record should have been on this particular line. The overhead wires on this and all other Midi electrified lines on the 1500 volt d.c. system are supported by artistic looking Gothic-shaped steel arches, a design not seen anywhere except on the Midi. The driving force in all this enterprising work

225

was Monsieur Jean-Raoul Paul, who had joined the railway in 1899, and in the short space of fourteen years had risen to be general manager. He retired in 1932, shortly before the merger with the Orleans. It was due to his foresight that the passenger electric locomotives were classified 'grand vitesse', and had a rated maximum speed of 130 km./h., higher than the legal speed limit then enforced throughout France. These locomotives were of the 2–C–2 type, that is three powered axles with individual drive, and a four-wheeled bogie, fore and aft. They had a one-hour rating of 1678 kilowatts.

The first Midi main line to be electrified is of course the important international express route from Hendaye to the Mediterranean coast, and from Bayonne the through express trains call at Puyoo (where the line from Dax joins in), Pau, Lourdes, Tarbes, and Montrejean, to Toulouse. It is a beautiful route, at times almost brushing the foothills of the Pyrenees. In these days the modern developments of the early electric locomotives make fast time between the stops, and come into Toulouse from the southwest. Strangely enough one of my own most lasting recollections of railways in Toulouse is that of lunching at the station buffet. In Chapter Seven of this book I have told how such meals can become protracted. Well, the smart decor and gastronomical delights of the buffet at Toulouse are such as to receive honorable mention in at least one travel book, and when in a short interval between some locomotive tests my French companion headed smartly for this buffet, I feared the worst — dashing out leaving a half-eaten meal, because the return train could on no account be missed! But it has been said that 'even on Judgment Day a Frenchman will not miss his lunch', and on entry my companion spoke so rapidly that I did not catch a word. Things then began to happen with equal rapidity. A four course lunch was served with such speed that in less than forty minutes we strolled out, exceedingly replete, and sauntered up to the locomotive with ten minutes to spare. It can be done!

Returning now to Bordeaux, the main line to Paris is not one of the most scenic routes in France, and the gems of architecture that can be glimpsed from the line have to be pinpointed, and looked out for, or they will be missed. But for enthusiasts of the stop watch, it was a great place even before the tremendous electrics of today, the

'Capitole', 'Etendard', and 'Aquitaine', began running lengthy stretches of the journey at 200 km./h. Equally there can be few major express routes on which the principal stopping stations serve places of such historical and architectural interest: Angoulême, Poitiers, Tours, Blois, and Orleans. Compare, for example, Rugby, Crewe, Preston, Carlisle, and Carstairs! It is true that not much of these beautiful French towns and cities can be seen from the train; but each of them is worth a stop-over. At Tours the line enters the valley of the Loire and soon afterwards, going north, we must be on the lookout for Amboise, on the right hand side of the line to see to good advantage one of the finest of the great chateaux of France. From Tours to Orleans, or more strictly from Saint Pierre des Corps to Les Aubrais, is always a very fast stretch, where the modern super-flyers will be doing 200 km./h. Whatever its place in French national history may be, and whatever its present charms as a city, Tours will be forever famous in railway history as the birthplace of one of the greatest ever of locomotive developments, initiated by André Chapelon, and described in the next Chapter. As the train slows down a little from its hurricane pace, and nears the city of Orleans, there is a fine distant view of the magnificent cathedral. Then on to another spell of 200 km./h. running over a grand straight line until the track dips down towards Etampes and enters upon the winding final stretch beside the river Juine, and the approach to Paris.

The beginning of the Chapelon steam locomotive development took place at a time when the Paris-Orleans Railway had definitely embarked upon a programme of main line electrification intended to embrace, as quickly as practicable, the whole of its two principal main lines, to Bordeaux, and to its point of junction with the Midi, at Montauban. The system of traction was 1500 volts d.c. in accordance with the Ministerial Decree of 1920, and in December 1926 the first section, over the 200 kilometres from Paris to Vierzon, was brought into operation. The choice of Vierzon as the terminal point of the first stage was interesting, as it marked roughly the changeover point between level and hilly running on the main line to Toulouse. It meant also that trains on the Bordeaux line would be electrically hauled as far as Les Aubrais. The original express locomotives were of the 2–D–2 type, very powerful units, while a number of general purpose all-adhesion type on two four-wheeled bogies were also put into service. On heavy trains these were often used in pairs. It is however of great historical interest to record that the Paris-Vierzon scheme was not the first undertaken by the Orleans Company. There had been a section electrified at 600 volts d.c. since 1899.

By the end of the nineteenth century it had been found that the original terminal station in Paris, on the Quai d'Austerlitz was becoming inconvenient and unpopular with travellers because of its distance from the centre of the city, and because there had been a marked movement of the residential population towards the western boundaries. Accordingly the company embarked upon a westward extension 3700 metres in length, and 3100 metres in tunnel beneath the left bank of the river Seine to the new terminus at the Quai d'Orsay. It was a difficult and expensive job, and the new station opened in 1900 was built in a magnificent style worthy of its situation in such a distinguished area in the city. But from the outset it was determined that on such a line, almost entirely in tunnel, and to be used by the most important express trains on the railway, steam traction was out of the question. It was electrified from the start, at 600 volts d.c. using the third-rail system of current collection, as later standardised on the Southern Railway in England. The original locomotives were of the centre-cab type, with neatly sloping forward casing as on the original electric locomotives of the Metropolitan Railway in London. Electric traction was used initially only between the Quai d'Orsay and Austerlitz stations, which became known as the *Nouvelle Gare d'Orleans* and *Ancienne Gare d'Orleans* respectively. The promoters of the great project optimistically envisaged that changing engines from electric to steam at Austerlitz would take no more than two minutes. Contemporary observers have said that never to their knowledge had the change been made so quickly, though a time of exactly three minutes had sometimes been observed. It seems that four minutes was generally nearer the mark; that was smart working enough — in all conscience!

The station at the Quai d'Orsay was a magnificent affair. The circulating area, vestibule, and grand hall were at street level, from which one descended to the lower level of the platforms. There was none of the basement-like atmosphere that pervades the platforms of certain great Canadian stations that are arranged in this way. From the platforms the lofty arch of the roof, fully glazed, gave a tremendously spacious air. Another unusual feature for France, and one much appreciated, was that the platforms were level with the floors of the carriages, and passengers were spared that steep climb up steps which is normally needed. There were nine platform lines, four used by suburban trains, and five by main line expresses. The circulating area and vestibules were designed in the most grandiose manner, while the river frontage on the Quai d'Orsay itself was extremely impressive. When the station was opened eight electric locomotives dealt with between 150 and 200 trains per day.

CHAPTER NINETEEN

The climax of French steam

I have told in Chapter Six how, during the First World War, the French Government ordered 400 4-cylinder compound 'Pacific' engines of the Etat design as a first step towards what was hoped to be a general standardisation of railway rolling stock. The Orleans however, no more than the Nord, had no enthusiasm for such a trend, and when the time came for post-war development, they went their own way. The need was urgent. In working up to pre-war standards of speed and frequency of service, it was not merely a case of restoring the *status quo*. There was a demand for much better rolling stock, and all-steel carriages were being introduced. Unfortunately this could not be done overnight, and for a time many trains ran with a mixture of heavy all-steel bogie stock and a proportion of the old wooden four-wheelers. In several serious accidents, arising from arrears of maintenance in the aftermath of the war, wooden coaches were crushed between heavier new vehicles, with grievous loss of life, and the outcry against this veteran stock demanding its complete replacement became a national issue. In consequence locomotives were called upon to pull much heavier loads.

Among locomotive men of the Orleans it was generally agreed that the 'Pacifics' had been a disappointment. Compared to the de Glehn 'Atlantics' of 1903 which could sustain 1342 kilowatts in the cylinders, the 'Pacifics' could barely reach 1500 kilowatts. While this had been adequate with pre-war loads, it was not enough for the conditions of the 1920s. Although the Orleans had been allocated 40 of the Government sponsored 'Pacifics' of the Etat type, the investigations towards improved performance that began in the locomotive department at Tours were directed almost entirely upon the pre-war Orleans designs. The first step came in 1923, when one of the '3551' class was slightly modified, by substitution of Trick ported valves for the original low pressure valves. In these early stages of the development it was clear that improvement in performance was being sought by the minimum of alteration, and unlike the other French railways major capital expenditure on new locomotives was ruled out by the policy of introducing main line electrification. The steam locomotive men had to make do as best they could, and improvement was vital otherwise unfavourable comparisons would be made between performance north and south of Les Aubrais, and to a lesser extent on the Toulouse line north and south of Vierzon. The substitution of Trick ported valves gave little improvement, and the next step was towards poppet instead of piston valves.

An enquiry made in Austria by Monsieur Garsonnin, engineer of material, aroused interest in the Lentz type of valve, and authority was given for the rebuilding of two further engines of the '3551' class. By the year 1926 the officer, who in Great Britain would be called Chief Mechanical Engineer but who in France was designated Ingénieur en Chef du Matérial et de la Traction, M. Lacoin, had determined that every possible means should be sought to improve the performance of the 'Pacifics', and M. Billet, Ingénieur Principal, Chef du Service du Matérial, put one of the brightest younger men of the department, the ever-famous André Chapelon, in charge of the investigation. Chapelon had already won distinction by his adaptation of the Finnish Kylala type blastpipe to French needs, embodying its principles in a twin-orifice arrangement. In France, and everywhere else subsequently, it became known by a combination of the two names KYL(ala)-CHAP(elon), though an English humorist suggested that a device with the name 'kill-chap' sounded dangerous! Anyway, following up the interest in poppet valves M. Lacoin sent a deputation to London in 1926, consisting of Messrs. Billet, Chapelon, and Willoteaux — the last named a specialist in valve design. Their principal aim was to discuss poppet valves with the Paxman Company, who were the licensees of the Lentz patents.

In the meantime the 'Pacific' engine No. 3579 was rebuilt with poppet instead of piston valves and tested on the line; but the mere substitution of valves produced little result, and a much more extensive rebuilding was applied to engine No. 3566. By systematic indicating of the cylinders Chapelon had found that inadequate cross-sectional areas of steam passages were having a most restrictive effect. These were entirely re-designed, and streamlined internally. Then attention was given to improving the steam raising capacity of the boiler itself, particularly with an improved design of superheater giving higher steam temperatures. Lastly the rebuilt engine was fitted with the Kylchap twin-orifice blastpipe, which provided a greater cross-sectional area for exhaust of the steam, without reducing the entraining action of the blast in sustaining the necessary draught on the fire to produce rapid combustion, and a high rate of steam generation. The final refinement was to include Nicholson thermic siphons in the firebox, to promote rapid circulation of the water. The results of this rebuilding were phenomenal, but though every detail of it was due to André Chapelon it is equally important to appreciate than when the rebuilding was done, in 1929, he was still in a subordinate position. There was another factor that helped to set the seal upon this highly successful development, and that was the basic chassis design of the nigh-twenty year old Orleans 'Pacifics'. That company, like the Nord and unlike the Est and the PLM, built their locomotives like battleships. There was no flexible frame theory there. The main frames were 318 mm. thick, and in anticipation of their having to transmit greater power than when originally designed they were reinforced at all the critical points. This proved a most wise provision, because when No. 3566 was taken out on the line and tested, her maximum output was found to be 50 per cent. greater than originally — *fifty per cent*!

Curiously enough the rebuilding attracted little attention at first. By the time No. 3566 began trials, the electrification between Austerlitz and Vierzon had got well into its stride, and was claiming most of the general publicity so far as the Orleans railway was concerned. It was however a point of deep significance that the engine made her first runs between Tours and Poitiers within a few days of the centenary of the historic Rainhill trials on the Liverpool and Manchester Railway, in England. It would perhaps be overstating the case to suggest that the running of No. 3566 ushered in an epoch of equal

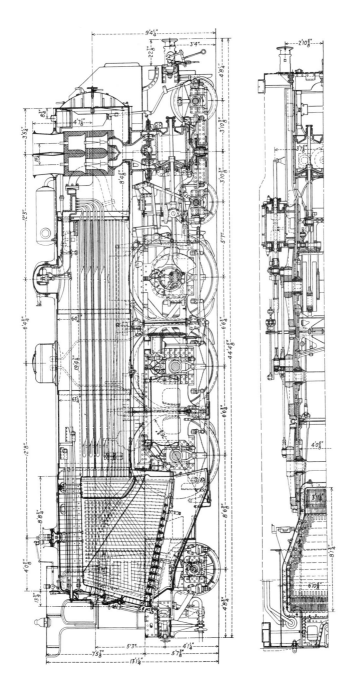

30. Chapelon rebuilt Orleans 4–6–2 locomotive — 'Transformation'!

233

importance in the history of railway traction to that following the successful running of Robert Stephenson's 'Rocket' in 1829, but the coincidence of the dates is impressive. The Paris-Orleans Railway was singularly modest in publicising the tremendous achievement of its locomotive department, and it was not until May 1930 that any indications were made public, and then again in a most modest way. In that month there was an international exhibition at Liege, and three of the French railways sent examples of their latest locomotives. There, while the Est and the PLM exhibited huge 4–8–2 locomotives in the flesh, and the Nord sent one of their very successful Bréville 'Pacifics', the Orleans merely displayed two graphs. But to those who were in the position to appreciate them, those graphs contained data that took some believing.

Both graphs showed the gradient profile of the line between Poitiers and Angoulême, 113 kilometres, and the two runs had been made with loads of 360 and 555 tonnes. On the first run the engine was quickly accelerated to 120 km./h., on the gradually rising gradient from Poitiers, and then on reaching the foot of the Couhé-Verac incline, 5 kilometres at 1 in 200, the speed was *increased* on the gradient to 125 km./h., and the complete run to Angoulême completed in 60³/₄ minutes, an average of 111.3 km./h. This was good enough, especially in the brief demonstration of exceptional power on the 1 in 200 gradient; but then the second run was found almost incredible by those who studied its details, for the big load of 555 tonnes was hauled from Poitiers to Angoulême in 62³/₄ minutes — an average of 108.5 km./h. The Couhé-Verac incline was mounted at a minimum speed of 112.9 km./h. It was indeed a transformation from the original engines of the '3551' class, for against the indicated 1530 kilowatts which those engines could just manage at their best, the rebuilt 3566 reached 2328 — a fifty per cent. increase. Furthermore, at 120 km./h., the kilowatts at the drawbar had been stepped up to 1342, again a fifty per cent. increase over the previous best.

The British technical press had always taken a keen and enthusiastic interest in French locomotive practice, ever since that great observer Charles Rous-Marten had extolled the work of the de Glehn compound 'Atlantics' on the Nord, in the early years of the present century. But so positively surreptitious were the initial activities of the Paris-Orleans 4–6–2 No. 3566 that it was not until October 1931, almost two years after her first emergence from the works at Tours, and then in *The Railway Engineer*, that the British railway world learned of the transformation and of the astonishing performance that the engine was putting up. In an article most succinctly presented by another noted engineer-journalist, Charles S. Lake, indicator diagrams, taken in comparable conditions on one of the original engines and on No. 3566, revealed with startling clarity the success of the modifications made by Chapelon. His original investigations had shown how little work was being done in the low pressure cylinders of the original engines, and the following numerical comparison is quite astonishing:

Indicated kilowatts comparisons

Engine No.	3579	3566
Speed 105 km./h. nominal		
actual km./h.	105	102.2
Kilowatts high pressure cylinders	1088	1004
low pressure cylinders	291	992
total	1379	1996
Ratio kW. high pressure cylinders		
kW. low pressure cylinders	3.74	1.01
Speed 120 km./h. nominal		
actual km./h.	126.5	118
Kilowatts high pressure cylinders	984	978
low pressure cylinders	153	628
total	1137	1606
Ratio kW. high pressure cylinders		
kW. low pressure cylinders	6.4	1.55

It will be seen that when working really hard at around 105 km./h. the rebuilt engine was producing almost exactly the same power in

235

both sets of cylinders — an ideal state of affairs — whereas the original engine was doing no more than one fifth of the total work in the low pressure cylinders. At maximum legal speed the performance of the original engine was even worse, with only 153 kilowatts out of a total of 1137 contributed by the low pressure cylinders. There were many other features that a locomotive engineer could extract from that memorable article in *The Railway Engineer*, and appraise the astonishing work of transformation that had been effected on engine No. 3566.

In February 1932 the locomotive received its first mention in *The Railway Magazine* when Cecil J. Allen, writing under one of his pen names, 'Mercury', commented upon the test details previously published in *The Railway Engineer*, and gave particulars of other excellent runs; but up to this time there had been no mention of the man whose genius lay behind the success of No. 3566, André Chapelon. At this stage also the twin-orifice blastpipe was referred to as the 'K.C.' type, and not the Kylchap. It was not indeed until he had contributed a masterly paper to the Société des Ingénieurs Civils de France in 1936, and it was reviewed in *The Railway Gazette* in the following May, that the vast majority of British railwaymen and railway enthusiasts first heard of his name. It was his chief, the genial Marcel Bloch, who in 1938 on the nationalisation of the French railways went to the Service Central du Material, as Chef de la Division des réparations du material moteur. Chapelon himself still continued in a subordinate position. Long before this however the fame of the rebuilt Orleans 'Pacifics' had spread like wildfire through France. In 1933 the Nord organised a fascinating series of competitive trials between Paris and Calais, briefly referred to earlier in this book in Chapter Seven, in connection with the enormous Est 4–8–2s. In these trials the Orleans 'Pacific' scored a most resounding triumph.

Matched against Est 4–8–2s, a Collin super-Pacific of the Nord, and the experimental '241.C.1' 4–8–2 of the PLM it completely outclassed the Nord and Est engines, and equalled the maximum efforts of the much larger '241.C.1' but on much lower running costs. The Nord were so impressed that they straight away ordered 20 'Paris-Orleans-Transformations' as they became known, from the Orleans company. The extension of the electrification from Les

Aubrais to Tours had made a considerable number of Paris-Orleans steam locomotives surplus to requirements and the order from the Nord was welcome. At the same time the Etat, the Est and PLM all began experimenting with improved front-ends on the Chapelon principles, and the addition of feed water heaters and higher degrees of superheat. The standards of performance improved everywhere but not to the same phenomenal extent as on the former Paris-Orleans engines rebuilt wholly on the Chapelon lines. The first example of this most historic design that I saw myself was one of those newly acquired by the Nord, when I visited the La Chapelle running sheds in 1934. The engine was then resplendent in the traditional chocolate brown livery, and made something of a contrast to another Paris-Orleans 'Pacific' which was on the shed. This was one of the Etat type allocated from the wartime Government order for 400, which in 1934 was in the grey livery of the Orleans Company.

Having achieved such success with the rebuilding of the '3551' class larger-wheeled 'Pacifics', attention was next transferred to the smaller wheeled '4500' class, the very first European 'Pacifics'. The rebuilding in this case, as at the time the locomotives were first introduced in 1907, was directed towards the Central France line which, in 1933, was still operated by steam south of Vierzon. I have emphasised in the preceding Chapter what a difficult line this is over which to operate heavy trains. It is not only a matter of climbing heavy gradients. The curves greatly increase the haulage effort required, while the fact of some of the heaviest trains running during the night and early morning often leads to bad rail conditions. It was no use rebuilding the old 'Pacifics' to provide fifty per cent. more tractive power if the adhesion was likely to prove insufficient for the increased power to be utilised; and so the momentous decision was taken to rebuild the '4500' class, not as 'Pacifics' but as 4–8–0s. I must not at this point be tempted to interject my own ideas on locomotive design, except to say this was one feature of the Chapelon development that did not have the widespread influence that it deserved. In response to the instigations of certain close friends I once ventured, in one of my monthly articles in *The Railway Magazine*, to suggest how I thought the steam locomotive might have developed and in this essay, under the sub-title 'Sticking my neck out', I thought that for heavy express work where steep gradients were concerned, we in Great Britain might have done better to develop the 4–8–0 rather than the 'Pacific' type.

Enough of my own views, however. The plain facts are that the Orleans Railway, in applying Chapelon principles to this second 'transformation', scored if anything an even greater success. They were intended for no 'kid gloves' operation. Tremendous loads were taken over the Central France line, and although the saw edge character of the gradient profile did not demand continuous heavy steaming for any great length of time, the power output needed when climbing the sharply curved 1 in 100 inclines was such as to require intense firing for half hours at a time. Where the transformed 'Pacifics' had sustained outputs of 1492 kilowatts at the drawbar, and 2238 kilowatts in the cylinders when going hard the 4–8–0s of the '4700' class were found capable of 2238 kilowatts *at the drawbar*. This of course required plenty of coal, and the tenders were equipped with steam operated coal pushers so that the firemen did not have the additional labour of getting coal forward. Had this facility not been available to them, there is no doubt the feat I am about to relate would have been impossible. One might, for example, scarcely believe that with an enormous 15-coach train of 650 tonnes, the 63.5 kilometres from Montauban to Cahors were covered in $51^1/_2$ minutes. The minimum speed on the 1 in 100 gradient being 58 km./h. On the second toilsome ascent the train was slowed to 30 km./h., at Souillac, over a viaduct under repair, and engine and crew had to fight back against the heavy gradient. In 9 kilometres of 1 in 87 the speed had risen to 60 km./h. — a marvellous piece of work with such a load.

News of a performance like this was not long in reaching the Nord, and again arrangements were made for trials with the dynamometer car between Paris and Calais. The prime object in this case was to try one of the Orleans 4–8–0s on the heavy intermediate express trains; but then the tests were concluded with a truly 'all out' run in each direction on the Golden Arrow schedule, with a train of empty coaching stock, 640 tonnes. Not only this, but on this special occasion in 1935, the speed limit was temporarily relaxed to 140 km./h. This might have seemed a little strange with a locomotive having coupled wheels of only 1850 mm. diameter, and which in its original condition had rarely exceeded 105 km./h. In the event, the engine concerned, No. 240–707, made two of the greatest runs in the entire history of the steam locomotive. A stop was made at Amiens in each direction, and the four sections of the test can be summarised thus:

Section	Distance km.	Actual Time min.	Net Time min.	Net Av.Sp. km/h.
Paris (Nord) — Amiens	130.8	$68^3/_4$	$67^1/_4$	116.4
Amiens-Calais (Maritime)	166.5	$87^1/_2$	85	117.5
Calais (Maritime) — Amiens	166.5	$85^1/_2$	$85^1/_2$	116.8
Amiens-Paris (La Chapelle)	129.2	$70^1/_2$	69	112.4

On the outward journey, for the 32 kilometres of dead level track between Noyelles and Etaples the speed was held steadily at the maximum speed permitted, 140 km./h., and on the final stage of the run home, descending from Survilliers towards Paris the speed was allowed to rise briefly to 147 km./h. To say that British observers were impressed by the news of such a performance was an understatement. The idea of a 4–8–0 locomotive weighing no more than 109 tonnes, hauling 646 tonnes at 140 km./h., on level track was something entirely new.

The Chapelon developments on the Orleans sparked off other researches, and one of the Nord engineers attached to the Nord–Belge group of lines, Lemaitre by name, designed a different form of multiple jet blastpipe. The ultimate aim was similar to that of the Kylchap, to provide a greater cross-sectional area at the top of the nozzle, and thus a freer flow to exhaust without reducing the draught on the fire. So, while Chapelon achieved this by simply having two nozzles, one behind the other, Lemaitre had a ring of five nozzles at the periphery, and one in the centre. The diameter of the last mentioned could be varied by the driver according to the needs for steam production. The outward sign of an engine with the Lemaitre blastpipe was a chimney of larger diameter than normal, in contrast to the narrow elongated chimney of the Kylchap. The Lemaitre

239

blastpipe gave excellent results and was immediately adopted by the Nord, and applied to some of the veteran de Glehn 'Atlantics'. These engines were put on to the 'Blue Bird' Pullman express running non-stop between Paris and Brussels. What they could do was amply shown by a run observed by Baron Vuillet, when the first 202 kilometres out of Paris took no more than $112^1/_2$ minutes; but for dense fog encountered in Belgium the 310 kilometres from Paris to Brussels would have been completed in 176 minutes, an average speed of 105.5 km./h., with a load of 296 tonnes.

The Lemaitre blastpipe was a considerable factor in improving the performance of a British locomotive class, which had proved unreliable and generally disappointing. It was also a class heavily concerned with the London-Paris service of the 1930s between Victoria, Folkestone, and Dover, namely the Southern 4-cylinder simple 4–6–0, of the 'Lord Nelson' class. These engines had proved curiously variable, the same engine sometimes making a good run on the outward journey to Dover, and doing poorly on the return. After becoming Chief Mechanical Engineer of the Southern Railway, O.V.S. Bulleid rebuilt these engines, utilising Chapelon principles in redesigning the cylinders, valves and steam passages, and they were equipped with the Lemaitre multiple jet blastpipe. The incorporation of these French features worked like a charm, and the engines thereupon became entirely reliable, and at times brilliant performers. Unfortunately their stay on the Continental boat expresses was brief, because the outbreak of the Second World War in 1939 brought the suspension of cross-channel passenger services. The war itself, and the German occupation of France from May 1940 onwards caused much interruption of normal railway engineering activity in France; but I have referred in Chapter Six to the rather remarkable feat of the Nord in getting the streamlined de Caso 4–6–4 locomotives built. Elsewhere, the rebuilt Paris-Orleans 4–8–0s performed prodigies of heavy load haulage, but in so doing they seemingly overtaxed their strength, and began to suffer from cracked frames. Despite the traditional robustness of Orleans locomotives one can hardly expect frames to stand up to power outputs practically *double* that for which they were originally designed; but that is what the 4–8–0s actually achieved!

In 1944 when the eventual outcome of the war seemed no longer in doubt a French mission was sent to the U.S.A. with specifications for a new 2–8–2 locomotive design, and authority to discuss its production with the leading American manufacturers. It was to be a general service type, pooled, for maximum utilisation in contrast to pre-war French practice in confining engines to individual crews. Eventually the Baldwin Locomotive Works were entrusted with the design, and early in 1945 orders for a total of 700 new locomotives were placed with Alco, Baldwin and Lima. A further order for 640 units, some from the Montreal Locomotive Works was afterwards passed, but actually only 1323 engines took the road in France, because 17 were lost at sea, when the ship conveying them foundered in a gale. They were typically American in their design, with massive well-designed working parts, bar frames, liberal use of roller bearings, feed-water heaters, and all the coal-fired units had mechanical stokers. Six hundred of them were oil fired, and of these I have written briefly in Chapter Seventeen. They had no teething troubles, and immediately upon arrival in France gave an excellent account of themselves. The quality of French enginemen was never displayed better than in their immediate and enthusiastic reception of these engines — so different in their details and their action to anything they had had before. The French *mécanicien* and his *chauffeur* had always been among the very élite among locomotive footplatemen, and in the '141 R' class, 'Les Americaines', they realised they had a magnificent tool for the post-war job.

The role of steam from 1947 onwards was however no more than transitory on the French railways. While locomotives were urgently needed to get the system going again after the fearful destruction in the last year of the war, electrification of the entire main line network became the fixed policy. In the years of transition some very fine work was done by the new '241 P' class 4–8–2s referred to in Chapter Seventeen. After the elecrification of the main PLM line to Marseilles they were transferred to the Western Region, and worked between Le Mans and Rennes, and between Le Mans and Nantes. Also as progressive electrification proceeded to Lyons and ultimately to Marseilles a number of the PLM 'Pacifics' were transferred elsewhere, mostly to the Northern and Eastern Regions. In the latter days of steam the English boat trains to Boulogne and Calais were shared by ex-PLM 'Pacifics' and Chapelon engines of the 'Paris-Orleans-Transformation' type. Towards the end, when electrification had been extended to Amiens, the running of the boat trains to Calais partook of a nostalgic interest for many British locomotive enthusiasts, though to minimise maintenance costs and make the engines last as long as possible without the need of heavy repair they were handled very gently. When starting from rest they were allowed to make their own way rather than be flailed away in the fiery style of the old Nord, in the years between the two World Wars. The Calais crews all had their own engines, and the work they did was beyond praise, in the way of skilful enginemanship; but it was rarely spectacular.

These days were really something of an anticlimax in the long and distinguished story of French steam. During the latter stages of the war André Chapelon worked out new designs for standard steam locomotives, and all were to have been 3-cylinder compounds, in the style of the original Smith-Johnson compounds on the Midland Railway of England, dating from 1902. Three cylinders were proposed, because with the tremendous power he was proposing to develop there would not have been space between the frames to get in crank webs of sufficient strength. The four types proposed were:

Type	Duty	
4–6–4	super express passenger	maximum speed 200 km./h.
4–8–4	express passenger	to haul 950 tonnes up 1 in 200 at 120 km./h.
2–8–4	heavy mixed traffic	to haul 1200 tonnes up 1 in 200 at 90 km./h.
2–10–4	heavy freight	to haul 2000 tonnes up 1 in 200 at 70 km./h.

As it turned out only an experimental unit of the 4–8–4 type was actually built; the magnificent '242.A.1'. This great engine did some wonderful work, and developed 3730 indicated kilowatts, with good economy of fuel. For a new, experimental engine it was remarkably free from trouble, and in working one particular test journey from Paris to Dijon and back with a load of 861 tonnes, it showed clearly

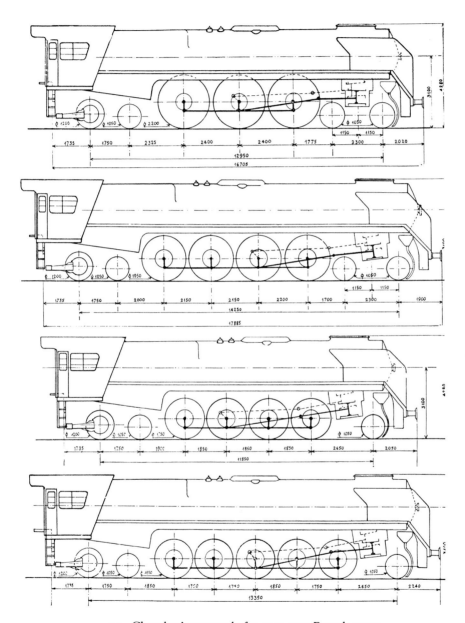

31. Chapelon's proposals for post-war French steam

that M. Chapelon's target of performance was comfortably attained. But the decision to terminate steam locomotive working on the French railways made this great project virtually stillborn, and the one engine actually built — '242.A.1', was scrapped in 1960 after a life of only 14 years. It was a tragedy, but one that in all the circumstances was almost inevitable.

CHAPTER TWENTY

200 km./h. and more!

In making its zig-zagging tour on the railways of Western Europe this book has so far alternated between experiences of modern travel, spells of nostalgia, and glimpses of the work of great men, with steam, diesel and electric locomotives taking the stage in turn, and the often quaint operating methods of earlier days giving place to modern computerised methods. In this last Chapter in describing the build-up, mainly in France, towards daily commercial running at 200 km./h., with the prospect of still faster trains before many years are out, the saga leads inevitably to thoughts of where the latest railway engineering technology could be leading us, and how it fits in with the general evolving sociological situation as the world itself draws nearer to the twenty first century. From the mid-1950s the French railways have been in the van of this movement, though as earlier Chapters of this book have told, extensive plans for new high speed lines are well advanced now in both West Germany and Italy. In the years between the two World Wars French policy towards electrification was to some extent constrained by strategic considerations, and the major schemes actually put into effect were on routes extending away from her eastern frontiers, rather than those like the Nord, which carried the heaviest traffic. But the experience of the 1920s and 1930s on the Midi and on the Orleans formed the basis of the major works undertaken after 1945.

Nationalised railways all over the world are existing on what has been called 'deficit budgeting' and in some countries, some with among the longest experience of railway operation of any in the world, there was at one time a facile assumption that once steam traction was eliminated, the bank balance would, as if by magic, change from red to black, almost overnight. Some schemes for large scale electrification reached an advanced stage of planning with no provision whatever for acceleration of service. There was to be merely a change from steam to electric traction. It was confidently thought that what has elsewhere been called 'the sparks effect' would bring back the lost traffic. In France this view never prevailed, and I can add that the fallacy of it was realised in England before planning for the electrification of the West Coast main line had gone too far. Early in the 1950s there was a rapidly growing awareness in France of the serious competition arising in first class passenger business from the internal airlines, and the management of the Société National des Chemins de Fer, SNCF, concluded that the only way to meet this competition was by speed — but essentially speed combined with comfort, exactitude of performance, and above all impeccable standards of safety.

There was no magic formula for success. Every single engineering facet involved in the running of trains had to be studied and developed to yield higher performance. The track, the coaching stock, and the systems of traffic control were of an importance fully equal to the more spectacular job of making locomotives run faster, and pull heavier loads. This latter point needs some emphasis, because from the very outset the French, unlike the West Germans, accepted the situation that some of their heaviest and most popular trains must be singled out for substantial acceleration. It had been found that with skilful bogie design the new 'all-adhesion' types of electric locomotive, the 'CC 7100' series and the 'BB 9000' series could be run safely at the highest speeds then envisaged in ordinary traffic, 140 km./h. The prototype locomotive, numbered 'CC 7001' built by the French firm of Alsthom, was introduced in 1949, and incorporated a form of body suspension that dispensed with the conventional bolster and pivot. Instead the body was connected to each bogie by two vertical swing links. They move in opposite directions to permit the bogie to turn relative to the body on curves, or both tilt the same way to allow some lateral displacement of the body from the bogie centre line. It proved extremely successful in a series of tests carried out on the Paris-Orleans-Midi in 1949; among a great variety of traffic demands these included high speed trials between Paris and Blois in which a maximum speed of 180 km./h. was attained. The SNCF had set their sights considerably higher than this, and in March 1955, on the magnificently straight line of the old Midi Railway between Bordeaux and Dax they went *really* all out, with locomotive No. 'CC 7107', and with a 'BB', No. 9004, on the following day.

It was not simply a case for taking a locomotive out, with a load of only three coaches, and seeing what could be done. The aim was to run at 300 km./h., and previous tests had indicated that to achieve such a speed it would be necessary to develop something like 7460 kilowatts. That would mean picking up from the overhead line something in excess of 4,000 amperes. The ordinary pantographs fitted to the 'CC 7100' and 'BB 9000' locomotives would not carry such high currents, and so special pantographs were designed for the tests. Both locomotives had their gear ratio modified to adapt them for a speed of at least 300 km./h. and all working parts on the locomotive that had to rotate were laboratory tested up to an equivalent of 450 km./h., to ensure that the exceptional centrifugal forces generated at high speed did not cause disintegration of the rotating parts! The section of line chosen for these epoch-marking speed attempts was that between Facture and Morcenx, where the line from Bordeaux has turned south and is virtually straight for nearly 66 kilometres. The two locomotives made railway history, each attaining the tremendous speed of 332 km./h., which remains a world record still today. It was with a feeling something akin to awe that I travelled over this same line, albeit merely as a passenger, on the morning express from Paris to the Spanish frontier not very long afterwards. Our locomotive had been a standard example of the same 'CC 7100' class, and had brought a modest load of 19 coaches down from Paris. The same locomotive continued through to Hendaye. From the start at Bordeaux we covered the first 39 kilometres to Facture in $24\frac{1}{2}$ minutes, and had covered 25 kilometres at an average of 125 km./h. up till then; but once round the curve and into the long straight we really got going, and the 70 kilometres from Facture to Morcenx were run at an average of 133 km./h. through an almost interminable forest of pine trees.

I remember no less vividly a journey over the electrified PLM line from Paris to Dijon, when my wife and I were travelling with a party of the Institution of Railway Signal Engineers. We had crossed by the early service from London, and by the time we reached Paris most of our party were getting rather travel-weary. A close friend then in the service of the London Midland Region of British Railways and much involved with the electrification works between Manchester, Liverpool and Euston then in progress, was clearly impatient as we trundled round the Petite Ceinture line to the Gare de Lyon, and referred to our programme. 'Another $2^{1}/_{2}$ hours to Dijon', he snorted, 'what are they doing, putting us on to a goods train'! I had to tell him that from the Gare de Lyon to Dijon was just about as far as from Euston to Liverpool. He was mildly impressed, and rather more so when we saw that splendid evening train 'L'Aquillon', that contained our reservations: 16 coaches and one fourgon, 622 tonnes, without passengers, and a little 80 tonne 'BB' of the '9200' class to haul it. This type was developed from the record-breaking 'BB 9000' of 1955. We covered 128 kilometres in the first hour out of Paris, and passed Tonnerre 196.5 kilometres in $89^{1}/_{4}$ minutes — a brilliant average of 132 km./h. from the start. For 182.5 kilometres we had averaged 139 km./h. A very long slowing for permanent way work between Tonnerre and Lezinnes cost us 13 minutes in running, but we reached Dijon nevertheless in $155^{3}/_{4}$ minutes, and on that heavy ascent from Les Laumes to Blaisy Bas that figured so prominently in Chapter Eighteen this 80 tonne electric locomotive took its train at an average of 132 km./h. My London Midland friend was no longer talking about goods trains when we arrived at Dijon!

Such running, which had become standard by the end of the 1950s, was however not good enough for the SNCF. By the superb engineering built into the reconstructed track, trains like 'L'Aquillon' were able to ride smoothly at full speed through big junctions like Melun, Montereau, and Laroche, and the very fast overall times could be maintained without exceeding 140 km./h. But the SNCF was already looking to continuous running, over comparable distances, at 160 km./h., and in 1969 the most impressive 'CC 6500' class locomotives were introduced. Apart from their enormous power they represented a notable advance in French locomotive design. Hitherto electric locomotives, externally, had not developed far from the shapes that caused the steam enthusiasts' jibe that they were nothing more than 'tin boxes'. The 'CC 7100' and 'BB 9000' classes that made such staggering speed records in 1955 were certainly more smoothed and shrouded than any of their predecessors, but they were still 'boxes', and it was in this respect that the great new 'CC 6500' class made such a departure. They formed part of a series of new designs all of 5968 kilowatts, of which there were three varieties:

1. the 'CC 6500' to operate on 1500 volts d.c.
2. the 'CC 14500' to operate on 25000 volts a.c.
3. the 'CC 21000' to operate on either of the above.

The first two types have a total weight in working order of 114 tonnes, and the third, because of the additional equipment involved, weigh 120 tonnes.

Apart from any technical considerations however these new locomotives are strikingly styled externally. The cab windows are inclined backwards, to minimise glare, while this shaping is repeated in the bold application of strong colours to the basic grey in which these locomotives are painted. The side panels and louvres are finished in what an English railway enthusiast could well describe as 'Midland Red', with a border of orange. This style has been applied to the variety of high power electric locomotives of the SNCF. No less striking is the style developed for the large main line diesel electric locomotives now being used on the non-electrified sections. On these the set-back front window style is also used, but the colour motif applied to the basic grey is a sky blue as distinct from the red of the electrics. These locomotives were used briefly on the easternmost part of the line along the Cote d'Azur, after the steam '141 R' class had been removed and before the electrification was completed. They are now extensively used on the Western Region of the SNCF.

The 'CC 6500' electrics are most impressive locomotives to ride. As related two Chapters earlier I had some experience of them on the former PLM, where on the southbound 'Mistral' I came nearest in my railway travelling experience so far to covering 160 kilometres in a single hour. But it was my journeys on the Orleans routes in 1974 that provided experiences that are likely to remain as long lasting memories. It is deeply moving, almost to the point of calling it awe-inspiring, to stand at the outer ends of the 'Grandes Lignes' departure platforms at the Gare d'Austerlitz, and see the two 'CC 6500s' at the head of the 'Capitole' and 'Etendard' respectively, and to reflect that these two great trains, leaving within five minutes of each other, will soon be racing south, still only five minutes apart, at 200 km./h.! And these two trains are no light weights. On the days I travelled each of them was made up of 11 of the huge 'grand confort' coaches, with a gross trailing load of 622 tonnes.

It would perhaps be invidious to suggest that the French 'grand-confort' coaches are the finest railway passenger vehicles that have yet been introduced on any railway, anywhere, but 'great comfort' is no mere catch word for designating these coaches. The accommodation is luxurious, backed up by extremely efficient air conditioning, tasteful decor, and huge 'picture' windows. All the same, I well remember the remark of a frequent traveller between my own home station of Bath, and London, when a new so-called luxury train at inflated prices was put on. He said: 'Oh yes, it's a lovely train until it starts'! Indeed, the riding of that train was at times execrable. Not so the French 'grand confort' coaches. Their riding is superb, and one can be less conscious of very high speed in these than on many a slower train that I know. When reserving seats one has the choice of the open saloon type of car, or of compartments providing seating for six passengers, three a side. These huge cars measure 25.5 m. over buffers, and provide seating in great luxury for 46 or 48 passengers. There are separate dining cars, so that one has a short walk before and after a meal. Great skill has been exercised in their mechanical design so that, although so large and having such sophisticated equipment, they are not unduly heavy. A rake of 11 of them, as running on the 'Capitole' and the 'Etendard', weighs 578 tonnes without passengers and luggage.

Having said that one can be almost unconscious of the speed inside these beautiful carriages, there will naturally be some curiosity as to what it is like to ride the head of the train at 200 km./h. The Orleans road, and particularly the Bordeaux line has some magnificent racing stretches. The first comes after one has mounted the rise out of the river valley at Etampes, with the speed rising from the '130' restriction through Etampes itself, while climbing, to 160 km./h. at Guillerval. Here the line comes out on a level open countryside, and we really begin to 'fly'. In response to the driver's adjustments the speed mounted rapidly, and once the speedometer needle was on the '200' mark, there it was kept. It was a 'grand confort' locomotive too! The riding was wonderfully steady and smooth, and one soon began to lose all sensation of speed. It is true we nipped through country stations pretty smartly. Trains going in the opposite direction were travelling on a relative straight track, in a very open countryside. The real sensation came as we neared Orleans and slowed down to run through the junctions at Les Aubrais. We seemed to be crawling, but when I looked at the speedometer we were still doing 110 km./h. — 68 m.p.h.!

It was on the 'Capitole', bound for Toulouse that in the course of a timekeeping journey I surpassed my previous record for the number of kilometres covered in a single hour, by train, in Europe. We ran the 170.3 kilometres from Bretigny to Vierzon in $59^{1}/_{4}$ minutes, 172.5 km./h. The 'Etendard' making its first stop at Saint Pierre-des-Corps (Tours), continues with the fastest booked start-to-stop run in Europe, and the first at an average speed of more than 160 km./h. — 101 kilometres on to Poitiers in 37 minutes, an average of 163.8 km./h. Astonishing though it may seem this section of line is far from level, although splendidly straight, and the first 25 kilometres is mostly climbing at 1 in 200 — the kind of gradient on which steam locomotives of the inter-war generation would be doing well to hold 100 km./h. Yet up this gradient the 'CC 6500' on the 'Etendard' stormed at 180 km./h. and passed Villeperdue, the top of the hill in 10 minutes from Saint Pierre, 22.8 kilometres. After that it was easy, at 200 km./h. all the way, except for a brief easing to 150 through Chatellerault.

The 'Etendard', and 'Le Capitole du Matin' are early morning expresses, giving arrivals in Bordeaux and Toulouse by lunch time; but in recent years the SNCF has developed a timetable philosophy of providing very fast services leaving Paris in the early evening, and reaching all distant destinations before midnight. These are mostly heavy restaurant car expresses of which 'Le Capitole du Soir' is one, leaving Paris at 18.00, and making the same speed as the morning train. Another remarkable train on the Orleans road is 'L'Aquitaine', leaving at 17.51 and running the 582 kilometres to Bordeaux non-stop in the level four hours — an average of 145 km./h. In the morning the 'Etendard' takes only five minutes more, but with three intermediate stops. These are indeed brilliant locomotive performances, and to cities like Limoges, Dijon, Tours and even to Lyons, where the journey time is $3^1/_2$ hours, or less, such splendid trains provide a very effective competition with internal airlines just as the electrified services in England have done from London to Liverpool and Manchester. When the journey time becomes extended to the $6^1/_2$ hours of the TEE trains to Marseilles, or the 5 hours to Lausanne, the case becomes marginal, as indeed with the British 5 hour run from London to Glasgow. Then one cannot disregard road competition. I know of a certain French lady motorist, admittedly a very expert and intrepid driver who, suddenly advised of the serious illness of a relative in Nice, and being too late for the 'Mistral', got in her car in Central Paris, and arrived on the Cote d'Azur before the train!! I admit this was a somewhat exceptional case.

In September 1976 some further accelerations were made on the Bordeaux line, but to compete regularly and effectively with the internal airlines still faster running than 200 km./h. is considered necessary, and in accepting this view there is the realisation that even if much higher speeds could be made safe, trains making such speeds would be difficult to fit into the timetable network of busy existing lines. Furthermore while incurring the expense necessary to improve still further junction layouts, and curves, there is also the question of power consumption. The high speed tests between Bordeaux and Dax in 1955 amply confirmed the enormous increase in power involved in exceptionally fast running. Even as things are today, the increase in general running speeds on the Orleans lines is frequently proving a tax upon the electrical power supply network which was designed now nearly 50 years ago, when speeds and the density of traffic were considerably less than those of today, but from these considerations came two decisions of major importance. The first was that to provide much faster services from Paris to French provincial cities the bulk of the track must be entirely new to enable running speeds to be increased from 200 to 300 km./h., and enable city to city average speeds of 220 km./h. or more to be scheduled regularly. Secondly, the traction would have to be the 25,000 volt a.c. system.

To enable super-express trains to be run between Paris and Lyons in the level two hours, that is at a start-to-stop average of 210 km./h. a new line is now being constructed. This will diverge from the existing PLM main line at Combs-la-Ville, 27 kilometres from Paris, and will connect into the existing railway network around Lyons at Sathonay, 18 kilometres from the present main station. By taking an entirely new alignment, and avoiding the considerable eastward salient of the existing line to pass through Dijon, the distance from Paris to Lyons will be reduced from 512 to 420 kilometres. There are to be only two intersections with the existing line: one at Montbard, roughly half way between Combs-la-Ville and Dijon, and the second at Macon. The new line itself is being engineered for running at a maximum speed of 300 km./h., and the junctions with the existing line are being laid so that they can be traversed, over the deviations, at 160 km./h. The completion of this line, and the introduction of the Très Grandes Vitesse (TGV) trains, will reduce the present fastest time between Paris and Lyons, $3^3/_4$ hours to the level 2 hours, and even without further acceleration south of Lyons, the fastest time between Paris and Marseilles will come down from $6^1/_2$ to $4^3/_4$ hours and become definitely competitive with the air lines.

The prototype high speed train, the 'TGV-001' was completed in 1972, and has already some notable achievements to its credit. Working to broad specifications laid down by the SNCF a consortium of the leading French manufacturers of mechanical, electrical, and turbine railway traction equipment designed this remarkable train, and it was built at the famous works at Belfort where, 75 years earlier, Alfred de Glehn developed his celebrated 4-cylinder compound steam locomotives. 'TGV-001' made its trial runs on the fine road of the Alsace-Lorraine main line between Mulhouse and Strasbourg, and before leaving its native Alsace it had made a spectacular run at 240 km./h. Then the site of the continued testing was transferred to the existing racing track of the old Midi, between Bordeaux and Dax. This is not only favourable from the viewpoint of alignment but it is also a less densely occupied route, furthermore having the advantage of shelter from the pine forests and thus less likely to interference from strong adverse winds.

The experimental train consisted of a power car at each end, and three trailing cars intermediately. It was articulated throughout, with the five vehicles carried on six bogies. The use of gas turbines, with electrical transmission is interesting, because it is the first of its kind anywhere designed for ultra-high speed rail traction. In its planned commercial version with electric traction the train will provide seating for 382 passengers, and unlike the TEE and other luxury trains, it will carry both first and second class. There will be full bar facilities, but at the speed 'TGV-trains' will go, there will be no time for full restaurant car meals in the elegant style customary on the SNCF. In addition to the Paris-Lyons service in two hours, a service between Paris and Lille, 252 kilometres in exactly one hour is planned. The trials that have been conducted between Bordeaux and Dax have fulfilled all expectations, so far as pure speed is concerned. By July 1972 a run at 300 km./h. had been made, and on December 8, 1972, travelling north on the Midi racing stretch a maximum of 318 km./h. was attained between Labouheyre and Facture.

During the autumn of 1976 I was able to see some of the tests in progress, and to ride in the cab at high speed. Some alterations to the bogie suspension were being examined, and maximum speed was limited to 250 km./h., but that was exciting enough. Even so the riding in the driving cab and in the train was so smooth that the actual travelling did not provide the supreme thrill. It was to stand at the line side, see it approach, and still more to see it flash away into the distance at the full 250 km./h. that left one rather breathless.

In the meantime this zig-zagging tour of railways in Western Europe is nearing its end. On one of my recent journeys north from Bordeaux I was not for once in the locomotive cab, and I sat back and just watched the pastoral landscape of south-western France roll smoothly by: Libourne, Coutras, Angoulême, Poitiers — our 'BB 9200' was making good time, but however brilliant the modern 'electrics' may be, and however sensational the speed records made among the pine forests of the Landes, this line for me will be forever linked with the exploits of the Chapelon 'Pacifics'. And from Chapelon the mind passes swiftly to others whose fame is written in the pages of European railway history. As an engineer myself, I must be forgiven if I have given most prominence to engineers; to men like Du Bousquet and de Glehn; to Conrad, Walschaerts, Belpaire,

254

Schmidt; to Gölsdorf, Giesl-Gieslingen, and Caprotti. Today, even with the integration arising from TEE services, the increasing standardisation of freight rolling stock, and the pooling of technical knowledge through U.I.C. (Union Internationale des Chemins de Fer) there is still a striking individuality among railways in the countries of Western Europe.

Years ago my great friend, David L. Smith, writing of the immortal Glasgow and South Western Railway, said that for the enginemen of Ayr the trip to Carlisle seemed to savour of an Awfully Big Adventure, neatly lifting the capital letters from *Winnie the Pooh*. Today I always think it is still something of an adventure for an Englishman or a Scotsman or a Welshman for that matter, to make his unaided way around Europe. I find it so, as much as when I first set foot in France very, very many years ago. May it always remain so; and if my ramblings in this book tempt any island-bound railway enthusiast to cross the Channel, and venture for himself, I shall be more than happy.

255

Les Chemins de Fer. Pierre Weil. Librairie Larousse, Paris, 1964

Continental Main Lines. O.S. Nock. George Allen & Unwin Ltd., London, 1963

English and Foreign Express Trains. E. Foxwell and T.C. Farrer. Smith, Elder & Co., London, 1889

A Manual of Locomotive Engineering. W. F. Pettigrew and A.F. Ravenshear. Charles Griffin & Co. Ltd., London, 1899

'Type Pacific' from *Les Locomotives a Vapeur Francaise.* L.M. Vilain. Vigor Frères, Paris, 1959

50 Jahr Lötschberg Bahn. R. Bratschi. Bern-Lötschberg-Simplon Railway, Bern, 1963

Narrow Gauge Railways of Europe. Sir Peter Allen and P.B. Whitehouse. Ian Allan Ltd., London, 1959

On the Old Lines. Sir Peter Allen. Cleaver-Hume Press Ltd., London, 1957

Preserved Steam Locomotives of Western Europe. P. Ransome-Wallis. Ian Allan Ltd., London, 1971

Railway Reminiscences of Three Continents. Baron G. Vuillet. Thomas Nelson and Sons Ltd., London, 1968

Switzerland's Amazing Railways. Cecil J. Allen. Thomas Nelson and Sons Ltd., London, 1953

Swiss Federal Railways, Electrification Completed. Swiss Federal Railways, 1960

Unsere Triebfahrzeuge (Swiss Locomotives). Paul Winter. Orell Füssli Verlag, Zurich, 1959

Van d'Een Honderd Roe naar Lombardijen (125 Years of Dutch Stations). Marie-Anne Asselberghs. Kruseman's, Den Haag, Holland, 1968

Verkehrshaus der Schweiz (Swiss Transport Museum). Swiss Transport Museum, Lucerne, 1962

A World on Rails (German Railways — in English). Kalb Ossig Röver. German Railways, Frankfurt, 1968

Periodicals:

The Railway Magazine. From 1897, London

The Locomotive Magazine. From 1896, London

The Railway Gazette. London

La Vie du Rail. Paris

Revue de l'Association Francaise des Amis des Chemins de Fer. Paris

Index

INDEX